The Power of the Between

The Power of
the Between

An Anthropological Odyssey

PAUL STOLLER

The University of Chicago Press   Chicago and London

PAUL STOLLER is professor of anthropology at West Chester
University and the author of ten books.

The University of Chicago Press, Chicago 60637
The University of Chicago Press, Ltd., London
© 2009 by The University of Chicago
All rights reserved. Published 2009
Printed in the United States of America
17 16 15 14 13 12 11 10 09   1 2 3 4 5

ISBN-13: 978-0-226-77534-0 (cloth)
ISBN-13: 978-0-226-77535-7 (paper)
ISBN-10: 0-226-77534-8 (cloth)
ISBN-10: 0-226-77535-6 (paper)

Library of Congress Cataloging-in-Publication Data

Stoller, Paul.
   The power of the between: an anthropological odyssey / Paul Stoller.
       p. cm.
   Includes bibliographical references and index.
   ISBN-13: 978-0-226-77534-0 (cloth: alk. paper)
   ISBN-13: 978-0-226-77535-7 (pbk.: alk. paper)
   ISBN-10: 0-226-77534-8 (cloth: alk. paper)
   ISBN-10: 0-226-77535-6 (pbk.: alk. paper)   1. Stoller, Paul.
2. Anthropologists—Niger—Biography. 3. Anthropologists—New York
(State)—New York—Biography. 4. Songhai (African people)—Niger—
Religion. 5. Songhai (African people)—Niger—Social life and customs.
6. West Africans—New York (State)—New York—Social life and customs.
7. Harlem (New York, N.Y.)—Social life and customs. I. Title.
   GN21.S79A3 2009
   301.092—dc22
   [B]   2008032886

♾ The paper used in this publication meets the minimum requirements
of the American National Standard for Information Sciences—
Permanence of Paper for Printed Library Materials, ANSI Z39.48-1992.

We concluded that there is no single, inevitably correct procedure. It is as if in our travels a party of us came upon the remains of a camp fire. Some of us might simply wish to examine it minutely, to discover what manner of people had used it—where they came from, where they were going and when. Others, on observing that some of the ashes were still warm, might be more inclined—and might even have requisite know-how—to stir through the embers in order to kindle the flame which would form the basis for another campfire, which was no longer "theirs, then," but "ours, now."

FROM THE TRANSLATOR'S FORWARD OF *A GLOSSARY OF SUFI TECHNICAL TERMS* (ISTILAHAT AL-SUFIYA), COMPILED BY QASHANI AT THE BEGINNING OF THE FOURTEENTH CENTURY

Contents

Acknowledgments

The narratives in this book are based upon more than thirty years of living anthropology in the Republic of Niger and in New York City, as well as in the U.S. medical system. I am grateful to the many institutions, both public and private, that have over the years have granted me funds to conduct ethnographic research. These include the National Science Foundation, the National Endowment for the Humanities, the John Simon Guggenheim Memorial Foundation, the Wenner-Gren Foundation for Anthropological Research, the American Philosophical Society, the School of Advanced Research on the Human Experience, and West Chester University. In many instances, the chapters in this book are reconfigured from bits and pieces of previously published essays. Parts of the prologue and epilogue appeared in "The Work Must Go On," which was published in *American Anthropologist* 107, no. 1 (2004): 123–26, in *Rouge* 3 (2004), and will be published as "Jean Rouch and the Power of the Between," in *Three Documentary Filmmakers*, edited by William Rothman (Albany: State University of New York Press, forthcoming). Portions of chapters 16–20 have previously appeared in my book *Stranger in the Village of the Sick: A Memoir of Cancer, Sorcery and Healing* (copyright © 2004 by Paul Stoller; reprinted by permission of Beacon Press, Boston). I thank my friends at Beacon Press for their willingness to publish a memoir on the anthropology of health and illness. Portions of other chapters have been adapted from "Embodying Knowledge: Finding a Path in the Village of the Sick," which I presented at a symposium, "Ways of Knowing," held at St. Andrews University in January 2005 and published in *Ways of Knowing: Anthropological Approaches to Crafting Experience and Knowledge* (New York: Berghahn Books, 2008), 158–181. I thank Mark Harris for inviting me and the other participants (Michael Herzfeld, Tristin Platt, Amanda Ravetz, Huon Wardle, James Leach, David Riches, Joanna Overing, Jonathan Skinner, Greg Downey, Trevor Marchard, Kai Kresse, Dominic Boyer, Christina Grasseni, Peter Gow, Richard Fardon, and David Parkin) for their constructive comments. Portions of other chapters have been fashioned from "Remissioning Life/Reconfiguring Anthropology," a paper presented at a 2006 School of Advanced Research (SAR) on the Human Experience advanced seminar, "Cultural Perspectives on Cancer: From Metaphor to Advocacy." I thank Diane Weiner and Juliette McMullin for inviting me to participate in the SAR seminar. Their comments, as well as those of the other participants (Simon Craddock Lee, Suzanne Heurtin-Roberts, Holly Mathews, Anastasia Karakasidou, Deborah Erwin, and Leo Chavez, and Marjorie Kagawa-Singer), provided much-needed depth and breadth to the essay. A later version of that essay, "Remissioning Life: West African Wisdom and the Power of the Between," was presented in April 2007 at a University of Chicago combined workshop in African Studies and Medicine, Practice, and the Body. I thank Nicholas Harkness for inviting me as well as Ray Fogelson, the workshop discussant, for his insightful comments. Portions reprinted by permission from *Confronting Cancer: Metaphors, Advocacy and Anthropology*, edited by Juliet M. McMullin and Diane Weiner. Copyright © 2008 by the School for Advanced Research, Santa Fe, New Mexico.

Chapters 8–10 are adapted from an essay, "Sensuous Ethnography, African Persuasions, and Social Knowledge," which was published in *Qualitative Inquiry* 10 (2004): 817–35. I thank Norman Denzin for encouraging me to submit an essay to the journal he edits. Chapters 10–14 are based on "Circuits of Art/Path of Wood: Exploring an Anthropological Trail," which was first published in *Anthropological Quarterly* 76, no. 2 (2003): 207–35. I thank Roy Richard Grinker, editor of *Anthropological Quarterly*, for his comments on that essay. Chapters 20–24 were adapted from "Ethnography/Memoir/Imagination/Story," are reprinted from a special issue, The Art of Ethnography, in *Anthropology and Humanism* 32, no. 2 (2007): 178–91, with the permission of the American Anthropological Association, Arlington, VA. I thank Russell Sharman for encouraging me to submit the essay and Edith Turner for her comments.

I am indebted to many people at West Chester University who went out of their way to facilitate my ongoing research. For their efforts on my behalf I thank David Buchanan and Jenny Skerl, past deans of West Chester University's College of Arts and Sciences, and Edmundo Morales,

Anthony Zumpetta, and Susan Johnston, past and present chairs of West Chester University's Department of Anthropology-Sociology. Friends and colleagues have read and commented on various parts of this book. For their constructive efforts, I thank Christine Mullen Kreamer, John Chernoff, A. David Napier, Tord Olssen and Christina Lengyel. Their comments have aided me immeasurably. T. David Brent of the University of Chicago Press patiently encouraged me to develop the ideas for this work, and the book is much the richer for it. Jasmin Tahmaseb McConatha read the entire manuscript with characteristic care, making the text all the more accessible and all the more coherent.

I am most deeply indebted to the many West African men and women who have consistently taken the time to answer my persistent questions. Throughout the years their answers have been incredibly enlightening. I thank them for their great patience, for their grace, and for their ever-present humanity.

Prologue: The Power of the Between

In October 2006 I took the New York City subway to Harlem to visit my West African friends at the Malcolm Shabazz Harlem Market. I got off the train at 116th Street and exited on the south side of the station. Walking up the steps into a mild fall morning, I glanced to the right and saw the silver dome of the Malcolm Shabazz Mosque, founded by Malcolm X in the 1960s, glimmering in the morning haze. Turning left, I strolled down a wide, liter-strewn sidewalk, passing a drab corner grocery store, a vacant lot, and a seafood market in which a wide assortment of fresh fish had been arranged on beds of ice, their dead eyes fixed on the high ceiling. Just beyond the fish market a surreal vision: two multicolor minarets, fashioned from plastic stretched over metal skeletons, rose majestically toward the sky. Shaped like an arc, a yellow sign buttressed the two minarets, creating a gateway to a shopper's paradise. The sign's red letters read Welcome: Malcolm Shabazz Harlem Market.

Beyond the gateway, the market was separated into two sections by an open space filled with several picnic tables. Each section consisted of a series of stalls that lined three wide aisles enclosed by plastic sheeting attached to an extensive network of tent poles. On any given day you could find a variety of goods: Dutch wax cloth, African statues, masks, drums, and baskets as well as seasonal accessories like ski caps, baseball caps, gloves, and scarves. You could also find silver jewelry from Mexico, Indonesia, and West Africa as well as pungent oil-based perfumes and incense, the continuous aroma of which usually laced stale city air with the sweet bouquet of jasmine or sandalwood. These sights and smells have always reminded me of West African markets—convivial places filled with the palpable excitement of market exchange and the infectious mirth of market bonhomie.

It was cloudy in Harlem on that October day, but the vibrant colors of print cloth draped over market display poles like so many flags brightened the dull gray of hazy air. I entered the market and strolled toward the Wamba Store, a leather bag shop owned by Boubé Mounkaila, a man from Niger, one of the many merchants I befriended during fifteen years of ethnographic research among West African immigrants in New York City. As I walked down the central aisle, my friends showered me with a cascade of greetings. Malian and Guinean traders greeted me in French. Liberian traders asked after my health in English. The Nigerien merchants chanted their salutations to me in Songhay and Hausa, the two major languages of the Republic of Niger, the site of the first stint of my ethnographic research among the Songhay people. In the background, the syncopated rhythms of the West African lute, the *mollo*, competed with the sonorous voice of a local talk radio host going on and on about personal responsibility and the war in Iraq.

Because it had been months since we had seen one another, Boubé, who was busy arranging his goods, dropped a bag and came forward to shake my hand.

"How is your health?" he asked. "And how is the health of your house?" he asked in the typical West African manner.

"It's good," I responded.

Boubé pulled out two metal folding chairs. "Sit. I'll go and find you some coffee." Carrying their own folding chairs, other traders joined us. Issifi Mayaki, a Nigerien who sold jewelry, sat down next to me as did Moussa Boureyma, another Nigerien who sold hats and shawls.

We greeted one another and began to catch up. I talked to them about my work and travels. They talked about the business climate and their travels to African heritage festivals across the United States. Issifi had just returned from Atlanta, Moussa from Chicago. A few minutes later Boubé returned with coffee. Our talk ranged from U.S. and African politics, one of our favorite topics, to the considerable curiosities of life in the United States.

As our discussion unfolded, other West Africans merchants walked over to join us. Soon we had become a group of eight men and one woman. When a passerby demonstrated some interest in a product in one of the shops, the shopkeeper would peel away from our conversation, converse with the customer, make a sale or not make a sale, and return to the group.

The Malcolm Shabazz Harlem Market has been one of the few places I know in the United States where people still take time to engage in unhurried conversation. True to form, our discussions continued for hours. As our talk progressed so did our consumption of coffee and tea. When a late afternoon lunch materialized, we moved from the stall area to the market's open space where we found an available picnic table. Grimy-windowed apartment buildings towered over us to the left and right, giving our picnic space a distinctly urban feel. And yet, when Boubé passed out plastic spoons and opened two Styrofoam containers, the pungent aroma of African food transported me to rural West Africa. Even though we found ourselves in central Harlem, the sharp smells of Senegalese *thébudan,* a rice pilaf with fish and vegetables, and *sauce gombo,* a viscous okra sauce with a few chunks of beef, temporarily took me back to my early days in Mehanna, Niger, where, during initial fieldwork, I ate so well that after six months I had gained twenty-five pounds!

We didn't converse very much while we ate. In West Africa eating is a serious business that should not be interrupted by talk. As we ate in relative silence, an African American man approached.

"How's it going, brothers?" he asked.

Issifi Mayaki, who knew the man, asked him to join us.

"Thanks, but I already ate."

"But there is food here," Boubé protested. In most West African societies, if someone invites you to eat, you should accept. If you are full, it is enough to take one or two spoonfuls of food. This gesture demonstrates respect and reinforces social relations. "Sit and eat," Boube insisted.

"That's okay," he said. "Thanks." He looked at our group and then focused on me, the white person at the table. "Who's your friend?" he asked Issifi.

"Paul," Issifi said, pointing at me, "is one of us."

"He doesn't look like one of you," the man interjected.

"But he is," Boubé insisted. "He speaks our language. He lived many years in Niger. He knows my village and my relatives. He knows our customs."

"Is that so?" the man asked me.

"It is true," Boubé stated on my behalf.

"Paul is our brother," Issifi said.

The man stared at me. A large space separated our spheres of understanding, our orientations to the world. "My relationship to these men," I said, "is complicated. We say we are 'brothers' because I have lived in their world and they have lived in mine." I paused a moment for effect. "In West Africa the elders like to say: 'Even if it floats in the river for one hundred years, a log can never become a crocodile.'"

My African friends nodded their agreement.

"What does that mean?" the man asked.

"It means," I answered, "that even though I've lived in Africa, speak an African language, and respect African customs, I'm not an African and will never become one. I am between Africa and America."

———

Indeed, anthropologists are always "between" things—between "being-there," as the late Clifford Geertz put it and "being-here," between two or more languages, between two or more cultural traditions, between two or more apprehensions of reality. Anthropologists are the sojourners of "the between." We go there and absorb a different language, culture, and way of being and return here, where we can never fully resume the lives we had previously led. In this book, I attempt to write about how living anthropology can transform its practitioners, changing our conception of who we are, what we know, and how we apprehend the world.

Living between things can have several existential repercussions. It can simultaneously pull us in two directions so that, in the end, to quote a ritual incantation of the Songhay people of Niger, "you don't know your front side from your back side." This state usually leads to indecision, confusion, and lethargy. The between can also carry us into the ether of what Jean-Paul Sartre famously called "bad faith," a systematic and continuous denial of who we are in the world. In bad faith our vision is so obscured by webs of self-contained illusion that shades of difference are shut out and the brightness of wonder is dimmed. In bad faith we see, as David MacDougall has recently written, but we don't look.[1] If, however, we find a way to draw strength from both sides of the between and breathe in the creative air of indeterminacy, we can find ourselves in a space of enormous growth, a space of power and creativity. For me, that is the power of the between and the subject of this book.

———

During a televised interview, Robert Gardner, the highly regarded and highly provocative documentary filmmaker, posed this question to Jean Rouch, one of the most creative spirits in the worlds of anthropology and

Jean Rouch and the author at Rouch 2000, a retrospective of his work at New York University. Photograph by Françoise Foucault.

cinema. "Jean Rouch," he asked, "are you an anthropologist or are you a filmmaker?"

"Well," Rouch smiled, "anthropologists think I'm a filmmaker and filmmakers think I'm an anthropologist."[2] He smiled at Gardner and said nothing further. For Rouch, that boundary-defining question was beside the point. Just as the Songhay sorcerer lives in a space between the village and bush, between the world of social life and the world of the spirits, just as the cancer patient in remission lives in a space between health and ill-ness, so Rouch lived between France and West Africa, between ethnogra-phy and fiction, between anthropology and film—a liminal figure par ex-cellence. Rouch understood the creative power of being between things.

The idea of the between is a central concept in Moroccan mystical thinking. In his thoughtful and elegantly argued book, *Imaginative Hori-zons*, Vincent Crapanzano describes how Moulay Abedsalem, his Moroc-can friend and mentor, thought of "the between." For Moulay Abedsalem, the between is "*barzakh*, and *barzakh* . . . is what lies between things—be-tween edges, borders, and events. He likened it to the silence between words and to dreams. 'The dream is between waking life and sleep,' he said, using the expression 'little death' for sleep to emphasize, I believe, the absence (*ghaib*) he, like other Moroccans, associated with sleep and dreaming."[3] The notion of the between has deep roots in Sufi thought. It is a central tenet in the philosophy of the Andalusian Sufi, Ibn al-'Arabi (1165–1240). Al-'Arabi says that the between is . . .

something that separates . . . two other things, while never going to one side . . . , as for example, the line that separates shadow from sun light. God says, "he let forth the two seas that meet together, between them a *barzakh* they do not overpass (Koran 55:19); in other words one sea does not mix with the other . . . .Any two adjacent things are in need of *barzakh*, which is neither one nor the other but which possesses the power . . . of both. The *barzakh* is something that separates a known from an unknown, an existent from a non-existent, a negated from an affirmed, an intelligible from a non-intelligible.[4]

In al-'Arabi's mystical world, the imagination, like the between, like the state of disease remission, is indeterminate. "At times it appears to be 'between' the spiritual and material—the sensuous—world; at others 'between' being and nothingness, as somehow equivalent to existence. The important point is that the imagination is an intermediate 'reality,' inherently ambiguous, and best described as 'it is neither this nor that or both this and that.'"[5] Put another way, the imaginative interstices of the between become, for many of us, spaces of ambiguity that can generate fear and anxiety, as when the cancer patient attempts to negotiate the indeterminate space between health and illness. And yet, dwelling in the between, or what Arnold Van Gennep and then Victor Turner called the liminal, can also be illuminating. Reconnecting the liminal to the nuanced medieval Sufism of al-'Arabi, Crapanzano wrote:

The liminal has often been likened to the dream . . . It suggests imaginative possibilities that are not necessarily available to us in everyday life. Through paradox, ambiguity, contradiction, bizarre, exaggerated, and at times grotesque symbols—masks, costumes, and figurines—and the evocation of transcendent realities, mystery and supernatural powers, the liminal offers us a view of the world to which we are normally blinded by the usual structures of social and cultural life.[6]

The liminal, then, can be a space of creative imagination, of provocative linkages, of *barzakh*, of personal empowerment. When anthropologists, filmmakers, or writers mix these elements into a narrative, their stories not only evoke the things most deeply human, but do so in way that underscores the existential multiplicities of social life in a complex world.

———

My first full exposure to being between things took place in Tera, Niger, in the spring of 1970. I had joined the Peace Corps in the summer of 1969 and, because I had studied French in college, was assigned to Francophone Africa. From a choice of seven countries, I picked Niger, perhaps the poorest and most "traditional" nation in West Africa. "Traditional" meant that only a small percentage of the Nigerien population spoke French, a fact that would compel me to learn an African language. Peace Corps Niger posted me to Tera, an isolated town west of the Niger River, where I was to teach English as a foreign language at the regional secondary school.

Even if you had a private car, which I didn't, it took a long time to travel the 180 kilometers from Niamey, Niger's dusty capital, to Tera, the largest Nigerien settlement west of the Niger River. Between Niamey and Tera none of the roads were paved, which meant that flat tires and broken axels were not infrequent roadside occurrences. You also had to cross the Niger River on an old ferry whose engine broke down at least once a week. Given its isolation, many people in Tera had little experience with Europeans, let alone Americans.

When I first arrived in Tera in October 1969, I embraced this set of "traditional" conditions. I was twenty-two years old and had led a relatively sheltered life in the suburbs of Washington, D.C. Because I wanted to be a novelist, I thought that my immersion in "traditional" Africa would inspire me to write fiction. In due course, I installed myself in a three-room cement villa on the secondary school campus. Through exposure to sand and dust, the villa's whitewashed exterior had been dulled to a brownish hue. Inside, the dwelling had whitewashed walls, smooth cement floors, shutters rather than windows, ceiling fans that, due to the absence of electricity, did not work, and "running" water that "ran" from a hose siphoned to a rusty water-laden 100-liter metal barrel that been secured onto the tin roof.

Despite my literary ambitions, I fell into an expatriate kind of life. Mornings and afternoons I taught my classes. At noon and at sunset, I ate with my French colleagues—soups, pastas, couscous, much mutton, and a great deal of cheap Spanish wine. At night I retired to my villa, where I studied French and Songhay in the dim glow of a kerosene lantern.

My favorite time of day was the late afternoon. As the heat subsided at the end of the school day, I'd go with my French friends to the only bar in Tera, Chez Jacob, a small mud-brick room that housed a kerosene refrigerator. Outside the entrance to Chez Jacob were two wooden benches, where we would sit, savor the late afternoon breezes, and drink large bottles of Kronenbourg beer. As we quenched our thirst, we would talk about the rundown condition of the school, the strengths and weaknesses of our students, and the politics in Niger, France, and the United States. After several beers, we might even talk about feelings of loneliness and alienation, our loves won and lost, and our dreams for the future. Separated by space, culture, and social standing, we knew little about the lives of the men, women, and children, mostly Songhay, among whom we lived. So much for cultural immersion!

An incident in April 1970 changed everything—at least for me. By that time, my Songhay had improved and I was able to have rudimentary conversations with my neighbors. On a particularly hot Thursday afternoon I went with my French friends, a skinny math teacher from Paris and a burly geography teacher from Toulouse, to drink beer at Chez Jacob. A crowd of people had gathered in a dusty open space opposite the bar. In the distance, I could hear music: the clack of drums and the whine of what seemed to be a violin. In response to the rhythmic music, people danced, kicking up clouds of dust.

A short, thin old man dressed in a white tunic that covered white trousers walked by and smiled. He had wrapped a black turban around his head.

"What's taking place over there, Soumana?" I asked him in Songhay. When I came to town, I would often talk with this man.

"They are looking for the spirits to come, Monsieur Paul," he stated.

"Spirits?" I asked.

"You know," Soumana said in a raspy voice, "they live in the bush and sometimes come to the village and take a body."

"I see," I said with some no small amount of skepticism.

Soumana nodded and wandered into the crowd.

I told my French friends what Soumana had said.

"I've heard that the Songhay have spirit possession," the burly geography teacher stated.

Having never seen or imagined anything like a spirit possession dance, I looked on with keen interest. Suddenly the music stopped. From the dance grounds, deep groans could be heard. I stood up on the bench and tried to see what was going on. Amid the crowd, I saw a young man, dressed in a white laboratory coat, twirling around. Saliva that had oozed from his mouth had dried on his chin in patches. Like a soldier, he saluted people in the crowd and then offered to shake hands.

Meanwhile, Soumana rushed back to Chez Jacob. He pointed to the figure in the laboratory coat, "He wants to meet you, Monsieur Paul."

My heart pounded. "I don't think I want to meet him," I said, a bit breathlessly.

A medium possessed by a Hauka spirit, Tillaberi, Niger, June 1977.
Photograph by the author.

"But if you don't," Soumana insisted, "it will be very bad for us in Tera. He will sicken our children." He grabbed my forearm. "Please."

Soumana led me to the open space. People in the crowed greeted me. The man in the laboratory coat held a syringe and talked to a woman and her child in the mixture of Songhay and broken French. He turned and saw me standing with Soumana. His eyes blazed with a feverish power. The vein in his forehead was swollen and throbbing. He then goose-stepped in my direction, planted his feet squarely in front of me, and extended his open hand

"Enchanté," he said.

"Enchanté," I responded, not knowing what else to say and afraid to take his hand.

"Your mother," he shouted in Songhay, "has no tits."

"Yes, she does," I said instinctively.

Laughter erupted.

"Your father has no balls."

"Yes, he does," I protested.

More laughter shot through the air.

"Enchanté," the man said once again as he extended his open hand.

When we shook hands, his touch somehow sent shock waves through my body as if I had touched a live wire.

Soumana tugged my arm and led me back to Chez Jacob. "Thank you for meeting him," he said.

"Who was that man?" I asked, still stunned from the handshake.

"He is a Hauka spirit—not a man. We call him *lokotoro* (the doctor).[7]

This "shocking" encounter turned my carefully constructed world upside down. The Hauka, I discovered that evening, were a family of Songhay spirits that mimicked Europeans and European culture. Why would such mimicry exist in Niger? Why would the "spirit" make fun of my mother and father? Was there a world of the spirits, as most Songhay believed, that mirrored the everyday world? More fundamentally, how could a "spirit" take over the body of a man? How could a "spirit" make people sick? Why did his handshake send shock waves through my body?

In 1970 I had no idea how to think about these questions. I told myself that what I had seen was nothing more than theater, the construction of an artful illusion. The so-called world of the spirits, I said to myself, was an elaborate fiction. Spirits could not possibly exist; they could not make people sick. Given my cultural socialization, these rational explanations made perfect sense. Even so, a sense of existential uncertainty lingered in my mind. I had seen—and felt—something so shocking that my assumptions about the world had been challenged. Although I couldn't verbalize it at the time, my encounter with the Hauka had thrust me into the indeterminacy of the between. For the first time in my life, I had fully experienced the uncertain feeling of being between things, of being neither this nor that. My otherworldly meeting with the Hauka palpably put me between Niger and the United States, between Songhay experience and American culture, between spirit and substance, between illusion and reality.

The discomfort of being between things in Tera impelled me to begin my explorations of the Songhay world. That year, I studied the Songhay language, talked with elderly men and women, and attended spirit possession ceremonies whenever I could. The following year, Peace Corps Niger reassigned me to the secondary school in Tillaberi, a town on the east bank of the Niger River some 120 kilometers north of the Nigerien capital. In Tillaberi, the late afternoon sounds of spirit possession music eventually led me to the dune-top home of Adamu Jenitongo, who invited me to attend ceremonies in his compound. I became a frequent visitor. At the end of my Peace Corps tour in June 1971, I wanted to study and ultimately understand" the Songhay spirit world. In retrospect, it was my "meeting" with the Hauka in Tera, the first of many experiences of being in the between, that marked the beginning of a scholarly path that has taken me far and wide in search of explanations, knowledge, and wisdom.

––––––

This book is a kind of disciplinary memoir in a different key. It is the story of my life in anthropology, of my attempt to understand the social and cultural complexities of contemporary life, of my struggle to write about life in the world. In this book I suggest that acknowledging the power of the anthropological between is an insightful way to make better sense of the quandaries of human being.

The Power of the Between consists of a series of relatively short chapters that in various ways explore the vicissitudes of contemporary social and intellectual life. None of the chapters take the form of academic essays that can usually be found in scholarly journals. These are often written in an unencumbered impersonal style. In this book, I attempt to blend personal narrative and analytic discourse, for living and doing anthropology, no matter how obliquely we represent the experience of "being there," is intensely personal. In one way or another, then, the chapters in this work attempt to integrate "being there" with "being here" to consider the central issues in the social sciences—culture, power, social change, and human resilience—issues that underscore those things—love, fear, pain, courage—that define the human condition.

1

Seeking Truth

Soon after my return to the United States in 1971, I began graduate studies. At that time, I hoped that my studies would one day get me back to Niger so that I might understand better the mysteries of the Songhay spirit world. In the 1970s social science generated a great deal of excitement in the academy. Many social scientists of this era believed that through the application of sound methods and theory you could discover principles that governed social behavior. Many linguists suggested that by understanding the "deep structures" of syntax, they could unlock the mysteries of human cognition. Many anthropologists, especially in Great Britain, thought that if you engaged in the rigorous comparative analysis of the structures of society, you could discover "deep" rules that would explain the inner workings of social life. In France, Claude Lévi-Strauss argued—quite persuasively, I should add—that the comparative study of kinship, art, and myth would reveal universal principles of cognition. Once revealed, these might solve the mystery of how people think. Ethnomethodologists like Harold Garfinkle and Gail Jefferson used the study of conversation to isolate "rules" that seemed to govern how people interact. No matter the approach that the scholars of this era followed, most of them believed that systematic analysis could scrape away the highly variable surfaces of social reality to reveal the deep truth of things. Like their cousins in the natural sciences, most social scientists of that time engaged in what John Dewey called "the quest for certainty," the rigorous and systematic attempt to transform social chaos into cultural order.[1]

I was first exposed to the excitement of seeking truth as a linguistics student at Georgetown University. In the late 1960s and early 1970s Georgetown was a center of great innovation in linguistics. At the venerable School of Languages and Linguistics, graduate students received rigorous training in morphology, phonology, semantics, and transformational syntax. We read the classics of structural linguistics—Bloomfield and Trubetzkoy—as well as the "new" more "radically" conceptual linguistics of Noam Chomsky and his students.[2] The divide between the structuralists and transformationalists became palpably evident during plenary sessions of the annual Georgetown Round Table on Languages and Linguistics. Indeed, the spatial allocation of Walsh Hall auditorium demonstrated generational, intellectual, and sartorial division. Scores of young males of the "transformationalist" persuasion, for example, sat on the left side of the room, many of us having grown long hair and beards, most of us dressed in jeans, tee shirts, and sweaters. Scores of older men of the die-hard structuralist persuasion, by contrast, sat on the right side of the room, the buzz cutter having left many of them fuzzy-topped. Most of them sported what seemed like lumpy dark suits, white shirts, and narrow ties. Transformationalist women tended to have long hair and wore jeans or slacks. Structuralist women usually had short hair and wore skirts and white blouses.

The professors in my program, sociolinguistics, demonstrated an infectious enthusiasm for their research on vernacular Black English. Scholars like Roger Shuy, Ralph Fasold, Walt Wolfram, and William Labov of the University of Pennsylvania, who would sometimes come to lecture, used sociological data to refine the linguistic theory of their day, suggesting that syntactic rules, like those described by Chomsky and other transformationalists, could not exist in a context-free ether. They argued that social context had to be computed into the matrix of linguistic rules. Meanwhile, Dell Hymes, who at the time also taught at the University of Pennsylvania, had developed the ethnography of communication, a research framework within which scholars considered how the socio-cultural context might shape culturally specific linguistic interaction.

Having already had a two-year West African experience in the Republic of Niger, the ethnographic approach to the study of language very much appealed to me. And so I left Georgetown and found myself an advanced graduate student at the University of Texas at Austin. There I learned about French structuralism, debated the whys and wherefores of ethnomethodology, and renewed a longstanding interest in existentialism and phenomenology. During my years in Austin, I had the chance to meet such scholars as Erving Goffman and Mary Douglas. The late Annette Weiner, who was then an assistant professor at the University of Texas conducting ongoing fieldwork in the anthropologically famous Trobriand Islands, insisted we read anthropological classics—among many others, Malinowski's Trobriand work, Radcliffe-Brown's work on the Andaman Islands, Raymond Firth's ethnography of the Tikopia.[3]

Infused with this rush of anthropological theory, I set off in the fall of 1975 to attend for the first time the annual meetings of the American Anthropological Association. Determined to drive straight through to our destination, four of us—starving graduate students all—piled into an unheated, rusted-out Volkswagen Bug and made our way from Austin, Texas, to San Francisco. We drove west on Interstate 10 across the Permian Basin, crossed the Pecos River at sunset and headed toward El Paso and New Mexico. In the middle of the cold night, somewhere between Winslow, Arizona, and Phoenix, we all got stoned, which, I suppose, is what you were supposed to do on a cold night in the desert back then. Indeed, our altered state quickly made our difficult travel circumstances a bit easier to bear. Soon enough hunger pangs gripped us, forcing a much-needed exit to a Phoenix diner, where we ordered a table full of pancakes. Our detour, though, didn't radically derail our plan to drive to San Francisco. We devoured our food in short order and were once again headed west. We soon discovered, however, that in our collective altered state, no one had remembered to fill up the gas tank. At dawn we ran out of gas in the middle of the Sonora Desert. With the help of two retirees in an RV, we siphoned enough gas to make it to the next service station. After a minor engine breakdown, we finally limped into San Francisco, unloaded our gear at a cheap hotel, and made our way up Nob Hill to the Fairmont Hotel, the site of the anthropology meetings. Excited, we entered the hotel.

My friend took in a deep breath. "Can you smell it, Paul?"

"Smell what?" I asked.

He smiled. "Structuralism," he said. "There's structuralism in the air."

During the four days of the meetings, I presented my first paper—on the "logical rules" of Songhay greetings, but unfortunately never sensed the aromatic contours of structuralism.

One year after the 1975 trip to San Francisco, I returned to the Republic of Niger to conduct fieldwork among the Songhay people. By that time, my training in the social sciences was, or so I thought, fairly well developed. I knew how to do phonetic transcriptions and how to write the grammar of an unwritten language. I knew how to compile a demographic census, construct and administer an interview instrument and do a qualitative analysis of its results. I intended to use this tool kit of methods to generate data that would describe Songhay sociolinguistic processes. I wanted to understand how the ritual language of spirit possession ceremonies played in the game of local Songhay politics. These data might then be used to refine knowledge of how language is used in the competition for power, which, in turn, would make a small contribution to social and linguistic theory. In the larger scope of things, the research results might bring us a small step closer to the truth, which, in turn, would help me to understand the whys and wherefores of spirit possession. I was well on my way to becoming a Seeker of the Truth.

The rigorous pursuit of the truth, I discovered through long hours of graduate school reading, thinking, and debate, has had a long history in the academy. It is part and parcel of the concept of rationality, which, in its universal form, suggests that you can isolate Truth through the precision of language and logic. In this view finding the Truth, which was then my goal, is a matter of analyzing statements for coherence and logical consistency. Rational beliefs, for example, would be those that would adhere to the universal rules of coherence and logical consistency.

Logical inconsistency may seem the core of our concept of irrationality, because we think of the person who acts irrationally as having the wherewithal to formulate maxims of his action and objectives which are in contradiction with each other.[4]

Viewed in this manner, you could say that a universal rationality is an extension of the Enlightenment project in which universally applied reason is used to constitute "truthful" knowledge.

Although there has been considerable agreement about the centrality of logical consistency to the constitution of universally rational statements and beliefs, I discovered that there is divergence on three related issues about how rational thought might explain human behavior, how it might account for human choices:

1. Can rational intentionality explain social behavior?
2. Do individual predispositions affect rational choice?
3. Is rational choice free of social context?

The first two questions are fascinating but less germane to a discussion of rationality in anthropology than the third question, which confronts the seemingly unending debate about relativism in the human sciences.

As already stated, the universal rationalists, like my early heroes Chomsky and Lévi-Strauss, believe in a singular rationality founded upon transcendent principles of logic that are universally applicable no matter the sociocultural context.[5] Armed with these context-free rules, scholars like Chomsky believe they could make sense of any phenomenon they encounter. Further, using logical criteria, they attempt to measure the relative rationality/irrationality of a system of belief. Assessing evidence that consists of a set of statements about belief, they make judgments. In the end, universal rationalists seek to transform the tangle of irrational beliefs into a coherent set of logical explanations. I found many examples of anthropologists who followed this well-worn path.

Consider the ideas of Robin Horton, an anthropologist who has lived for many years in West Africa. In his writing, Horton admits that African systems of thought are capable of what he calls cohesive "theoretical" thinking. He suggests that African traditional thought is rational but wonders if it is rational enough. "At this stage of the analysis there is no need for me to insist further on the essential rationality of traditional thought. I have already made it far too rational for the taste of most social anthropologists. And yet, there is a sense in which this thought includes among its accomplishments neither Logic or Philosophy."[6] For Horton, African systems of thought are sophisticated but closed, unable "to . . . formulate generalized norms of reasoning and knowing."[7] Horton's take on African thought is somewhat similar to that of E. E. Evans-Pritchard in his work, *Witchcraft, Magic and Oracles among the Azande.* Both scholars applaud the previously overlooked sophistication of African thinking, but in the end they maintain a universal take on rationality in which they find African systems of thought logically and philosophically inferior.

Dan Sperber, also an anthropologist, unequivocally embraces a universal rationality that he seeks to refine.[8] He pinpoints weaknesses in what he calls the intellectualist orientation (a strict universalism). Surveying the ethnographic literature, Sperber finds many cases that defy a strict universal rationality. By expanding the horizons of a universal rationality, Sperber contends, one can make sense of "apparently irrational beliefs." Sperber's primary criticism of relativists is that they are blithely unaware of the psychological ramifications of their views.

Sperber's scheme gets rather complicated, for he proposes a universal rationalist approach that embraces both propositional and semipropositional representations as well as factual and representational beliefs. Propositional representations, according to Sperber, are fully understood ideas; the semipropositional idea is one that is partially understood. Factual beliefs are the sum of representations in a person's memory as well as the representations that he or she is able to infer from that which is stored in memory. Representational beliefs, by contrast, consist of a nebulous set of linked attitudes that usually lack universal application. Sperber uses a matrix of these elements to assess the rationality of reported beliefs. Factual beliefs based upon propositional content are rational. Factual beliefs based on semipropositional content are irrational. Representational beliefs based on propositional content are weak candidates for rationality. "That cultural beliefs are representational is almost tautologous; that they are semi-propositional is implicit and even sometimes explicit in the way people express and discuss them. There are many implications to this view of cultural beliefs . . . but only one concerns us here: relativism can be dispensed with."[9] In sum, Sperber goes to elaborate lengths to clear rational space for cultural beliefs within a rigidly formulated universal rationalist paradigm. In the end, however, Sperber's project is a psychologically sophisticated extension of Evans-Pritchard's and Horton's universal positions on rationality.

Although the work of Horton and Sperber has been significant in anthropology, it is the extraordinary work of Claude Lévi-Strauss that extends the project of universal rationality to all of the human sciences. Although Lévi-Strauss's work has concerned such diverse subjects as kinship, totemism, myth, and art, the central goal of his structuralism, the "aroma" of which had so permeated the atmosphere at the 1975 meetings of the American Anthropological Association, is to uncover "elementary forms," abstract structures of categorization that underlie all social and cultural diversity. In structuralism, Lévi-Strauss extends the structural methods of linguistics, something familiar to me, to cultural analysis. In phonology, for example, an individual phoneme, /p/, is meaningless in and of itself. Its meaning is contingent upon its relation to the other phonemes in a language. By extension, an individual cultural datum—the power of an individual shaman or a particular kinship or marriage practice—is an isolated element, the true meaning of which becomes clear only when it is situated in a system of relations.

In his first major work, *The Elementary Structures of Kinship,* Lévi-Strauss presents a mind-boggling array of kinship and marriage practices. In his thorough analysis, he seeks unity in diversity, and at the end of the volume he isolates what he calls the "atoms of kinship," a core, universal structure to which all forms of kinship and marriage can be reduced. In his influential essay, "The Sorcerer and His Magic," Lévi-Strauss argues that the various individual acts of sorcerers are less important than how they fit into a system that relates sorcerer, patient, and group traditions of health and sickness. In his study of myth, Lévi-Strauss suggests "if there is a meaning to be found in mythology, it cannot reside in isolated elements which enter into the composition of the myth, but only in the way those elements combine."[10] In analyzing how the elements combine, Lévi-Strauss isolates in mythical thought a "kind of logic . . . as rigorous as that of modern science."[11] He suggests further that the only difference between mythical and scientific thought lies "in the nature of things to which it is applied."[12] Although human thought patterns, like human practices of kinship, marriage, and sorcery, may vary considerably, there exists for Lévi-Strauss abstract universal structures of human cognition.

In sum, Lévi-Strauss's structuralism constitutes one of the most powerful arguments for a universal rationality. Although Lévi-Strauss does not deny sociological difference, he reduces its specificity to theoretical insignificance. In his scheme the diversity of local nuance is lost in the unity of universalism.

———

For me, structuralism became the perfect machine for seeking the truth of social life. It fit well with my previous training in linguistics. If you plugged in carefully collected sociocultural data—kinship and marriage practices, the symbolic array of non-Western art, and structural patterning of myths, the machine spat out universal principles that transcended culturally specific data. Once isolated through structuralist analysis, these pristine principles took us many steps closer to a systematic understanding of ritual symbolism—of the Hauka, for example. On a broader plain, it promised to give us a better understanding of the processes of human cognition and, by extension, a deeper comprehension of the human condition.

Alternative Truths

Considering the very good fit between structuralist sensibilities and my graduate training in linguistics and social anthropology, imagine my elation at the news that I had been awarded a grant to spend the 1977–78 academic year in Paris at Claude Lévi-Strauss's Laboratoire d'Anthropologie Sociale (LAS). Because there was much about structuralism that I didn't understand, I thought that one year chez Lévi-Strauss would certainly refine my awareness of important binary oppositions that would, in turn, give me the wherewithal to make better sense of my spirit possession data from Niger, especially my notes on Hauka spirit possession. What's more, the year would give me time to read, think, debate, and write.

In 1978 the LAS was housed in the most prestigious of French academic institutions, Le Collège de France, founded in 1530 by King François I. The LAS could be found on the second floor of a classically styled building on the rue des Écoles, constructed in 1779, that housed the offices and classrooms of the Collège de France. A walk into the courtyard of the College de France is a physical confrontation with an extraordinary intellectual history. There were statues or plaques that preserved the memory of intellectual giants, past Collège professors all, who like Maurice Merleau-Ponty, lectured to the public—truly free and open events. Once through the courtyard, if you were going to LAS, you walked up two flights of creaky stairs and entered Lévi-Strauss's domain, which had an extensive library, a small conference room, and, I was told, a very good photocopying budget.

BIBLIOTHEQUE DU MUSEE DE L'HOMME

Nom : STOLLER   Prénom : Paul

Nationalité : Américaine

Adresse : 11, Place Marcelin Berthelot
PARIS 5°

Profession : Chercheur: Professeur

Société :

Diplômes possédés : Anthropologie, Sociol.

Travaux en cours : Projet sur la langue
et la magie Songhay.

Signature du Titulaire :

Le Conservateur en Chef :

F. Weil

1979

The author during his year chez Lévi-Strauss.

My sponsor at LAS was the indefatigable Madame Suzanne Bernus, a wonderful woman who, like me, did ethnographic work in Niger. Although her early research focused on the urban relations of Niger's capital city, the bulk of her work described the social life of the Tuareg nomads of northern Niger. When I met her in 1978, Suzie, who died tragically in a car accident in Mali in the early 1990s, was a robust woman in her midforties. She wore thick glasses that partially obscured the brilliance of her green eyes. When you met her you sensed immediately that she was the sort of person who tirelessly extended herself to others.

In our initial conversations, we talked a great deal about Niger, spirit possession, and the plight of the Tuaregs, but never broached the subject of structuralism or anthropological theory.

"Well, Suzie," I said, after several of these purely ethnographic conversations, "I have to ask a most important question."

"Which is?" she asked, leaning forward in her chair in the Section Africaniste, a cramped office at the top of the aforementioned creaky stairwell, just to the right of the LAS entrance.

"Since I am in the house of Lévi-Strauss," I paused for effect," I have to ask: What is structuralism?"

Suzie Bernus burst out laughing. "Well," she said taking in a breath and smiling. "No one around here really knows, Paul. Only Monsieur Lévi-

Strauss knows the answer to that one." She smiled at me and fumbled at some papers. "By the way, as a research associate, you will, of course, have to meet with Monsieur Lévi-Strauss. He'll want to know about your research plans."

"When do I meet him?" I asked.

"In fact, you meet him tomorrow at 10:00 a.m. I'll take you in." She fumbled more papers. "Don't be late. Monsieur Lévi-Strauss is very conscious of time."

The next morning, Suzie Bernus took me through the massive leather-padded double doors that opened to Lévi-Strauss's corner office, which that day was awash in late September sunlight. The austerity of the space struck me—very few books, a few spare wooden tables covered with neatly arranged papers. Arranged on a corner bookshelf was an array of photographs. The largest of these was a portrait of the late Maurice Merleau-Ponty, Lévi-Stauss's close friend and a philosopher of rather unstructuralist sensibilities. To the left of the double doors, there was a salon-like space—a small coffee table atop a small Persian carpet, atop a parquet floor. Several comfortable leather chairs made the salon seem downright cozy.

Lévi-Strauss, who that day wore a dull gray suit, a white shirt, and a thin black tie, was taller than I had imagined. He asked us to sit down. Seconds later, his assistant entered with coffee. Although I had been nervous about meeting such a famous scholar, Lévi-Strauss put me immediately at ease. He graciously welcomed me to his research group and invited me to use the facilities. He asked about my previous research and my plans for future publication. Then he asked me about life in the United States. We talked about New York City. He encouraged me to attend the public lectures at the Collège de France. To my disappointment, he said not a word about structuralism, and I was far too intimidated to ask him my "most important" question.

I did attend many lectures in the ground-floor auditorium of the Collège de France. Although Lévi-Strauss's rather dry presentations were quite interesting, I found the public lectures of his Collège de France colleagues much more intriguing. That year, I sat in on Roland Barthes' lectures on photography and witnessed the performances of Michel Foucault, who, for his famous lectures on the history of sexuality, would sometimes float into the packed auditorium wearing a fabulous black cape. These more dynamic considerations of history, culture, and representation seemed to provide better theoretical frameworks for the data from Niger that begged far more context-sensitive explanations of the poetics and power of Songhay sorcery and spirit possession.

When I arrived in Paris I had thought that structuralism might tame the shocking wildness of Songhay sorcery and spirit possession, especially the case of the Hauka. Ironically, my exposure to the world of structuralism had the opposite effect; it led me to cast critical doubt on rationalist projects in which universal principles rendered invisible and insignificant local cultural realties.

———

My year in Paris convinced me that there was no singular rationality, but several alternate rationalities, based upon diverse sets of rules, distinct Wittgensteinian language games, specific "ways of worldmaking," many of which might prove to be inconsistent.[1] In time, I began to think critically about a central tenant in cultural anthropology—relativism. Over time, here's what I discovered.

Relativists seek to understand the nuances of local context in the hopes that they avoid making insensitive analytic errors. Given the density of other systems of belief, they believe that it is best not to make judgments of relative rationality/irrationality. One of the great achievements of Evans-Pritchard's Azande work on the logics of magical practices is that it was the first scholarly treatise to consider a set of non-Western beliefs as something more than a jumble of irrational superstitions. In so doing he demonstrated that non-Western systems of beliefs, like those that many Songhay hold about sorcery and spirit possession, could be highly sophisticated in their own right. Although many contemporary scholars who are relativists no longer adhere strictly to an absolute relativism, they remain consistently critical of an absolute universal rationality. This move is an attempt to temper relativism with good sense.

Stanley Tambiah is one anthropologist who tempered relativism with good sense. Like many contemporary relativists, he considered an uncritical cultural relativism untenable. Using Hilary Putman's quip that if all is relative, then the relative is relative too, Tambiah suggested that in radical relativism critical judgments are impossible. Can we excuse, he wondered, the Holocaust or apartheid in the name of cultural relativism? In contrast with Dan Sperber, however, Tambiah believed that all symbolic expression or action cannot be transformed into some form of logical proposition, a key criterion for a universal rationality. He cautioned scholars about the dangers of using the criteria of Western rationality as a judgmental yardstick: "[T]he universal rationalist should beware of too cavalierly underrating the difficulties that have to be surmounted in the process of translation between cultures, or of artificially overrating the status requirement that all discourse be reduced or transformed intro the verifiable propositional format of logicians."[2] Given these difficulties, Tambiah steered a moderate course through the debate. He believed that scholars should strive for comparisons and generalizations where they are appropriate, but, like the Songhay sages, he urged patience. He wrote that "to declare that two phenomena seem incommensurable in our present state of knowledge does not automatically put you in the relativist camp or deny the possibility of measurement at some future time."[3] Such a position enables the scholar to maintain that religions adhere to a set of existential universals and constraints and yet differ in fundamental ways.[4]

Clifford Geertz, for his part, was less ecumenical in his assessment of a universal rationality. In his well-known and much-cited essay "Anti-anti Relativism," he criticized the attempts of Sperber and Horton to erase relativism from the anthropological landscape. Although he believed that relativism is an ill-defined and tired concept, he objected to the intellectual moves of Ernest Gellner, another well-known rationalist, Horton, and especially Sperber "to save us from ourselves."[5] Evoking the universality of cognitive processes, rationalist antirelativism for Geertz was the attempt to undermine cultural diversity. "As with 'Human Nature,' the construction of otherness is the price of truth. Perhaps, but it is not what either the history of anthropology, the materials it has assembled, or the ideals that have animated it would suggest."[6] "The objection to anti-relativism is not that it rejects an it's-all-how-you-look-at it approach to knowledge or a when-in-Rome approach to morality, but that it imagines they can only be defeated by placing morality beyond culture and knowledge beyond both. This speaking of things which must needs to be so, is no long possible. If we wanted home truths, we should have stayed at home."[7] The major projects of a universal rationality, like those of Lévi-Strauss, have been by and large developed, according to Geertz, by scholars who had indeed stayed at home. Can a universal rationality be reconciled with experience? Geertz said no.

How might we apply this thoughtful relativism to explain my encounter with the Hauka in 1970? In his thoughtful essay "Witchcraft and Selfcraft," Terrance M. S. Evens spoke to the epistemological importance of experience. He thought that the anthropological record productively—based upon (field) experience—confounded the neat and tidy distinctions drawn by universalists like Sperber. For him the otherness of the Hauka, for example, should not be obliterated by narrowly drawn rules of reason. Evens would like for scholars to approach the quandaries of otherness through the philosophy of Emmanuel Levinas in which the difference between self and other is "no less reducible than relative, such that it can be meaningfully engaged but not finally resolved."[8] Distancing himself from the universal rationalists, Evens placed himself in the between. In such exotic systems of belief as the Azande, he found a truth worth knowing. It was, however, an inassimilable truth that was beyond our world, beyond our reason, which exacted a fundamental cost—"the cost of the world as we know it, which is to say, not the enrichment, as one may used to hearing, but the veritable transformation of our-selves."[9] Here Evens took the relativist position that other systems of knowledge contained much wisdom, that we have much to learn from the likes of the Azande or the Hauka, and that such learning could well be personally transformative.[10]

———

Evens made a powerful point, a position that resonated with my experience as a field anthropologist. Even so, I soon discovered that the great problem that underscores the unending debate about rationality is that it ultimately boils down to whether you can accept some version of relativism or universalism. This either/or impasse, a patch of quicksand that you find often in the indeterminate spaces of the between, often resulted in published hand-wringing. Relativists complained that universal rationalists were insensitive, Eurocentric, or even racist. Universal rationalists chided the relativists for their scientific naïveté and epistemological imprecision. The hand-wringing has continued to this day as many anthropologists continue to debate the "scientific" status of anthropology. In this ongoing debate unapologetic universal rationalists still criticize the fuzziness of the radical relativists whom they continue to label as postmodernists. For their part, relativists have often considered the intellectualist "scientific" principles of the universal rationalists as mere illusion. Even the more thoughtful considerations of Geertz, Tambiah, and Evens have not advanced our comprehension beyond the narrowly defined boundaries of the original debate.

What's an anthropologist to do?

Embodiments

By May 1977 I had been doing fieldwork for more than eight months in the town of Mehanna, which is on the west bank of the Niger River, some 150 kilometers north of Niger's capital city, Niamey. Mehanna stands in a place where the westernmost branch of the river carves its way through tawny sand dunes that sometimes rise abruptly from river's edge. There are places just to the north and south of Mehanna where 100-foot-tall wind-contoured dunes tower like monumental sculpture over the river.

Like most Songhay villages in the 1970s, Mehanna had neither running water nor electricity. With the exception of the health dispensary, which featured cement walls, a tin roof, and mostly empty shelves, the other structures in Mehanna consisted of mud-brick walls and leaky daub roofs. These mud-brick compounds, which housed Mehanna's more well-to-do families, lined seven dirt pathways that fanned out from a central square that bordered the river. The poorest residents lived in grass huts they built toward the outskirts of town. By Songhay standards, though, Mehanna was a relatively prosperous town. Its market, held on Thursdays, would draw hundreds of customers of various ethnicities: Tuareg men wrapped in indigo turbans; Fulan women, encased in rough-textured homespun indigo cloth and bedecked with heavy silver earrings that stretched out their earlobes; Yoruba men wearing long shirts fashioned from brightly patterned Dutch Wax cloth that covered a matching set of balloon trousers. People came by dugout, truck, camel, horse, or donkey to sell their goods, buy necessities,

The author during early fieldwork in Mehanna, 1977. Photograph by Sidi Ibrahim.

and spend what was left on a bar of fragrant soap, a Coca Cola, or perhaps on a snack of delicious fried fish.

The town's felicitous proximity to the Niger River usually provided an abundance of food. Men tending riverside gardens routinely harvested lemons, guavas, and mangoes, not to forget manioc and tobacco. You could usually buy fresh meat, slaughtered daily, for reasonable prices from the market butchers. No matter the day, you could cheaply savor the taste of roasted mutton and goat and enjoy the pungent flavor of fish stews.

Like most field anthropologists I worked hard to establish rapport with Mehanna's residents. As the months passed, some people professed to be my friend. Others treated me with indifference. Still others said that they didn't like the presence of an infidel "European" bent on writing a book about their village. In time, though, my work on the strategic use of language in local-level politics took shape. One afternoon, though, an unexpected event compelled me to change course. As I typed my field notes in my two-room daub-roofed mud-brick house, two birds, which had persistently nested in the rafters of my ceiling of sticks, shat on my head. Had I been alone, this event would have simply been yet another field annoyance. But on that day, a rice farmer named Djibo, who happened to be in my house, saw what happened. Djibo, who was a *sorko*, a sorcerer among the Songhay people, interpreted this excretory act as a sign that I should become his apprentice.

"Paul," he said, after proclaiming his thanks to God, "I have seen a sign. I am a sorko," he stated, "and you have been pointed out to me."

"No kidding."

"Tonight you must come to my compound and begin to learn."[1]

Deciding that this was an opportunity I could not pass up, I began a sometimes contentious apprenticeship with Sorko Djibo. He taught me incantations and showed me where to find plants used to treat people for physiological problems ranging from rheumatism to malaria. In time he introduced me to the plants that sorkos mixed in potions to counter attacks of witchcraft. Fate had given me the opportunity to learn about sorcery "from the inside." Although my confrontation with the Hauka had exposed me fully to being between things, learning about sorcery "from the inside" planted me more permanently between America and Africa, between science and religion, between reality and illusion. At the time, of course, I was too busy learning about sorcery to reflect critically about the between. I considered sorcery to be an illusionary means to some sociocultural end. The efficacy of the curative plants was easy enough for me to understand. The isolation of a chemical compound in the plant "explained" how a "tea" might combat malaria or rheumatism. The treatment of witchcraft, which I thought of as a psychological state, seemed symbolic. I hadn't yet learned how to live in indeterminate states, how to empower myself from both sides of the between.

But the anthropological odyssey is full of unexpected surprises that challenge sacred assumptions, which brings me back to May 1977. Sorko Djibo asked me to come with him on a healing mission. A prosperous shopkeeper who had made the pilgrimage to Mecca had been ill for months. This man, one of the most pious Muslims in Mehanna, had been treated at a regional hospital and had been a patient at the National Hospital in Niamey, where he had undergone a battery of tests, none of which had identified his illness. Concluding that the shopkeeper suffered from a psychosomatic illness, the physicians at the hospital sent him home. No one could explain how this psychosomatic disease had caused him to lose so much weight. By the time the shopkeeper had returned to Mehanna, he could no longer walk. Confined to what he thought was his deathbed, the shopkeeper summoned Sorko Djibo, who asked me to assist him in a curing rite.

Early in the morning we walked into shopkeeper's expansive compound that featured his own three-room mud-brick house, three one-room houses, one for each of his wives and their children, two large mud-brick rectangularly shaped granaries set on stilts for millet and a smaller cone-shaped mud-brick granary in which he stored rice. Three cows and a small flock of sheep and goats had been tethered to wooden poles. We found the shopkeeper outside lying like a beached whale on a bed fashioned from sticks. A large acacia protected the bed from the relentless Sahelian sun.

Sorko Djibo in Mehanna performing a sorcerous rite, 1977. Photograph by the author.

From within their deep sockets, the man's eyes blazed with fever. He looked at us with the uncomprehending gaze of the doomed. Gasping for air, he said, "I don't agree with any of this, but what choice do I have?"

"He suffers from witchcraft," Sorko Djibo stated. "His soul has been stolen, and we have to bring the stolen soul back to his body."

"How do you do that?" I asked both with admiration and skepticism.

Sorko Djibo asked one of the man's wives to bring us a basin filled with water. In short order, he kneeled next to the basin, sprinkled an array of powdered plants and barks on the water's surface. Then he poured some perfume into the basin and recited an incantation called "water container."

Turning to the shopkeeper's wife, he said, "Wash your husband with this ablution. Make sure to use up all the water." He turned to me. "We must go and find the man's soul."

Curious of his next step, I followed Sorko Djibo. We took one of Mehanna's seven paths toward the outskirts of town. Mud-brick walls that protected the privacy of people in mud-brick houses soon gave way to fences made of millet stalks that shielded people who lived in grass huts. Trudging through dune sand we slowly made our way to the edge of town, a place where women would pound millet plants, separating the precious seeds from their husks. They would then rake the empty husks into piles that looked like large ant hills.

Without saying a word, Sorko Djibo got down on his knees and crawled though one particular hill of millet husks. In an instant, he jumped up and said: "Praise be to God." He turned to me, a deep smile creasing his face. "Do you see it?" he asked.

"See what?" I asked.

"Did you hear it?"

"Hear what?" I asked again.

"Did you feel it?"

"Feel what?" I asked with increasing frustration.

Sorko Djibo brought his face, which was square and as smooth as a perfectly chiseled piece of black granite, very close to mine. The whites of his eyes glowed a dull red as if someone had backlit a fire somewhere in the recesses of his brain. Slowly he shook his head. "You look," he said, "but you don't see. You listen, but you don't hear. You touch, but you don't feel." He shook his head once again. "Maybe in twenty years," he concluded, "you'll learn to see, hear and feel."[2]

——————

The Songhay people believe that there are certain peak moments in life when the sojourner reaches a fork on the path, a point, they say, of misfortune. This point marks the space between the world of social life and the world of the spirits. It is a space of danger that you must negotiate. Finding oneself at such a point you must choose to go to the left or the right and bear the existential consequences of your choice. At that moment, I did not fully understand the existential importance of Sorko Djibo's approach to the sensory world, but I did reach one important conclusion: I needed guidance along the anthropological path. This revelation compelled me, as mentioned in the previous chapter, to study structuralism and poststructuralism in France. After a year of intense reflection,

I had found those orientations inadequate. I had then grappled with the limiting permutations of relativism. Like the assumptions that give shape to universal rationality, I had also found the principles of relativism wanting. Having drifted into the spaces of the between, I hoped to find a middle path that would enable me to understand the Hauka, an approach that would teach me how to see, hear, and feel.

This middle path eventually led me to consider rationality from a phenomenological vantage that would engage the issues of multiple realities and experience. Phenomenology started with Edmund Husserl, who charted a rigorous methodology, the *epoché,* which would enable observers to apprehend lived reality. This process, which takes several steps, enables the observer to move through several levels of consciousness until he or she grasps the immediacy of the object of observation.

The strategy for beginning, in Husserl's case, was one which called for the elaboration of a step-by-step procedure through which one viewed things differently. His model was one of analogy to various sciences, often analytic in style; thus he built a methodology of steps: epoché, the psychological reduction, the phenomenological reduction, the eidetic reduction and the transcendental reduction. At the end of this labyrinth of technique what was called for was a phenomenological attitude, a perspective from which things are to be viewed.[3]

In the end, the epoché was an effort to return "to the things themselves," to let things speak, to let them show themselves.[4] Put another way, phenomenology "is an attempt to describe human consciousness in its lived immediacy before it is subject to theoretical elaboration or conceptual systematizing."[5] Indeed, in some of the most influential work in religious studies, scholars like Mircea Eliade have employed the phenomenological epoché to assess data from the history of religion.

And yet Husserl's ideas proved to be problematic. Although Husserl influenced a whole generation of philosophers, many of his descendants rejected his inattention to how one lives in the everyday world. They wondered how observers might so purify their perception to experience "lived immediacy." Taking many of these criticisms into consideration Alfred Schutz transformed Husserl's ahistorical abstractions into a set of concrete conceptions that would enable observers to apprehend the chaos of what he, like Husserl, called the "lifeworld."

For Schutz the description of social reality involves neither a singular intellectualist move to transform sets of beliefs and behaviors into universally verifiable propositions that mirror reality nor the naïve relativist move to accept the complete incommensurability of differing systems of belief. For Schutz the individual's interpretation of any event entails the apprehension of multiple realities. The most essential of these is what Schutz called the "natural" attitude, which consists of the socially conditioned mechanisms we use to experience the immediacy of everyday life. The natural attitude shapes the contours of interaction between self and other and is therefore mediated through culture as well as a person's "biographically determined situation." The natural attitude focuses on intersubjectivity. It also enables us to make sense of what Schutz called the "paramount" reality.

Although Schutz problematically privileges the everyday as paramount, he also writes about other attitudes that flesh out our experience of social reality. These other "attitudes" include dreams, fantasy, science, and religion. Schutz demonstrated how these various "attitudes" interpenetrate as we experience the flux of social life.[6]

Critics have faulted Schutz for placing too much emphasis on the "paramount" reality of everyday life. Such logic parallels the rationalist contention that there is a transcendent reality that is prior to other realities. If we equalize the weights of the various "attitudes," however, the epistemological flexibility of Schutz's approach becomes constructive. By employing a multiple realities approach to the question of rationality, one can avoid the niggling problem of how to evaluate what is and what is not rational. In a world of multiple realities, there are several paths, as Sorko Djibo tried to teach me, to the apprehension of social reality.

An Azande following the interpretive procedures of the poison oracle, for example, might employ personally and culturally conditioned aspects of the natural, scientific, and religious attitudes in trying to grasp the social reality of witchcraft. By the same token, an anthropologist, like Evans-Pritchard or Terrence Evens, would also need to apply a range of personally and culturally contoured attitudes to make sense of Azande witchcraft. The quality of social description, then, would depend on how well the Azande and anthropological multiple realities of the Azande world might be reconciled.

Multiple realities, of course, exist within distinct and permeable universes of meaning. From a phenomenological perspective, the nature of your experience, like my experiences as Sorko Djibo's assistant, is the key to reducing distances between universes of meaning. As experience expands with time, the boundaries of the universes may begin to intersect, creating an arena of shared space and interpretation. Some critics argue, of course, that experience may or may not result in increased awareness, let alone personal transformation. And yet, some of the best and most challenging descriptions of cultural practice come from scholars, like Evans-Pritchard, who have spent long periods in the field.

Evans-Pritchard's book *Witchcraft, Oracles and Magic among the Azande* is marked with textual equivocations that may well have resulted from the troubling nature of his experiences among the Azande. He admits to using Azande logic to run the day-to-day affairs of his household. He waffles about the "soul of witchcraft," writing passages filled with the very logical contradictions he denigrates. Perhaps Evans-Pritchard kept his silence about what Evens states directly: that there is a profound truth about the world as the Azande know it and that truth exacts a high price, a personal transformation.[7] Given the irreducible nature of these kinds of experiences, the world we thought we knew may no longer exist.

Such a realization does not mean that there is no place for universal rationalists or relativist practices in the apprehension of the social worlds of diverse peoples; rather, it means that there are several interpretative moves scholars can employ to make sense of the multiple realities of their experience. Such a practice compels scholars to be humbled by the kind of complex forces to which Sorko Djibo first exposed to me in 1977.

But there has been great resistance to an experience-centered approach to the human sciences. Lévi-Strauss, for one, found the phenomenological foregrounding of experience troubling. He thought that reality and experience must remain discontinuous. Pierre Bourdieu criticized the ahistorical nature of the phenomenological epoché, which, he suggested, ignores the historical and cultural context of the social.[8] Although Bourdieu's conception of the habitus seems similar to the phenomenological notion of the lifeworld, he saw the move to phenomenology as a descent into the solipsistic subjectivism of the autonomous subject. Indeed, one central tenet of poststructuralist thought involves the problem of the subject. In Michel Foucault's work, for example, the idea of the episteme, the formation and structure of historically situated discourses, excluded the autonomous subject.

Many of these criticisms, however, focused on such classical phenomenological practices as the epoché, which many phenomenologists have also criticized. They also mistakenly believed that phenomenologists retained outmoded concepts derived from the Romantics. As Michael Jackson has argued, "no matter what constituting power we assign the impersonal forces of history, language and upbringing, the subject always figures, at the very least, as the site where these forces find expression and are played out."[9] From Jackson's vantage, phenomenology is more than simply a philosophy of the subject: "Insofar as experience includes substantive and transitive, disjunctive and conjunctive modalities, it covers a sense of ourselves as singular individuals as well as belonging to a collectivity."[10]

Perhaps one of the most essential aspects of phenomenology for the study of contemporary social life is its emphasis on embodiment. First and foremost, phenomenological embodiment is the rejection of the Cartesian separation of mind and body. For Maurice Merleau-Ponty, whose work has become increasingly important to anthropologists, consciousness devolved from embodiment: "Consciousness is in the first place not a matter of 'I think that' but of "I can . . . [it is] a being-towards-the-thing through the intermediary of the body."[11] Although it could be argued that such a view of embodied consciousness is too subjective and ahistorical, it could also be argued that "the orderly systems and determinate structures we describe are not mirror images of social reality so much as defenses we build against the unsystematic and unstructured nature of our experiences within that reality."[12] It could be further argued that although one's embodied perception of an encounter might well be unsystematic and unstructured, it has always been historically, socially, and politically situated.

As Jackson suggested, scholars often avoid acknowledging the contingent nature of situated experience as when two small birds shat on my head in the presence of a Songhay healer. If you fail to acknowledge the contingency of experience, you avoid the indeterminacies of the between—the ambiguities of social life, the tangential contours of experience, and sensuous processes of our bodies. If you do accept the contingency of experience and present yourself fully in the vortex of the between, then your body—the scholar's body—demands a fuller sensual awareness of the smells, tastes, sounds, and textures of the lifeworld. Such an embodied presence also means that scholars open themselves to others and absorb their words.

Sorko Djibo's critical comments eventually led me to believe that embodiment is more than the realization that our bodily experience gives rise to metaphors that deepen the meaning of our experience; it is rather the realization that we too are consumed by the sensual world. Such is the scope of an embodied rationality.[13] If you accept an embodied rationality, you reject the conceit of control in which mind and body, self and other are disconnected. To accept an embodied rationality is to live anthropology and dwell in the between within which you recognize, like wise Songhay sorcerers and griots, that you cannot master sorcery, history, or knowledge; rather, it is sorcery, history, and knowledge that masters you. To accept such an embodied rationality is, like the Hauka spirit medium or diviner, to lend your body to the world and accept its complexities, tastes, structures, and smells. Such is the path toward seeing, hearing and feeling the world—with humility.

Such humility does not mean that scholars ignore historical and political contexts or relinquish their agency. An embodied rationality, I eventually realized, can be a flexible one in which the sensible and intelligible, denotative and evocative are linked through a profound respect for the world. It is an agency imbued with what the late Italo Calvino called "lightness," the ability to make imaginative intellectual leaps to bridge gaps forged by illusions of disparateness.[14] I wondered if an embodied rationality might trigger the anthropological imagination and expand the breadth and depth of anthropological inquiry. Could it really help us to better navigate the treacherous existential rapids found in the between.

Sufis are the masters of the between, of spaces that connect being and nonbeing. Here's a Sufi story that captures a central tension in "the between."

In a kingdom of long ago, there was a Sufi master from a very strict school who was one day strolling along a riverbank. As he walked, he pondered great problems of morality and scholarship. For years he had studied the ways of the Prophet Mohammed. Through the study of the Prophet's sacred language, he reasoned, he would one day be blessed with Mohammed's divine illumination and acquire the ultimate truth.

The master's ruminations were interrupted by a loud noise: someone was attempting to recite a common Sufi prayer. "What is that man doing? he wondered. He is mispronouncing the syllables. He should be saying 'Ya hu' instead of 'U yah u.'"

It was his duty, he thought, to correct his brother, to set him straight on the path of piety. He hired a boat and rowed his way to an island, the source of the errant incantation. He found an old man dressed in white frayed wool sitting in front of a hut. The man swayed in time to his rhythmic repetitions. He was so engrossed in his sacred incantation that he did not hear the Sufi master's approach.

"Forgive me," the Sufi master said. "I overheard your prayer. With all due respect, I believe you have erred in your prayer. You should say 'Ya hu' instead of 'U yah u.'"

"Thank you so much for your kindness," the old man said. "I appreciate what you have done."

Pleased with his good deed, the Sufi master boarded his boat. Allah, he reasoned, would take notice of his pious efforts. As it is written, the one who can repeat the sacred incantation without error might one day walk upon water. Perhaps one day he'd be capable of such a feat.

When the Sufi master's boat reached midstream, he noticed that the old man had not learned his lesson well. Once again the latter continued to repeat the incantation incorrectly. The Sufi master shook his head. At least he had made the proper effort. Lost in his thoughts about the human penchant for error, the Sufi master witnessed a bizarre sight. Leaving the island, the old man walked on water and approached the Sufi master's boat.

Shocked, the Sufi master stopped his rowing. The old man walked up to him and said, "Brother, I am sorry to trouble you, but I have come out to ask you again how to make the repetition you were telling me about. I find it difficult to remember."[15]

———·———

No matter the logical consistency of our propositions and semipropositions, no matter how deeply we think we have mastered a subject, the world, for embodied scholars, for Sufi masters, or for practitioners like Sorko Djibo, remains a wondrous place that stirs the imagination and sparks creativity. Those who struggle with humility, no matter their scholarly station, admit willingly that they have much to learn from forgetful old men and women who, at first glance, seem ignorant of the world. In the end these kinds of people not only have precious knowledge to convey but can teach us much about those unsettling places situated between things, places that challenge the foundation of our being-in-the-world.

4

Knowledge

In June 1977 I hadn't lived long enough to appreciate fully what I might learn from forgetful old men and women, who, at first glace, seemed to have little knowledge that might help me to better understand the modern world. Instead, I wondered why Sorko Djibo and Sorko Mounmouni, Djibo's father, had asked me to visit their compound so they might cast divining shells. When I reached their compound, they told me that they needed to look into my future. Filled with skepticism, I sat down in front of them. Blades of sunlight cut through the weave of thatch that roofed their conical grass hut. We sat on pure, fine-grained *wadi* sand that someone had hauled in from a dry riverbed in the bush somewhere beyond a dune that rose up like a camel's hump behind Mehanna. Sorko Mounmouni, a short, thick, craggy-faced man with fire in his piercing eyes, sat with his back against the hut's center post. Djibo and I sat facing him. The older man, Mounmouni, wore a soiled and frayed white cotton robe over a pair of soiled and frayed white cotton drawstring pants. He had decided to supervise my apprenticeship in Songhay sorcery from a distance. Since he did not know me that well or trust me that deeply, he preferred to use his son, Djibo, as the bridge between my apprenticeship and his knowledge.

Under his father's watchful eye, Sorko Djibo taught me how to recognize a witch. He described with reverence the spirit village under the Niger River, the home of Harakoy Dikko, the spirit goddess of the Niger River. Harakoy lived there, he recounted to me, amid countless fruit trees and unlimited amounts of food. He also told me about a place where the sorko, whose body is "of the water and of the river," could enter the river and follow a path through the water to Harakoy's village. "When you follow this path, you enter the water, but because you are of the water, you don't get wet. You and the water are one and you walk to the village and greet Harakoy who gives you power objects and hands you a container filled with the soil of her village, a soil that will not get wet when you put it in water."

But it wasn't enough to memorize incantations, learn about the healing power of plants, or participate in curing rites. In time, the apprentice must also be transformed. When my "path was ready to open," as the Songhay like to say, Sorko Djibo prepared me a batch of *kusu,* or magic cake. He said that the kusu, concocted from millet and a variety of powdered plants and tree barks and imbued with "old and powerful words," would transform me from an average person to a sorko. For the Songhay, he told me, the sorko is a person who follows a path that winds its way between the worlds of social life and the world of the spirits, or what the Songhay would call the "world of war." From the Songhay perspective, I became, to borrow from the title of the Tom Wolfe novel, "a man in full," a man who had eaten kusu.

This "full" man now found himself seated with his masters in the dusty dim light of a grass hut on the outskirts of Mehanna.

"The time has come for us to chart your path, young man," Sorko Mounmouni stated. "We shall see what the shells tell us."

Djibo handed his father a drawstring satchel made from black cotton cloth. The old sorko smoothed out the sand in front of him and threw the shells on the ground. He scooped them up and threw them again. This time he studied the configurations and nodded his head. He stared into my eyes.

"The shells do not lie," he stated. "They say you should leave Mehanna and travel to Tillaberi. In Tillaberi, you should seek out Adamu Jenitongo. Do you know of him?"

"I do," I answered. He was the same man I had befriended years before when I taught at Tillaberi's secondary school.

"He is our teacher. He is man of great power and knowledge. Go to him."

Following the path suggested by Sorko Mounmouni and the shells, I went to Adamu Jenitongo's dune-top compound, a round space encircled by a low fence made from millet stalks tied to tree branches pounded into the sand. The compound consisted of two mud-brick houses, each with a front and back room, and three grass huts shaped like beehives, one of which was the spirit house. I knew from my previous time in Tillaberi that Adamu Jenitongo used the spirit house to receive his patients.

Adamu Jenitongo was a short frail man, who had somehow been expecting me, graciously opened his world to me. He invited me to spend time in his compound during which a continuous stream of men and women of various ages brought their sufferings to Baba, which means "father" in Songhay and is used as a term of respect for older men. In each case Baba would diagnose the cause of their troubles and offer them some sort of treatment. Sometimes he prescribed a course of herbal medicines. Sometimes he suggested an animal sacrifice. Several times he staged a spirit possession ceremony to make offerings directly to the Songhay spirits.

Like Sorko Mounmouni, Baba knew how to read divinatory shells and shortly before my return to the United States in the summer of 1977, he saw trouble on my path. "There will come times when you fear for your life," he told me. "If that comes to pass, you must recite the *genji how*," which I had heard, was the most important incantation in Songhay sorcery. "It will help to protect you from your enemies." Concerned about the trouble on my path, Baba said he would teach me the genji how. "Come back in the middle of the night, and I will teach it to you."[1]

Determined to better understand Adamu Jenitongo's mysterious world, I set out at midnight to visit him. That evening was a black, moonless night. I left the house of a friend with whom I was staying and slowly made my way up the dune to Baba's compound. Guided by my flashlight and hoping to avoid vipers and puff adders, which liked to come out at night and enjoy the cool feel of the dune's crusty surface, I walked very carefully on the sand, hearing nothing except the whoosh of the wind and the crunch of my boots on sand. When I entered the compound, I saw the dim glow of a lantern in the spirit hut. I walked to the entrance of the hut and clapped to announce my arrival.

Baba invited me into the hut. The flicker of lantern light cast my mentor's face in a pattern of light and shadow. In this weak light his jet-black face remained obscure, but his eyes, always bright, shone like beacons, eyes that pierce through a person's defenses and immediate understand what he or she is about. Looking at his magnificent face, I sat down.

"The genji how," he said, "is very powerful; it balances the forces of the bush. Use it before you engage in sorcery or whenever you feel threatened."

Eager to get on with this important lesson, I nodded.

"These words come from my ancestors. They are sacred. They are stronger than you and me. You must respect them." He paused for a moment, eyeing me. "Do you hear what I'm saying?"

I said that I had, indeed, understood what he had said. In retrospect, I was too young and inexperienced to understand what he was to impart

Adamu Jenitongo in his Tillaberi compound, summer 1987. Photograph by the author.

to me that dark night. But Baba taught me the incantation. When I had learned it by heart, he asked me to recite it. And so I did—for the very first time.[2]

In the name of the High God. In the name of High God. I speak to the east. I speak to the west. I speak to the north. I speak to the south. I speak to the seven heavens. I speak to the seven hells. I am speaking to N'debbi and my words must travel until, until, until they are known. N'debbi lived before human beings. He gave to human beings the path. He gave it to Soumana. Soumana gave it to Niandou. Niandou gave it to Seyni. Seyni gave it Jenitongo. Jenitongo have it to Adamu and Adamu gave it to me. What was in their lips is in my lips. What was in their minds is in my mind. What was in their hearts is in my heart. Today I am infused with N'debbi and it is good for me. N'debbi has seven hatchets and seven picks. He gave the big rock, Wanzam, to Dongo. He gave power to the kings. He evades the capture of the blind. He evades the capture of the ancestors. The force—the force of heaven—protects all.[3]

Several days later, I left Tillaberi and returned to the United States. At the time, I had difficulty accepting the supposition that the genji how, a string of words, could protect me—or anyone—from sickness or the ill will of others. Instead, I found it a beautiful poem as well as an important bit of anthropological data that highlighted key themes of Songhay culture.

———

In time I came to understand and better appreciate the Songhay theory of knowledge, which is very different from our own theories. Songhay people, especially sorcerers, think that a person must learn something important through her or his experience. Put another way, you learn cumulatively by being in your body in the world.[4] This epistemology, then, is one that does not separate mind from body or experience from learning. The mind develops through the body's experience-in-the-world. In the Songhay view, the young mind is as undeveloped as the young body. Both need to be exercised to grow. Young apprentice sorcerers, bards, or weavers are not expected to master the nuanced intricacies of sorcery, poetry, or cloth design; rather, they are told to listen to their masters. By "sitting" with their masters, they slowly follow their paths to knowledge. They mix potions, recite poetry, or weave strips of cloth. Through time apprentices expand their practices-in-the-world. By way of these embodied practices, apprentices deepen their experience-in-the-world. As their bodies and minds develop, Songhay apprentices start families and travel to other villages, towns, or countries. This social experience, in turn, further deepens their experience-in-the-world. In the end cumulative experience-in-the-world slowly ripens the apprentice's mind, preparing it to receive powerful knowledge—what it means to weave the world, what it means to be the guardian of "old words," or what it means to understand death.

These truths are taught only to those apprentices who, through persistence and patience, have demonstrated the capacity of an elder to receive and understand that which is important—the knowledge that enables people to better their lives. These are philosophic lessons, then, that mark the final transition from apprentice to master. Masters like Moumouni

Kada, Kassey of Wanzerbé, a female sohanci of great power, or Adamu Jenitongo, use their total being to perform two primary tasks: (a) to practice judiciously what they have learned and (b) more importantly, to impart that knowledge-practice to the next generation of apprentices. In this way the dynamic tension among experience, knowing, and being generates knowledge that is learned, refined, and passed on in the classic and unending pursuit of wisdom.

Understanding a Songhay conception of knowledge, of course, begs a central question for those who live anthropology: how do we account for experience, knowing, and being in anthropology? Because fieldwork is an anthropological rite of passage, we, more than other social scientists, stress the link between doing and knowing.[5] When it comes to being, though, anthropologists, like most other scholars, tend not to write about how doing and knowing have shaped their lives. There is the aforementioned gap, as the late Clifford Geertz famously noted, between the aforementioned "being-there," the field experience, and "being-here," the institutional experience of the professional scholar.[6] Geertz's "being-there" is usually a sensuous, fully human experience filled with personal drama and life-changing events. "Being-here" usually compels us to adhere to a set of institutional rules that tend to separate "being there" from "being here." The result is that, more often than not, we excise much of the passion of "being there" from what we write. This absence, in turn, usually hides how doing and knowing ultimately shape being in anthropology. How can we understand the human condition if we place our own being in the margins of our professional discourse?

Like most anthropologists I, too, experienced the existential turbulence that you find in anthropological space between "being-there" and "being-here." As an apprentice anthropologist my admittedly limited experience-in-the-world steered me onto the path of "being-here." Despite an early detour through the Songhay world of sorcery, I subsequently avoided the topic of sorcery for almost twenty-five years. It was too painful, too embarrassing, too sensuous, and too "being-there." Having been stung by collegial ridicule in the past, I wanted to avoid it in the future. Like any scholar, I desired disciplinary respect. As my life course unfolded, personal events beyond my physical or emotional control compelled me to reconnect being to doing and knowing.

Sorcery

In December 1988 I traveled to Tillaberi, Niger, to participate in the funeral rites for my teacher, Sohanci Adamu Jenitongo, who had died in March of that year. At midday, we
left Baba's dune-top compound and silently walked single
file into the bush until we soon found a fork in the road—the
point, in the Songhay view of things, where the worlds of
social life and that of spirits intersect. The fork in the road is
a place of great existential uncertainty and danger, a reason
why the death rites of a man whose life exemplified how you
live in the uncertain, ambiguous space between the worlds,
would be staged in such a place.

At the fork in the road, one of Adamu Jenitongo's aged
cousins, also a sohanci, mixed in a large clay pot a concoc-
tion of water, pulverized plants and roots, and perfumes. He
then recited the genji how, for in the space of death, you
need to harmonize the forces of the bush. Covered completely in black robes, the dress that often identifies a person
as a sohanci, he recited other texts and then talked about
Baba. He spoke of Baba's tireless work as a sorcerer-healer
and his service as a spirit possession priest. "Most of you
here," he said, "were his mediums. You know that he was
a man of power, but also a man who was gentle, a man who
wanted the best for people, the best for our land." Women
began to wail as memories of Baba filled the air with sadness.
The aged sohanci asked Moussa Adamu and Moru Adamu,
Adamu Jenitongo's sons, and Daouda Godji, a monochord
violinist whose music, during spirit possession ceremonies,
lured the spirits to the bodies of Tillaberi mediums, to step

forward. He also called my name, an honor that both pleased and surprised me. The four of us stood facing the clay pot that marked the fork in the road. A few puffy cumulus clouds dotted a light-drenched sky. A hot wind hissed through the thorn trees.

The old man poured the solution into two clay pots and gave one small pot to Moru and me and the other one to Moussa and Daouda. "Go in the bush, take off all your clothes and wash with this special water," he said. "Go naked into the bush and wash from your bodies the filth of your Baba's death."

We washed the filth of death from our bodies, a cleansing that marked the end of the first phase of the funeral. Moussa, Moru, Daouda, and I then returned with the other mourners to Adamu Jenitongo's compound, where the aged sohanci directed the second part of funeral during which all of Baba's ritual objects were to be purified. The man in black asked that all the sacred objects in the spirit house—hatchets, spears, lances, small jars, cloth pouches, the tiny sandals "worn" by the Atakurma, the elves of the bush, and a score of spirit costumes—be brought outside. Once again, he recited the genji how, and then, taking fresh milk into his mouth from a bowl, he sprayed the objects with a milk mist, which washed from the objects the filth of Adamu Jenitongo's death.

Drummers and a monochord violinist played melodious spirit music and in short order several spirits violently took the bodies of mediums. The spirits twirled and swirled and sang the praises of "their" spirit possession priest, promising to bring good times to Tillaberi in the wake of Adamu Jenitongo's death. When the spirits finally left the bodies of their mediums late in the afternoon and people began to return to their homes, Moussa and Moru, now custodians of their father's precious power objects, put them back in the spirit house.

By the time all the mourners had left the compound, the sun was about to set. Moussa, Adamu Jenitongo's older son who was also a tailor, asked me into his two-room mud-brick house. In the dimness of dusk light, we sat down on a rough wooden bench that hugged the wall next to his sewing machine, which stood on a rickety wooden table facing the door.

Moussa took out a small cloth bag, opened it, and spilled onto his open hand two rings that had belonged to his father—a small finger-worthy copper ring, and a larger silver ring that you could slip onto an index finger. "Before he died," Moussa said, "Baba asked me to give you these objects. The copper ring was my one of grandfather's things. It is very old. Wear it on the third finger of the left hand."

"The finger of power," I interjected.

Moussa Adamu of Tillaberi, Niger, summer 1984. Photograph by the author.

"That's right. If you wear that one on the third finger of the left hand you will always be in contact with Baba. Sometimes, you'll hear his voice. When you sleep he may come to you in dreams and give you advice."

"And the silver ring?"

"You're not ready to wear that one. Baba said that you'll know when the time is right. For now, you must keep it in your ritual container." Moussa then gave me the rings.

"I'll take very good care of these," I said as I slipped the small copper ring onto the "finger of power."

"There's something else," Moussa said. "Baba said he taught you a great deal about plants and about origins of our spirit world."

"He did," I said.

"He didn't have a chance to teach us everything that he knew. He trusted you and said that you'd come back and teach us about plants and about the people of the past."

"I will come back soon and teach you what I know, Moussa," I said, finally understanding an important truth about my relationship to Baba. I had always wanted to know why he would reveal so many of his secrets to a white man. Sometimes, he said he did so because he liked me. Sometimes, he said he did so because he had confidence that I wouldn't abuse the power he had entrusted to me. Finally, I knew the real reason: his sons hadn't been ready to learn about important and powerful things. He therefore imparted some of this knowledge to me, trusting that I would one day return to complete their education. He also wanted to convey some of his wisdom to the outside world. That was one way that he would be remembered and his ancestors would be honored. For Baba, my "betweeness" ensured that his full knowledge would be transferred to the next generation and that his life-in-the-world would be recorded for posterity.

I returned to Niger March 1990 to honor Baba's trust in me. I flew to Niamey, got a ride to the Tillaberi bus deport, hired two boys to carry my gear, and walked over furrowed sands to the dune-top compound. For the first time in my field experience, I found myself relatively alone in the Songhay world of sorcery. What's more, I had reservations about Moussa, who, as Adamu Jenitongo's older son, had taken on the lifelong burden of being a sohanci. Moussa, who was tall and lean, had a face as beautifully proportioned as a realistic African mask: perfectly spaced black eyes, high symmetrical cheekbones, thin lips and a nose—neither short and fat nor long and angular—that complemented his other facial features. His was a face that never betrayed feelings.

Moussa welcomed me to the compound. In the afternoons we talked about plants and the people of the past. In the evenings we talked about Baba, the poisoned social relations in Tillaberi, and the genealogy of Moussa's family. Whatever he might have been thinking, Moussa professed his appreciation that I had traveled all the way from the United States to talk to him and his brother about plants and the history of the "people of the past." I wondered about his "appreciation," though. If I put myself in his place, I would resent someone like me, a white interloper who one day came calling only to be welcomed warmly into the powerful world of sorcery. I would have been disturbed if my father had entrusted his precious secrets to a stranger. I would have wondered if the white man chosen to impart powerful knowledge to the next generation of black men had purposefully omitted mention of the most important plants or the most central stories of the people of the past.

The night before my departure, Moussa suggested I eat *kusu,* the magic food that gives the sorcerer the power to walk the perilous path that separates the world of social life and the world of the spirits. "I've been throwing shells, and I've seen trouble on your path. You need to eat kusu," he stated.

Wanting to demonstrate my trust in Moussa, I consented. As I watched, Moussa led me to the side of his house where there was a wind screen fashioned from thatch. He spread out a small white cloth onto which he poured the powdered contents of three black cloth pouches. Using a sweeping counterclockwise motion, he spread the assortment of three powders on the surface of water that had been poured into small black pot. He recited the genji how and chanted incantations for strength and protection. Having completed the incantations, he spat three times into the pot. Then he built a small fire behind the wind screen and balanced the pot on three stones. "When the water boils," he said, "I'll add millet flour." In short order, the water boiled and Moussa began to stir the mixture until it thickened into a paste. Moussa handed me a spoon. "Are you ready to eat the food that requires no sauce?"

"I am."

"Good," he said. "Eat until you are full."

The next morning, I left Tillaberi and returned to Niger's capital city, Niamey, where I hoped to spend a few days before returning to the United States. That afternoon, the car I was riding in crashed into a Mercedes sedan that had suddenly stopped on the road. I hit my head against the sun visor—bruised but not battered. That evening, I attended a wedding. My head throbbed and I felt both feverish and nauseous. That combination of symptoms signaled the onset of malaria, a disease with which I had been all too familiar. I left the wedding early, returned to my friend's house, a large villa toward the northern outskirts of town. I knew the treatment for malaria: take extra doses of Nivaquin, the antimalarial drug then favored by the French. The next morning, however, my symptoms grew worse—high fever, weakness in the limbs, and dizziness. My friend's sister-in-law, a visiting physician from Togo, believed I had a drug-resistant form of malaria. She gave me another antimalarial drug, the sulfa-based Fansidar, to which I had an immediate allergic reaction.

That night malarial nightmares made me toss and turn. In one dream, I found myself a sorcerer-warrior in a battle to the death, which I lost. Then I felt a different sensation: searing pains raced up my leg, as if someone had stabbed me with a dagger. Fearing for my life, I recited the genji how and the leg pain slowly diminished.

From the rational standpoint, an orientation that I had assiduously developed during my training in linguistics and social anthropology, I tried to make sense of my situation. Yes, I probably had a severe case of drug-resistant malaria rendered even worse by an allergic reaction to sulfa drugs. And yet, given my fear of a painful and inexplicable death in a lonely room in an isolated town in a desolate and distant place, I also thought about my predicament in sorcerous terms. Someone, I sensed, had made me a victim of a sorcerous attack, an attempt to make me leave Niger. Sorcerous attacks, called *sambeli* in Songhay, take two forms—sending "fear" and sending "sickness." You send fear to your adversary, usually someone who is either a rival or a person who had brought you public shame, by winding copper wire around certain ritual objects as you recite the victim's name. In this way, the victim is consumed by your sorcerous power and thereby humbled into a deep respect for your sorcerous capacities. While many sorcerers I've known have sent "fear" to their adversaries, very few of them had the capacity to send "sickness." To send "sickness," you must possess a special bow and arrows associated with one family of Songhay spirits. You notch the arrow on the bow string and recite the victim's name as you spit three times on the arrow shaft. Then you shoot the arrow. If your aim is good, the victim will feel a sharp pain in her or his leg as if someone has stabbed it with a knife. Eventually, the "sickness" spreads throughout the body. If you don't have sufficient magical protection or magical antidotes, you will become partially paralyzed or you will die. If you possess protective amulets, which make you well "armed," the arrow harmlessly misses its target.

Later that morning I was barely able to walk. With difficulty and determination, I left the villa and took a taxi to visit Soumana, a herbalist and healer who lived in one of Niamey's outlying neighborhoods. With unblinking eyes yellowed by long exposure to Niamey's grit and dust, he listened to my story. Soumana wasn't a big man, but his square face, thick neck, and broad shoulders gave him an imposing presence. Despite this bulk, he moved through the world with a grace that suggested tenderness. Taking in a deep breath, he put his hand on my shoulder.

"Your path has been spoiled. Someone has sent sickness to you." He searched through his things and gave me resins to burn. He also gave me three small pouches that contained powders. "Go home and burn the resins every day." He pointed to the pouches. "Put three measures of each powder into tea or coffee in the morning and at night. Drink these teas until the powders are used up. Your Baba can no longer protect you from bad people. Go home and restore yourself."

Moussa, Adamu Jenitongo's older son, said that jealous rivals had sent me the arrow of "sickness." A number of people, including Nigerien scholars and civil servants, men and women with advanced university degrees, all gave me the same advice. 'When your path has been spoiled, go home."

Weak from sickness, I returned the United States. I saw a number of specialists in tropical medicine. They tested me extensively but found nothing. For almost two months I was too weak to leave my house. Everyday, I burned the resins Soumana had given me. As instructed, I drank the special tea morning and night. Slowly, strength returned to my legs and in time I was able to resume my normal activities.[1]

––––––––

My life in anthropology had once again thrown me into the turbulent space of the between and I did not know how to proceed. I had spent the decade of the 1980s seeking a way to incorporate my sorcerous experiences into anthropological writing. When I first tried to write about sorcery, I did so in a traditional fashion. The work of Claude Lévi-Straus and E. E. Evans-Pritchard structured the foundation of my early attempts to describe—and explain—my experiences with sorcery.

Despite my critical confrontation with Parisian structuralism chez Lévi-Stauss, the power of the theory remained seductive. The scent of structuralism still lingering in my consciousness, I considered writing about sorcery from a structuralist vantage. In his "The Sorcerer and His Magic," Lévi-Strauss argued that sorcerous ideologies were based on sociological fictions reinforced by magical sleight of hand. In the end, the power of the sorcerer, he argued, rested not in an intrinsic power but in the symbolic power of his or her relationship in the cultural continuum of illness and health.[2] As for Evans-Pritchard, his cultural approach to Azande sorcery and witchcraft seemed productively provocative. For him the ontological status of sorcery or witchcraft took a back seat to the description of a non-Aristotelian system of logic that reinforced a set of seemingly "irrational" beliefs. Although scholars have long attributed many differences between Lévi-Strauss and Evans-Pritchard, at a deep level they shared a disembodied, objectivist orientation to the world. I have already discussed Lévi-Strauss's quest for cognitive universals. Evans-Pritchard also used a disembodied theory of meaning and rationality to "comprehend" an exotic system of beliefs. Having thought about the elegant arguments of these monumental scholars, I found their analyses incomplete because they led me far from the sensibilities of the people I sought to understand. How could a disembodied analysis enable you to comprehend sharp pains that streak up your legs in the middle of the night?[3] How could a disembodied analysis make sense of a Hauka spirit's "electric" handshake? How could a disembodied analysis teach me, coming back to Sorko Djibo's challenge, how to see, to hear, or to feel?

As previously mentioned, the promise of phenomenology had steered me onto a middle course between rationalism and relativism. The views of scholars like Husserl and Schutz seemed sterile. The embodied approach advocated by Maurice Merleau-Ponty, however, seemed to be particularly apposite for someone attempting to learn how to see, to hear, and to feel the world. Although Merleau-Ponty brilliantly outlined his approach to an embodied phenomenology in his works *Structure of Comportment* and *Phenomenology of Perception,* it is his essay on art, "Eye and Mind," that captured my attention. In this short but probing essay, Merleau-Ponty suggested that the world consists of much more than observed objective reality. He said that "science manipulates things and gives up living in them."[4] For Merleau-Ponty the way back to the "there is" was painting. The painter could grasp the life that resided in objects. Unlike scientists, painters found their way back to the "there is" because they opened their bodies to the world.

As Andre Marchard, a painter, reflecting on the work of Paul Klee, wrote:

In a forest, I have felt many times over that it was not I who looked at the forest. Some days I felt that the trees were looking at me, were speaking to me . . . I was there, listening . . . I think the painter must be penetrated by the universe and not want to penetrate it . . . I expect to be inwardly submerged, buried. Perhaps I paint to break out.[5]

To paint the forest, Marchard said, you have to open your body to it and let the trees flow through your being. Reading these lines made me realize the vulnerability of the sorcerer and the painter, beings caught between science and the arts, between rationality and magic, between control and surrender. And yet, I felt strongly that anthropologists needed to write works that brought readers to dwell within them as they walked their solitary paths between there and here, exposing their hearts so full of excitement, fear, and doubt.

Merleau-Ponty's phenomenology of art filled me with confidence. Perhaps I could attempt to write about sorcery with the insight of a painter? Perhaps I could write a book that would bring readers to dwell within me along my sorcerous path between things? And yet the philosophical confidence that Merleau-Ponty's writing inspired provided a necessary but not sufficient rationale for writing about sorcery. For sufficiency I turned to the emerging scholarship on ethnographic representation—significant writing about ethnographic writing. Throughout the 1980s the arguments of George Marcus, Michael Fischer, James Clifford, Renato Rosaldo, and Mary Louise Pratt, among many others, cleared disciplinary space for "experiments" in ethnographic expression. They criticized an ethnographic realism that represented "the people" as objects of analysis. They advocated the partial presence rather than the total absence of ethnographers in the texts they wrote. In contrast to Lévi-Strauss and other rationalists, they suggested that ethnographic research could yield only "partial truths."[6] In the end, this intellectual move made it more possible to publish narrative ethnographies that featured dialogue, characterization, and plot.[7]

In this "experimental" climate, I began to write about sorcery but chose the memoir as a frame within which to represent my ethnographic experiences. In this way I could describe sorcerous rites not in some disembodied discourse but from the patchwork of social relations—fictive kinship, friendships, alliances—from which they emerged. This work brought me much writerly satisfaction, but no amount of satisfaction or discourse could reduce the uncertainty, pain, and fear brought on by what I thought to be a sorcerous attack.

Months later and thousands of miles away from Adamu Jenitongo's compound in Tillaberi, Niger, I came to a troubling conclusion about sorcery. My confrontation with "sickness" convinced me that sorcery was much like gunfighting in Hollywood westerns. Gunfighters practiced and dueled to become "the fastest gun in the West," which meant that their very presence injected fear—and respect—into any atmosphere. Gunfighters, like sorcerers, felt no sense of morality. They felt little or no remorse about the people they wounded or killed on their way to the top. Being top gun, though, seemed a mixed blessing. Out of fear, people paid them considerable deference. By the same token a skillful challenger could at any moment propose a gunfight, which could result in the top gun's death. In worlds of sorcery, there were "top guns" who were being continuously challenged—often with mortal consequences. Despite the power of my own weapons (potions, power objects, and the genji how), I possessed neither the stamina nor the psychological wherewithal to continue my pursuit of sorcery. Having regained my physical and emotional equilibrium in the safe haven of North America, I didn't know where my scholarly curiosity might take me next. I did know, though, that I would not return to Niger to continue my apprenticeship in sorcery. Weakened by "sickness," I left Niger in 1990. Since then, I have not been back.

New York City

In the spring of 1992 I received a phone call from my colleague and fellow Niger fieldworker, Wendy Wilson Fall. We had been friends a long time and our paths had sometimes crossed in Niger, where she worked among Fulan people to the west of Niger's capital, Niamey. A woman of boundless energy and intense curiosity, she had mastered more languages than I could ever possibly know, including, but not limited to Songhay, Hausa, Fulan, and Wolof. Wendy had recently been to New York City—to Harlem.

"Paul, you're not going to believe this, but there are Nigeriens on 125th Street in Harlem," she said excitedly when she phoned. "I was there with my friend and we went to Harlem. There's a street market there that looks very African. I spoke Wolof, Hausa, and Songhay to the traders—just yesterday. The traders are from rural villages, Paul. You should go up there and check it out."

I was excited about the call. As mentioned, I had not been to Niger in several years and very much missed the company and conversations of Nigeriens. The next week, I took the train to New York to spend a few days with my cousin who lives on the Upper East Side. From his apartment I took a bus uptown into Spanish Harlem and on 125th Street headed west toward central Harlem. It was Saturday and the mild spring temperatures brought people into the streets. Men milled about on the wide sidewalks, popping in and out of stores. Mothers strolled their children down the street. The crowds thickened considerably at the intersection of 125th Street and Lenox Avenue. Aromatic smoke from burning incense hung like mist in the air. A trader had arranged a line of brightly patterned Dutch Wax cloth on a chain-link fence. A glut of people clogged the sidewalk. The din of African languages—Wolof, Bamana, Fulan, and Hausa—brought back memories of the West African markets I had visited.

On the northwest corner of Harlem's most famous intersection, a man sat behind two rickety aluminum card tables that had been covered with bright print cloth. On this table, he had arranged a magnificent assortment of bead necklaces—deep burgundy beads with delicate white feather motifs that had been long ago shipped from Venice to the Bight of Benin; solid-colored beads shaped like barrels that had in precolonial times made their way from Bohemia to West Africa; round Dogon beads fashioned from the clay of the Bandiagara cliffs in Mali; multicolored beads refashioned from the pulverized remains of a wide variety of ornaments long ago traded on the West African coast.

Sensing that the bead trader was from Francophone West Africa, I spoke to him in French, asking after his health and that of his family.

"We are fine, thank you. And how is the health of your house?"

"All is well." We shook hands and I wished him success in business that day. "Sir," I said, "I'm looking for people from Niger."

He pointed down the street toward the west. "Ils sont là-bas," he said.

"Over there?" I asked, pointing uncertainly down the street.

He nodded. "Over there."

Weaving my way through the throng of shoppers and traders, I came upon a man whose angular face and long slender nose suggested that he might be from Mali or Niger. He looked me over.

I extended my hand, which he took.

"Mate ni go, ay boro?" he asked, in Songhay. "How are you, my friend?"

"I am well, thank you," I responded in Songhay, wondering why this man had chosen to speak to me in Songhay rather than in French or some variety of English. Perhaps he was expressing the linguistic frustration of being a West African in New York City? Perhaps he was monolingual? Perhaps he was playing with me. "How is the health of your compound? How go the people of your village?" I continued trying to be respectful.

He slapped me on the shoulder. "Great God!" A white man who speaks Songhay," he declared. "Where did you learn to speak Songhay?"

"In Mehanna," I said. "Have you been there?" I asked.

The man smiled. "Even in the absence of food, Mehanna is sweet," he said, reciting a well-known expression about the town where I conducted much of my early fieldwork. "Do you know my cousin, Abul Azziz?"

"I do," I responded. "I spent many nights sitting outside his shop

Two Nigerien traders on 125th Street, summer 1993. Photograph by the author.

listening to the BBC." How wonderful, I thought, to be in central Harlem talking Songhay to a man whose cousin—my friend—lived in Mehanna. Other men gathered around us on the sidewalk.

"Have you been to Sansanne Hausa?" one man asked. "Do you know Moussa Gado?"

As it turned out, I had spent time in many of the home villages of these men and knew a good number of their relatives. Some of them claimed that they had heard about me. Indeed, white people who speak Songhay are not numerous. But they could have heard about any number of "European" men or women who had spent time in western Niger. One of the men, Boubé Mounkaila, who came from Karma, a town that hugs the east bank of the Niger River some forty kilometers north of Niamey, asked me to sit with him behind his card table. At the time, Boubé sold baseball caps featuring the insignia of well-known sports teams: Chicago Bulls, New York Yankees, Georgetown Hoyas, Dallas Cowboys. We talked about the political and economic problems of Niger and the cultural curiosities of life in the United States. Other African traders strolled by periodically joining our multilingual conversation, which, depending on the circumstances, shifted from Songhay to French and from French to English and then back to Songhay or French. A women steering a shopping cart brought Boubé two large Styrofoam containers of rice smothered with what smelled like okra sauce. Boubé put the containers on the sidewalk and opened them. Six of us encircled the container with our chairs, and Boubé gave each of us a plastic spoon. After giving thanks for the food, Boubé said, "Nya kuungu," which means, "eat until you are full." And so a small circle of men, sitting on metal chairs unfolded on a sidewalk in central Harlem plunged their spoons into containers of rice and okra sauce. "Nya kuungu," Boubé said. "Nya kuungu."

When we finished eating, Boubé said that he and his friends would be pleased if I could return to 125th Street to engage in "fakarey," the Songhay term for informal discussion. Such an invitation is sweet music to the ears of any anthropologist.

"Whenever I come to New York," I told him, "I'll come uptown for a visit."

After phoning Wendy Wilson Fall to describe the transnational character of my lunch on 125th Street, I asked her if she planned to begin a research project there. Engaged in a long-term project of her own, she had no plans to initiate one in New York City.

"Well," I said, "I'd like to visit the traders when I can. I may even try to get funding for a project to study how the Nigerien traders have adapted to life in New York. What do you think?"

"Sounds like a good project, Paul. Good luck," she said graciously.

It took two years to get research funding to study intensively West African social and economic life in New York City, but that delay did not impede regular informal visits to 125th Street. From my home in the Philadelphia area, I could take the train and be on 125th Street in less than two hours. The visits reinforced my connection to West Africa and West African culture. I liked the market bantering in Songhay, French, and smatterings of English. I savored the West African food we consumed during sidewalk "fakarey" in central Harlem. Most of all, I enjoyed the fraternal ties I had begun to establish with my West African friends. No matter how crazy the market became, there was always time for talk, food, and laughter.

After more than one year of visits, some of the West African traders began to call me the *anasaara alfaggah*, the white cleric, a reference to the writing capacity of Muslim priests. In West Africa, literate clerics write letters for clients. During many visits to New York, I would often perform this service. Boubé Mounkaila would set up a metal table and two metal chairs in the empty bay of his Econoline van, which he parked on the street next to his sidewalk vending spot. When word got out that the anasaara alfaggah was in his "office," a line would form and people would pop into the privacy of the "office" and ask me to fill out job applications, complete immigration forms, or write letters to their relatives in Niger, Mali, or Burkina Faso. One of my first "clients" was a young man from Burkina Faso, Mounmouni, who brought in a job application for a security guard position.

"When do you want to begin the job?"

"As soon as possible," he said. He then provided his current address and phone number.

"They want to know about your job experience."

"What's that?" he asked.

"Have you ever been a security guard before?"

"I've been here for six weeks."

"Did you do this kind of work in Burkina?"

"There I worked, you know, in the fields and did, you know, commerce."

I wrote down "farming," and "commercial trading." "Do you have references?"

"Would you be my reference?"

"Of course," I said, writing my name and phone number on the application.

"And you can put down the name of my Uncle Abdou from Ouagadougou."

On a subsequent visit Mounmouni told me that he had gotten the security guard job. "I give thanks to Allah," he said. "The job is good and I am able to send money home to my family."

———

I never imagined myself becoming an anasaara alfaggah, filling out job applications in an "office" located in the carrier of an Econoline van parked on 125th Street in central Harlem! In retrospect this profound shift in field circumstances, of course, devolved directly from a set of economic, social, and cultural forces unleashed by processes of global restructuring. These processes, many of which have been triggered through the proliferation of communications technology, have, among other things, spurred the growth of multinational corporations, imploded notions of space and time, provoked the outplacement of manufacturing from the first to the third world, triggered the outsourcing of industrial parts and the down-sizing of corporate payrolls, undermined sectors of the U.S. middle classes, and have brought on the exponential growth of informal economies.[1]

The set of complex relations has also led to the polarization of the rich and poor, which, in turn, has led to mass migration from economically impoverished regions like Burkina Faso and Niger to spaces of unimagi-nable wealth like London, Paris, and New York City. The course of these developments has created highly complex and diverse transnational communities in North American cities like New York, which means that it is no longer unusual for someone like Mounmouni, a rural farmer and sometime trader from an isolated village in Burkina Faso, to show up one day in Harlem, looking for the Econline van "office" of the anasaara alfag-gah so he can get some help with his job application.

This shift in research conditions compelled a shift in my anthropo-logical sensibilities. As I have already recounted, my early fieldwork took place in the rural western region of the Republic of Niger, where I con-ducted fieldwork among the Songhay people, the majority population of this multiethnic region, who had been in residence for almost a thousand years. I found the glorious history of the Songhay people fascinating but was enchanted by the practices of such religious rituals as spirit posses-sion and sorcery. Given the set of previously described circumstances, including, of course, the marksmanship of two special birds, I decided to focus my work on non-Islamic Songhay religious practices. That decision meant that I backgrounded a whole set of important and significant top-ics: the political economy of multiethnic western Niger, the social and economic importance of Islam, and the impact of modernization on cul-tural identity and cultural production.[2]

My whiteness in a colonial-contoured space of blackness also had im-plications for field research. In the 1970s and 1980s whiteness gave me a sense of autonomy. Some of that sense came from a letter written by Niger's president at the time, General Seyni Kountché, which authorized me to conduct research among the Songhay. The autonomy also resulted from the legacy of colonial culture in Niger. Seventeen years before I be-gan research in Mehanna, Niger had been a French colony. Indeed, rural peasants as well as highly educated civil servants used categories of race to resent and revere the French. In some cases, Nigeriens would simultaneously express their admiration for advances of modern technology and denigrate the backward ways of Africans.

More often than not, it was impossible to cross the wide steam that colonialism had carved into Niger's arid steppes. Most people saw me as a rich white tourist seeking adventure in Africa who might be the source of a gift or a handout. I once thought that my ability to speak Songhay might narrow the gulf between the white American and his black African associates. My capacity to speak Songhay certainly amused people, but it didn't usually alter their colonial attitudes towards my whiteness and what it represented.

This set of historically derived conditions made most people consider me with some degree of suspicion. Even so, my whiteness and my research authorization also made me someone who had to be accommodated. People felt that they had to listen to my endless list of questions. There were a number of spirit possession priests who resented my presence at spirit possession ceremonies. There were also a number of sohanci who objected to my apprenticeship to Adamu Jenitongo. Despite their feelings, they did little to block my early research in Niger. After all, I had the support of the region's senior spirit possession priest as well as a letter from the president of the Republic. Powerless to do anything about my presence in the field, they kept their distance. In Niger I was morally but not politically accountable.

When I found myself as a sometime anasaara alfaggah on 125th Street in central Harlem my anthropological assumptions about doing fieldwork changed considerably. For starters, I had to rethink the intellectual context of my work. I realized that I could understand little about the lives of Issifi Mayaki, Boubé Mounkaila, or Moussa Boureyma if I lacked at least a partial understanding of the global forces that propelled them to emigrate from West Africa. I also realized that I would have to study the economic and social context—the transnational informal economy of New York City—to grasp how conditions of the New York street set the texture of their social and cultural lives in North America. On the streets of New York City I no longer had the illusionary luxury of focusing on one dimension of cultural life. To conduct an ethnographic study of West African traders in New York City, I concluded, I would have to immerse myself in immigration studies in addition to economics, geography, sociology, especially of the urban persuasion, and political science.

I also found definitively altered field conditions in New York. On the streets I worked amid a mix of peoples some of whom were in violation of city regulations, trade and copyright statutes, and immigration laws.

This tenuous situation made the traders wary of newcomers—even if they spoke an African language. Accordingly, I adopted a slow approach to doing fieldwork in central Harlem. I told the traders of my previous work and explained that I wanted to write a book about their experiences in New York City. They encouraged me to continue my visits, eat lunch, and talk about the events of day. Several years passed in this manner. After many lunches and many, many stories, the traders gradually invited me into their lives, sharing with me their successes, frustrations, loneliness, and insecurities.

This slow, periodic approach to fieldwork suited the political context of street ethnography in New York City. Undocumented West African traders did not want to draw attention to their activities because that might well engage—or so they thought—the attentions of local authorities. Keeping my research objectives in mind, I tried to be unobtrusively present for several hours a day during two- and three-day visits to Harlem. The sense of autonomy I felt in Niger never materialized in central Harlem. As in Niger, my whiteness on 125th Street sometimes triggered distrust and suspicion. Unlike the research context in Niger, though, my accountability in New York City was legal and political as well as moral. While many African American patrons of the street market perceived me as white man seeking "thrills" uptown in Harlem, when they saw me on a regular basis and heard me conversing in both French and Songhay, they'd ask the traders about me.

"Who is that white man?" they'd ask.

"Is he okay?"

"What's he up to?"

"He's our friend who lived in Niger," they'd say. "He comes here to visit and to eat African food."

"He's not a cop, is he?" people would ask.

"No, no. He's a teacher."

People on the street usually paid little attention to me. Even so, I quickly realized that street ethnographers in New York City needed to work within the limited scope of their historically conditioned situation. In my case, knowledge and experience in West Africa gave me some degree of access to the dynamic and unstable community of West African traders in New York City. At the same time, whiteness, cultural difference, and the politics of race limited that access.

Given the complexity of social and cultural conditions in transnational spaces, scholars, I realized, need to engage in long-term research to achieve even a modicum of ethnographic understanding. To meet this goal, some people have advocated using multidisciplinary teams that employ a wide assortment of research interventions.[3] In retrospect, I think the key to doing research in transnational spaces is not only a matter of methodological soundness but also stems from the suppleness of imagination. The traders I met in New York ingeniously found ways around regulatory roadblocks and were able to resolve seemingly intractable financial problems. In each and every situation they found themselves, they discovered imaginative and decisive solutions to their economic, political, social, and legal problems. In time, I knew that following their model would propel me productively forward on my considerably altered anthropological path.

———

This turn of events in New York City had steered my work away from the Songhay world of sorcery. Would my time in New York teach me how to see, hear, and feel? Would it deepen my existential depth? What would ethnographic research about West African immigrant life in New York teach me about the power of the between? At the time, I didn't care about these questions, for I felt intellectually renewed. I read new academic literatures, made new friends in New York, and confronted the complex world of transnational New York with newfound vigor.

Complexities

Along the considerably altered anthropological path that led me to the clogged thoroughfares of New York City, the complexity of West African immigrant social and cultural formations fired my intellectual curiosity. How could I make sense of West Africans in New York City? I discovered that the West African immigrants that I had befriended had evidently become prime players in urban theaters of social complexity. They had constructed, reinforced, abandoned, and reconstructed a variety of personal and economic networks that cut across New York City's already highly complex ethnic landscape.

In the early 1990s West African street merchants sold a variety of kente cloth products from their tables along 125th Street in Harlem. Kente cloth, which has a deep history, has long symbolized social and political prestige among West African peoples. Sewn in a complex weave of deeply and brightly dyed silk, traditional kente, worn like a toga, was donned on ritual occasions by the nobility of the Asante people in southern Ghana. Because of the long and complex process of its hand-loomed production, kente was expensive—the costume of rich patrons.

In the late 1960s and 1970s celebrities in the African American community began to buy and wear clothing and accessories fashioned from kente cloth. As African American identity became more and more connected to its African roots, the bright kente cloth patterns gradually became symbols of African American pride. Ghanaian kente remained too expensive for most buyers, so in the late 1980s enterprising Asian businessmen in New Jersey pinpointed a business opportunity: produce a print cloth copy of kente. They reproduced bolts of "kente" print cloth, which were reasonably priced, and shipped the textiles to Canal Street, the center of commerce in New York City's Chinatown. In time, African street vendors, also sensing a business opportunity, began to buy bolts of what they called "New Jersey Kente" from Asian traders on Canal Street. Soon thereafter, they offered "New Jersey Kente" to shoppers on 125th Street in Harlem. The "good prices" attracted buyers to their sidewalk tables.

This successful economic conclusion would be a logical place to end this narrative, but the story gets much more complex. News of the success of "New Jersey Kente" soon made its way to West Africa. In Ghana, proud kente weavers had long refused to produce "cheap" reproductions of their glorious cloth. Textile producers in neighboring Togo and Côte d'Ivoire, which had long produced kente reproductions, did not share the reticence of Ghanaian weavers. Seizing upon a new business opportunity, factories in these two West African countries began to ship to New York City a cheaper, higher-quality West African reproduction of a New Jersey reproduction of a West African original. The West African reproductions quickly undercut the sales of "New Jersey Kente." Accordingly, Asian entrepreneurs sought new business opportunities.

We here reach another logical end to the narrative, but the kente story continues. Because the price of the West African kente reproductions was attractive, Asian traders from Chinatown traveled uptown to buy the African reproduction of a reproduction of kente. Bolts of "kente" in hand, they returned to Chinatown, where they supplied sweatshops with the "African" cloth. Soon, Asian immigrants sewed kente scarves, shawls and hats, which enterprising West African street vendors bought in Chinatown to sell as "kente" in Harlem. And so in the summer of 1994, African American shoppers bought a "kente" cap from a West African who bought it from a downtown Korean trader with ties to a Chinatown sweatshop. Owners of the sweatshop had bought the "kente" from West African cloth traders in Harlem who had ordered many bolts of the West African "reproduction" of New Jersey "kente," itself a reproduction of Ghanaian kente. The multiple movements and reconfigurations of kente demonstrate powerfully how fluid transnational networks of people and products define contemporary social complexity.[1]

———

The social complexity that forms the foundation of West African immigrant life in New York City has also been revealed through tragic events.

In May 2003 the New York City Police (NYPD), for example, killed an un-armed West African immigrant at the Warehouse, a large repository of African art in Chelsea. The man, Ousmane Zongo, an immigrant from Burkina Faso, repaired statues and masks broken during transport from West Africa. He spoke little or no English and had little contact with Americans. His senseless death occurred during a police raid on a West African CD counterfeiting ring that stored its merchandise at the Ware-house. Zongo had not been part of the CD counterfeiting ring.[2]

This tragedy, which resembles the case of the unarmed Amadou Di-allo, who, in February 1999 was shot forty-one times by four New York City undercover policemen, devolves in part from the NYPD's ongoing campaign to regulate a key element of New York City's ever-expanding in-formal economy: the production and sale of counterfeit goods, including CDs and videos. In the case of counterfeit videos, so-called pirates extract roughly $250 million a year, according to conservative estimates, from the movie industry. Transnational networks have emerged to produce, distribute, and sell counterfeit videocassettes. Once the videocassette of a new film is procured—through theft at a distribution center or by using a camcorder at the film's premier—it is taken to a video factory capable of reproducing thousands of videocassettes a day as well as reproducing the film producer's packaging. In the 1990s New York organized crime fami-lies as well as networks of Dominicans, Arabs, and Israelis ran the counter-feit videocassette factories. Couriers from videocassette factories would then deliver boxes of counterfeit films to various drop-off points in the city, including, a Senegalese vendor in the Malcolm Shabazz Harlem Mar-ket at 116th Street and Lenox Avenue in Harlem. The Senegalese vendor, who displayed scores of videos at his market stall, wholesaled most of his stock to African American street vendors who put the videocassettes in knapsacks and hawked them in their neighborhoods—for a price slightly higher than wholesale. These networks of Dominican, Arab, and Israeli suppliers, Senegalese middlemen, and African American sellers worked smoothly for several years. But like many contemporary complex net-works, this one was ephemeral. In 1998 Blockbuster Video and the Mo-tion Picture Association of America pressured the city to crack down on unlicensed video sales, making it impossible for men like the Senegalese middleman to operate openly at the Malcolm Shabazz Harlem Market. Here again, the ever-shifting political economy of New York triggered the ongoing reconfiguration of a complex network of transnational social re-lations.[3]

As my research in New York City unfolded, West African immigrants became increasingly integrated into the economic life of Harlem. By 2006 there were an increasing number of African-owned businesses—restaurants, hair-braiding salons, clothing boutiques, craft shops, and import-export enterprises—in Harlem—especially on 116th Street. Most of the traders at the Malcolm Shabazz Harlem Market, also on 116th Street, were West Africans, many of whom had been in business for more than ten years. Despite this economic integration, most West Africans have retained a degree of social separation in Harlem, meaning that shared kinship, ethnicity, and to some degree nationality erects a series of sociocultural barriers that create sociocultural buffers among West Africans themselves and between West Africans and (African) Americans.

Many of these shifting barriers were already evident in 1994 when former New York mayor Rudolph Giuliani, keeping a campaign promise, shut down the informal African market on 125th Street. This decision provoked a flurry of political activity in Harlem. In response to the mayoral decision, a group of African American vendors and West African traders from Mali, Senegal, and Niger and the Gambia (the 125th Street Vendors Association) threatened to halt commercial traffic on 125th Street if the mayor dared to outlaw informal vending. Although the 125th Street Vendors Association was supported by the Nation of Islam, whose ministers preach a mixture of Islamic purity and African American self-sufficiency, some members of the association disliked and distrusted Nation of Islam leader Louis Farrakhan. Many of the West African members of the 125th Street Vendors Association wondered how such a man could call himself a Muslim.

The 125th Street Vendors Association was also supported by the Reverend Al Sharpton, who used his particular orientation to Christianity to voice his solidarity with hardworking African and African American people. Many African American and Asian shop owners on 125th Street supported the street vendors. Just as many African American and Asian shop owners, however, believed that the presence of street vendors hurt their businesses. Like the Nation of Islam, the Masjid Malcolm Shabazz, the mosque founded by Malcolm X, advocates Islamic austerity and African American self-sufficiency. Even so, the masjid indirectly supported the shutdown of informal trading on 125th Street. They promoted a plan to relocate the street vendors to their own regulated and city-sanctioned space on 116th Street, which, in the end, would make the vendors "legal" and maintain the cleanliness and security of Harlem's sidewalks. The Harlem Business Alliance and the Harlem Urban Development Corporation endorsed this plan. Both organizations promoted economic ties to West

African governments but did not like the cluttered, open-air African market on Harlem's major economic thoroughfare, a presence that symbolically belied Harlem's economic renaissance. The Giuliani administration also welcomed the masjid's plan, which would avoid a potentially violent racial confrontation and would also bring new business tax revenues into city coffers. In addition, the plan would enable Mayor Giuliani to claim that he was keeping his campaign promises.

As for the African vendors, they, too, had a view of Mayor Giuliani's crackdown on informal trade in Harlem. Consider the Senegalese traders, who had been in New York City since 1982 and were well represented among the West African traders in Harlem. Well-established Senegalese merchants, who owned boutiques or import-export enterprises, supported the dispersal of informal trade on 125th Street. Recently arrived Senegalese street merchants, by contrast, wanted to remain on the street where the continuous flow of goods and people translated into handsome profits. Most Malian traders wanted to continue their enterprises on 125th Street but refused to demonstrate with the 125th Street Vendors Association. Some of them decided to pay the Masjid Malcolm Shabazz to secure a stall at the new 116th Street market; others refused to pay the masjid and vowed to establish their businesses elsewhere. Few of the well-established vendors from Niger marched in the 125th Street demonstration. Some of them moved their businesses downtown to Canal Street; others agreed to become merchants at the new Malcolm Shabazz Harlem Market.[4]

The particular social configurations triggered by the Giuliani administration's decision to disperse the African market no longer exist. The 125th Street Vendors Association lost its raison d'être when its protest demonstration and boycott of 125th Street businesses proved to be ineffective. Since the demise of the 125th Street market, Harlem's major thoroughfare has attracted an influx of corporate capital. New office buildings have been constructed; franchises from major retail chains like the Body Shop have opened; Magic Johnson's multiplex movie theatre plays first-run feature films. Accordingly, business rents have risen and city tax revenues have increased—all part of the economic development plan that the Harlem Business Alliance and the Harlem Economic Development Corporation have espoused since the early 1990s.[5]

Since the dispersal of the 125th Street market in 1994, West Africans have reinforced their own political and economic organizations, some formal like the Association des Maliens aux USA, others informal like credit associations based upon ethnicity or region of origin. In various ways, these associations, which consist of a multiply embedded set of

The Malcolm Shabazz Harlem Market circa 1997. Photograph by the author.

ever-shifting networks, protect and promote the interests of West Africans in New York City. Many West Africans who once lived in New York City, however, have relocated to large metropolises like Atlanta and New Orleans and to smaller enclaves like Harrisburg, Pennsylvania, and Greensboro, North Carolina, the last being a thriving and expanding community of more than 2,000 Nigeriens.

In retrospect, these networks of West African immigrants—transnational, ethnic, economic, or personal—constitute a thin slice of the complex of social relations in contemporary New York City. Even so, impressive social malleability has enabled West African immigrants to shift and slide along the geographical and conceptual boundaries of urban space.

With apparent ease, they continuously configure and reconfigure their economic strategies, social positions, and personal identities in New York.

There are obvious differences between my field experiences in Niger and New York City. In Niger, I was able to experience worlds, as Jean Rouch liked to say, "not yet known to us." During my time in Niger, I struggled to understand the "truth" of sorcery and spirit possession, and in my representation of those phenomena I tried my best to reflect the wonder of those worlds. During my time in New York my West African friends invited me into a world of unexpected social complexity—copies of copies of original products that travel along the sinuous pathways of transcultural and transnational space. If there is one thread that connects these two strips of experience, it is my admiration for the resourcefulness of my African friends—people who can transform a barebones physical reality—be it in Niger or New York City—into a patchwork intangible and tangible wealth.

8

Family

The resourcefulness of my African friends, of course, has been fundamentally reinforced through ties of kinship, fictive kinship, and widespread networks of socioeconomic relations. From 1994 to 1997 I spent a good deal of my New York City field time visiting the Malcolm Shabazz Harlem Market. On each visit, my conversations with Boubé Mounkaila, Moussa Boureyma, and Issifi Mayaki underscored a key principle that is so deceptively simple that many scholars overlook its central importance: the fundamental centrality of social relations. Issifi Mayaki strongly exemplifies this principle.

Men like Issifi . . . have much to teach contemporary anthropologists. Their example reminds us of the central significance of understanding the nuances of kinship and social relations. For a person like Issifi, nothing is more important than his social relations—the viability of family, the maintenance of mutually nurturing friendships, the endurance of networks based and built on relations of mutual trust. With varying degrees of effectiveness, Issifi and his brother traders have continuously negotiated and renegotiated their social lives. In so doing they established new trading partnerships and have dissolved others. They have mastered the culture of capitalism as they have reinforced the traditions of long-distance African trading. They have staked out individual space in a market culture as they have engaged in a cooperative economics dictated by Islam and long-standing West African commercial practices. They have adapted to the unfamiliar stresses of city life in New York as they have reaffirmed their African identities.[1]

In January 1997 Issifi said that he missed his family in Niger and Côte d'Ivoire. By this time, Issifi had been in New

York City for five years. He talked about how much he missed his mother and his brothers

There are two important things in my life: family and the things that stir my heart. I sell my products to any person, Christian or Muslim, pastors and drug dealers, for if I am honest, money has no smell. If God grants me money in exchange for hard honest work, I must make sure that my family is okay, they're well fed, well clothed, well housed, and in good health. Then if there is something left, I buy things that stir my heart.[2]

When I visited Issifi's market stall in early March 1997 he was very much preoccupied with family matters. As always he had arranged his mostly silver jewelry in impeccably clean felt display cases. He kept his pricier objects, necklaces strung with large amber beads as well as silver necklaces featuring Tuareg crafted crosses, which represent the Southern Cross constellation, in a locked glass case. As he polished some of his silver rings, he told me that his father had been hospitalized in Abidjan, the former capital of Côte d'Ivoire. At the beginning of that month, Mounkaila Mayaki, Issifi's sixty-year-old father, a Hausa merchant from Niger, drove his car, an old but famously sturdy Citroën Deux Chevaux, to a market on the outskirts of Abidjan. He had wanted to buy sugarcane for his shop. Mounkaila Mayaki had been frequenting the market for more than ten years and had had a dry goods shop in Treichville, the *quartier populaire* (working-class section) of Abidjan, for more than thirty years. Like many Hausas, Mounkaila Mayaki, who was quietly proud of his Muslim faith and his culture, felt no fear of openly displaying his ethnic identity. He and his compatriots regularly wore one such display—the *grande boubou,* a billowing robe whose sleeves, neck, and back feature sweeping swirls of gold or silver embroidery.

Despite the fact that he was a foreigner whose language, culture, and religion were profoundly different from those of his Ivoirien neighbors, he had prospered during his thirty-year sojourn in Côte d'Ivoire. He shipped goods from Abidjan to the countryside. He also bought kola nuts, a stimulant that is savored throughout West Africa, and shipped them north to Niger. He brought his four sons, including Issifi, to Abidjan to learn about business. In March 1997 one of Issifi's brothers lived in Australia and worked in an African art boutique. Another taught elementary school in Niger. His youngest brother worked for the family patriarch in Abidjan. Indeed, Mounkaila Mayaki felt that he had much to be thankful for—until that March 1997 afternoon when a mob of Ivoiriens, identifying him as a Hausa because of his *grande boubou,* yanked him from his car and beat him within an inch of his life. No one, including the Ivoirien police, intervened.[3]

Mounkaila Mayaki's injuries, a severe concussion and several broken ribs, would necessitate a long stay in the hospital. Nevertheless, he had been lucky. In the Treichville section of Abidjan, the neighborhood of African immigrants to the city, a mob of Ivoiriens captured several Hausas and lynched them. As in Mounkaila Mayaki's case, a crowd that included police, witnessed the episode but did nothing. What Mounkaila Mayaki had not known that day was that a rumor had been going around that Hausas in Côte d'Ivoire possessed penis-shrinking sorcery. The rumor indicated that, if certain Hausas, who as foreigners had long played a major and profitable role in the Ivoirien economy, touched an Ivoirien man, the penis of the latter would shrink and eventually disappear. This rumor led to widespread beatings, including that of Mounkaila Mayaki, and to the aforementioned violence in Treichville.[4]

"Can you find out more about what happened to my father and the other Hausas?" Issifi asked on that day in March, knowing something of my past apprenticeship in Songhay sorcery. "I need to know if it is safe for my father to live in Côte d'Ivoire. Should he go back to the village in Niger?"

"I'll look into it right away, Issifi," I told him. It had been more than seven years since I had thought about sorcery in West Africa. And now, a transnational family connection had steered me back into that world—albeit from a very safe distance. I was eager to think more fully about the issues that precipitated this violence. What's more, the research about Mounkaila Mayaki's fate would in no way further implicate me into the matrix of sorcerous relations that I had fled in 1990. And so I launched myself into a small research project that temporarily took me away from my investigations of West African street traders—another example of how unexpected events in the between continuously shift the winds of your attention, propelling you down potentially rewarding detours.

———

The 1997 events in Côte d'Ivoire, I discovered, were not the only such incidence of putative penis shrinking. That same year mobs in Senegal tracked down, beat, and in several cases lynched suspected penis shrinkers. Like Mounkaila Mayaki, these victims were also from Niger. The previous year, 1996, people in Cameroon, according to an Associated Press dispatch, claimed that Nigerians, some of whom may well have been Hausas, had practiced penis-shrinking sorcery in Yaoundé. The story reported that "angry mobs . . . had lynched three men accused of using evil powers to cause male genitals to disappear . . . by shaking hands with their victims."[5] The phenomenon of penis shrinking has been cogently analyzed in Michael Jackson's noteworthy book, *Minima Ethnographica.* Considering the Cameroon incidence of penis shrinking, Jackson wrote that the epidemic "expresses . . . an existential loss of control over the boundary between one's own world (symbolically 'inside') and the world of the other ('outside') which in effect reduces people to the status of objects or things."[6] For Jackson, penis shrinking was in the final analysis

a challenge born of the human condition. Though a singular person exists with and through others, he or she may be diminished rather than strengthened in this relationship, eclipsed rather than fulfilled. Though this paradox of intersubjectivity finds expression in the political problem of how to strike a balance of power between different nations, it remains here as everywhere an existential issue of how the claims of any individual can be adjusted to the claims that others make on him or that he makes on himself on their behalf such that everyone finds validation and dignity in the man.[7]

In March 1997 the paradox of intersubjectivity had become more than an academic exercise for Mounkaila Mayaki; it had become life-threatening. How would he, I wondered, negotiate his existential between? During his father's two-month stay in the hospital in Abidjan, Issifi sent money for his care. He urged his father to return to Niger, where he would no longer be a foreigner who might be suspected of penis shrinking. In much of West Africa, the quality of one's stay at the hospital depends entirely upon his or her family support network. In many, if not most cases, it is the family's responsibility to make sure their relative receives the proper medicines. They also prepare the patient's food, which African hospitals rarely provide.

Upon his release from the hospital, Mounkaila Mayaki did, indeed, return to the central region of Niger where he rejoined his people.

Two months later on a warm, sunny day in May I once again visited Issifi at the Malcolm Shabazz Harlem Market. We greeted one another. I asked after the health of the other traders. When I asked after his father, Issifi told me that after two months of living "at home," Mounkaila Mayaki had returned to Côte d'Ivoire.

"Why would your father," I asked Issifi, "want to go back to a place where he was nearly beaten to death?"

"He was bored in the village," Issifi said. "He's lived in 'the big city' for thirty years." Issifi also explained that his father had also faced life-threatening danger in his homeland. "They're fighting a war in our region," Issifi stated. "You've heard about it, haven't you?"

"Are you talking about the Tuareg rebellion?" I asked, referring to the military activities of desert nomads in parts of central and north-central Niger.

"Yes. You see, the war brings to our village young government soldiers. They think they are big men who can do what they want. They are far away from the capital city and they have guns. So what do they do?" Issifi asked. "They beat local people," he said, answering his own rhetorical question, "take food from old women, and steal goods from merchants like my father." Mounkaila Mayaki also told his son that the young soldiers would frequently battle the aforementioned Tuareg rebels who lived in the countryside. Many people, including civilians, had died in these battles.

"Niger is a hard place," Mounkaila Mayaki said to his son, trying to explain his decision to leave home for a place where his status as a foreigner had precipitated a life-threatening assault. "Life is harsh in Niger," Mounkaila Mayaki said. "There is not enough food or water. People are hard there, also. Even though I am a foreigner in Côte d'Ivoire, it is a more peaceful place. Abidjan is not like Niger. In Abidjan you don't have to be vigilant everyday. Niger is my home, but as a country it is too hard."

Mounkaila Mayaki's words brought back to me memories of Niger's hardness. It is truly a hard country. The case of Mounkaila Mayaki reminded me of how we all negotiate our way through the intersubjective instabilities that constitute the between. For thirty years he negotiated and renegotiated his life as a foreigner and trader in Côte d'Ivoire—a man very much between things. One day that ongoing negotiated reality literally came crashing down on his head, and no one, including agents of the Ivoirien state, intervened on his behalf. Mounkaila Mayaki's relationship to Côte d'Ivoire's state apparatus had suddenly changed. He then returned to a dissatisfying Niger in which his indigenous status did nothing to decrease his vulnerability to the violent vicissitudes of the state—unruly soldiers who requisition—but also to the potentially lethal violence of his Tuareg rebel neighbors.

And so he returned to Côte d'Ivoire, where he renegotiated yet another matrix of all-important social relationships—some new, some old—that he refashioned to a sociocultural script that included new contours and textures. No one in Côte d'Ivoire had forgotten who the penis shrinkers might be, what had happened to them, or what might become of them in the future. The memory of Mounkaila Mayaki's beating was most certainly a sensuous one that he—as well as the people that beat him—thought about every day.

"How could my father ever forget that beating he suffered for simply being a Hausa?" Issifi wondered out loud that sunny day in May as he polished his silver rings.

I found Mounkaila Mayaki's story a complex one. It reminded me once again that doing contemporary social science is an enterprise in which the detour, to borrow from Wittgenstein, is usually far more interesting than the highway.

9

Sensuousness

My detour into Mounkaila Mayaki's world brought me back to questions that Sorko Djibo had first posed to me in the 1970s. Indeed, Mounkaila Mayaki's nearly fatal embodied experience of the politics of sorcery in Côte d'Ivoire made me wonder if I'd ever be able to "see," "hear," and "feel." Mounkaila Mayaki's physical apprehension of social life in Niger and Côte d'Ivoire led me toward a more deeply sensuous appreciation of the social. Where might such a path lead me?

It is ironic that sensuousness has remained tangential to the thinking of most social scientists, given its centrality in the human experience. This separation has been extended by an incomplete, if not flawed, comprehension of its assumptions and practices. Many thinkers have linked sensuousness to phenomenology and its putative ahistorical subjectivity.[1] On this detour, my purpose was not to present an exhaustive advocacy of a sensuous ethnography, but to pinpoint the key components of sensuous perception that might shed light on the turbulent relations among perception, power, and lived experience.

Perhaps one of the most essential aspects of a sensuous ethnography for an approach to the study of perception, power, and lived experience is its emphasis on embodiment. First and foremost, a phenomenological, sensuous embodiment is, as mentioned earlier in this book, a rejection of the Cartesian separation of mind and body. For Maurice Merleau-Ponty, consciousness devolves from embodiment.[2] Pierre Bourdieu and Claude Lévi-Strauss, as mentioned in previous chapters, have argued that such a view of embodied consciousness is too subjective and ahistorical. By the same token, it can also be argued that "the orderly systems and determinate structures we describe are not mirror images of social reality so much as defenses we build against the unsystematic and unstructured nature of our experiences within that reality."[3] It can be further argued that although our embodied perception of an encounter, like Mounkaila Mayaki's account of being beaten as a penis shrinker, may well be unsystematic and unstructured, it is always historically, socially, and politically situated.

From a more sensuously contoured, phenomenological vantage, perception—historical or otherwise—and sociopolitical behavior become unstable, nonlinear, and dynamic. For Merleau-Ponty history "is not an external god, a hidden reason for which we need only record our conclusions. It is a metaphysical fact that the same life, our own, is played out both within us and outside us, in our present and in our past, and that the world is a system to which we have various accesses."[4] In this light, history, perception, and political action are inventions that work "through a matrix of open and unfinished significations presented by the present. Like the touch of a sleepwalker, it touches in things only what they have in them that belongs to the future."[5] In this vein, history, memory, and perception are central elements that contribute to the instabilities of lived experience, for in the perception of past and present there

occurs a simultaneous decentering and recentering of the elements in our personal life, a movement by us toward the past and of the reanimated past toward us. Now this working of the past against the present does not culminate in a closed universal history or a complete system of all the possible human combinations . . . Rather, it produces a table of diverse, complex probabilities, always bound to local circumstances, weighted with a coefficient of facticity.[6]

Although Mounkaila Mayaki does not speak the language of sensuous ethnography, his story exemplifies the dynamically unstable nature of how the present animates the past and how that reanimation presents a matrix of possibilities and choices in his present—all of which have existential consequences for his future. This unstable matrix lies at the heart of an individual's embodied memories and perceptions and is a cornerstone of a sensuous ethnography.

Sensuous ethnography, which devolves from the embodied rationality that I mentioned in previous chapters, creates a set of instabilities for the ethnographer. Thinking about my own sensuous experience among the Songhay, I realized that by openly and modestly foregrounding local sensibilities I could construct social knowledge with an energy that better enabled me to identify elements in (African) social and political life that impelled men like Mounkaila Mayaki to return to Côte d'Ivoire to face an uncertain and dangerous life.

———

Mounkaila's Mayaki's story speaks to the instability of a one's personal path in Africa. Compounded many times, his story is a reflection of African politics in action that, according to Jean-François Bayart, bows to the logic of incompleteness as well as to the role of disorder.[7] In the face of such existential uncertainty, notions of solidarity, force, and vitality become socially important and politically prominent. The widely used sensuous metaphors that frame these notions, in turn, are negotiated and renegotiated. They can become, in short, tools of power as well as resistance.

Given the importance of vitality in African social circumstances that are, at best, uncertain, the metaphors in question usually hone in on elements of consumption in contexts of scarcity. Referring to the considerable political corruption in Cameroon, people often recite the proverb, Goats eat where they are tethered. Put another way, "the social struggles which make up the quest for hegemony and the production of the State bear the hallmarks of the rush for spoils in which all actors—rich and poor— participate in a world of networks."[8] These politically inspired— and inspiring—metaphors of consumption, of course, are often defined in terms of taste.[9] In other domains, they may also signify the "texture" of power (i.e., Mounkaila Mayaki's hardness), the "sound" of vital empowerment or the "vision" of political comportment.[10]

In their massive and magisterial account of the impact of colonialism on South Africa, John and Jean Comaroff considered how evangelists attempted to transform "naked" and "wild" Africans—the Tswana, in this case—into more controlled and "fashionable" colonial subjects whose comportment conformed to standards of "civility." In more realistic terms, European fashion and "taste" made the Tswana, at least in the eyes of the colonial administration, more compliant—better colonial subjects. Fashion, then, consumed the wild excess of Africans and sapped the (politically) dangerous vitality of the "locals."

The most carefully planned programs and/or policies in sensuous domains, however, almost always lead to unintended outcomes. Tswana manipulated the contours of evangelical (colonial) taste to meet their own social and political ends. The Tswana

had been absorbed into a nation-state in which they were not citizens; into a city-cen-
tered world that refused them a permanent urban home; into a universal "civilization"
that depicted them as tribal, parochial, different in kind. Although they had to work
with materials bequeathed them by the colonial political economy, they did not just
buy into the ready-made persona offered to them. In this, their attire was symbolic
of their general situation. And through it they represented themselves volubly: fabri-
cated largely from foreign materials, it nonetheless expressed a locally tooled identity
that elaborated on the vicissitudes of their history.[11]

Although this double-sided give-and-take of consumption—and its various metaphors—pervaded the colonial period, it has expanded exponentially in postcolonial Africa. It has become, in fact, somewhat predatory
and corrupt. The political news about Africa has been and continues to
be replete with countless headlines of waste, theft, corruption, and greed.
When the notoriously corrupt Félix Houphouet-Boigny was asked about
the multimillion-dollar price tag of the cathedral that he had built in his
Ivoirien home town, he proudly stated that funding for the structure had
not come from the Ivoirien state, but from his own pocket! In contrast to
popular belief, the "feeding frenzy" in contemporary African politics is not
limited to the elite; it is practiced by all segments of a population. The lon-
gest overhead power line in the world joining the dams at Inga and Shaba
serves as a perfect symbol of this truth: the corner irons of the pylons have
been appropriated by villagers to make beds, shovels, and other tools. The
daily cannibalization of the line is a modest and popular counterpoint to
the huge profits made by foreign civil engineers and Congolese decision
makers as a result of the construction of this grandiose and useless project.
Up, down, and across lines of seniority, politics, class, and ethnicity, men
and women are engaged in a fight for vitality—a continuously and variously waged battle for access and rights to limited resources.[12]

To amass and redistribute a fortune—by any means—is a sign par excellence of the contemporary vitality in much of Africa. Such action epito-
mizes popular notions of the African chief. Like Félix Houphouet-Boigny,
the shape of the African chief is almost always expansive, a symbol of
wealth. Such corpulent wealth rests deeply in the center of the sensuous
politics of postcolonial Africa. "The 'politics of the belly' carries a much
richer symbolic meaning than its polemical connotation might at first
suggest. In short, wealth is a potential sign of being at one with the forces
of the cosmos."[13]

When individuals "consume," however, they comport themselves in
various ways. As Bayart suggested, Africa "consumes" in a variety of ways.

"The regimes of political diet vary from the Nigerian or Zairois bulimia to the Tanzanian or Nigerien slimmer's diet, from the prophetic appetite of an Ahmed Sekou Touré or a Macia Nguema to the schizophrenic greed of Marxist-Leninist leaders, or from the redeeming austerity of a Jerry Rawlings or a Murtala Mohammed to the voluptuous appetite of a Félix Houphouet-Boigny or a Jomo Kenyatta."[14]

As I thought about Mounkaila Mayaki from yet another vantage in the between, I reconnected myself to the sensuousness of history and social life, which brought on a confrontation with "hardness," one of the core concepts of Songhay sorcery. If you are a "hard" sorcerer, you never retreat. In the most trying situations, you never betray your emotions. How did "hardness" have an impact on politics in Niger? How did "hardness" shape Mounkaila Mayaki's decision to return to Côte d'Ivoire?

Embodied Memories

One of the central myths of Nigerien political culture is that of Dongo, the mercurial thunder god, who is like the countryside of Niger: hard and unforgiving. When Dongo emerges in the primordial past he willfully burns villages, destroys crops and kills human beings. Faced by this celestial threat, Faran Maka Boté, the first praise singer to the spirits, intercedes and asks Dongo, the epitome of political hardness, for mercy. Dongo gives Faran the following choice: submit and coexist, flee, or die. The myth establishes that the king (of the sky) has control of supernatural elements—vitality—that he will use unflinchingly to burn, kill, and subjugate his subjects and consume the spoils.

Sonni Ali Ber (1464–91) used this very formula to free Songhay from the Kingdom of Mali to establish the Songhay Empire. Reputedly the greatest sorcerer of his day, Sonni Ali Ber was putatively capable of transforming himself into a vulture. From the sky, he surveyed his dominion and planned his attacks, which were murderously vicious. Like Dongo, he killed anyone who tried to resist him and then burned and pillaged the conquered villages, leaving in his wake a dust cloud of fear that did not dissipate. In this way, the power of Songhay expanded exponentially.[1]

Sonni Ali Ber's successor, Askia Mohammed Touré, used Islam as well as his magical capacities to dominate his subjects. Like Ali Ber, Askia Mohammed fought and won most of his battles. Like his predecessor, he was ruthless and hard. He forced newly conquered subjects to submit to his rule. Askia's soldiers killed those who contested his authority. He then consumed the spoils of his victory.

From the fall of the Songhay Empire in 1591 until the arrival of the French Expeditionary Forces during the last decade of the nineteenth century, there was a power vacuum in what is today the Republic of Niger. In the wake of the Songhay Empire there arose numerous chieftaincies and principalities that engaged in what the French call—quite wonderfully—*guerre intestin,* internecine war. These are small-scale wars of short duration and limited geographical reach. The major goal of these little wars was the capture of slaves. This period, of which there is little documentation in the historical record, featured ever-shifting alliances of chieftaincies within and between ethnic groups.

During these "hard" times, peasant farmers, as always, paid the dearest price. Marauding Songhay, Fulan, Tuareg, or Hausa chiefs burned their villages, stole their women and children, and requisitioned their food. These seasonal raids put these peasants between the forces of warring states, between nature and politics. This betweeness created much personal insecurity—except during the planting season (June through September) when all hostilities ceased. During this time, no one polity commanded complete power over the land. Unlike Sonni Ali Ber and Askia Mohammed Touré, men molded in the image of the deity Dongo, no one controlled celestial firepower, commanded unflagging respect, or exercised far-reaching authority.

By the turn of the twentieth century the French Army had filled this power vacuum. In their relentless military campaigns, they fired their pistols, rifles, and canons with as much brutal force as the mythical Dongo. Consider the early military record of the French Expeditionary Forces. In 1898 the French colonial authorities formed the infamous Voulet-Chanoine column, which pillaged its way through western and southern Niger, eventually defeating the Hausa army of Zinder as well as that of the Kel Elway Tuareg. Eventually the Voulet-Chanoine column joined another French Army column to engage and defeat Rebeh of Bornu, a feat that enabled the French to create in 1900 the Third Military Territory of Niger.[2] In 1906 William Ponty, governor-general of French West Africa, wrote in his official report:

The conquest of the Djerma is of recent date. It goes back about seven years and we should remember how rapid it was. After the passage of the Voulet-Chanoine mission, which had left blood traces in the villages it passed through, notably, Sansanne-Houssa, where 400 people had been massacred . . . the terrorized villagers let us establish ourselves when we decided upon occupation. Without a murmur, they helped us by providing the provision and porters we needed.[3]

Anthropologist Jean-Pierre Olivier de Sardan called these practices the "politics of terror." From the French military perspective, pacification "posed few problems." From the perspective of rural peoples in Niger, pacification meant burnt granaries, razed villages, summary executions, and devastating famines. "Thought of the Voulet-Chanoine column remained in all the memories. Fear reigned in the countryside."[4] At the end of the era of French pacification in Niger (circa 1915), what cultural attributes did *anasaarey* (Europeans) have in the eyes of the pacified? It can be reasonably assumed that Europeans were considered soldiers (*sodjê*). Soldiers took what they wanted: food and porters—spoils. Soldiers imposed discipline through terror: they fined, imprisoned, or executed those who disobeyed them. Soldiers were tough, merciless men who lacked courtesy and respect. And they were feared.[5]

This folk portrait of the French colonial soldier is curiously similar to that of Dongo and his relations with Faran Make Boté. Faced with Dongo's inconceivable firepower, Faran submitted to the greater power and authority of one who didn't care if he was liked, of one who would kill anyone who showed him disrespect. Like Dongo and his mortal models, Sonni Ali Ber and Askia Mohammed Touré, the French soldier became an unrelenting "hard" man who, as the Songhay ritual incantation says, won't step back, even when facing a lion. In Niger, the French reestablished an order based upon a sensuously hard politics of terror, an order that had not been known in Niger since the fall of the Songhay Empire in 1591. If peasants could neither flee nor disappear they had to learn how to coexist.

The dire need to submit and find a way to coexist with the French may have triggered the Hauka movement in 1925. According to Roger Bastide, spirit possession is manifested in times of precipitous change.[6] In western Niger, it emerged when the Songhay Empire consolidated under the tough rule of Askia Mohammed Touré. When the French ended hundreds of years of guerre intestin by terrorizing Nigeriens between 1898 and 1915, they set up in 1922 the Colony of Niger. They were "hard" soldiers who controlled firepower—a hard kind of vitality.

In this sociopolitical context new spirits emerged in Tondigandia in Niger. Hausa people called them *babulé* (Europeans). Songhay people called them *hauka,* which in Hausa means "crazy or mad." According to Nicole Echard,

[t]he Babulé begins during the 1925 harvest following the return to the village of a woman called Shibbo who had lived in a neighboring region. There, she had been

"attacked" by the "Europeanne," a female spirit of the brand new Babulé family, and she returned along with a few mediums of these new spirits as well as with musician-griots who knew their melodies and their demands. In one month the movement was organized under the guidance of Shibbo-the-Europeanne. About 100 people, considered as soldiers, formed a collectivity under the authority of a general staff that copied the French military hierarchy. The Europeanne ordered the manufacture of rifles: the blacksmiths were capable only of reproducing the form and only the bayonet was usable. During the day the men and women, who had abandoned the harvest after Shibbo's return, went to the bush to train for guerrilla war. Guard duty was organized, and lookouts were assigned positions in the village. Every evening there was a spirit possession dance during which the Babule came to hunt witches.[7]

The movement spread to other villages, where the "outlaws" were banished. New Hauka villages were founded. Finding the movement a threat to its authority, the Nigerien colonial government brutally crushed the movement and banished its leaders. They exiled Shibbo to what is today Burkina Faso. Faced with prison or forced exile, many of the adepts fled to the colonial Gold Coast where Hauka spirit possession flourished. It was in the colonial Gold Coast that Jean Rouch made perhaps his most memorable film, *Les maitres fous,* which depicts with a brutal and straightforward honesty the mimetic power of the Hauka spirits.[8]

How might Hauka spirit possession provide Nigeriens a way to coexist with French colonial rule? Among many West Africans, including Songhay and Hausa people, as we have already seen, when one is faced with insurmountable power, one first submits to it and then finds a way to coexist. In Faran Make Boté's case, he coexisted by becoming Dongo's praise singer. Conquered by the armies of Sonni Ali Ber and Askia Mohammed Touré, peasants paid tribute as they kept their distance from centers of power, authority, and abuse. During the era of guerre intestin, peasants attempted to become "invisible" to their oppressors. In the colonial period, Songhay and Hausa people may have used what Michael Taussig has called the "mimetic faculty" to coexist with French colonial authority.[9] The mimetic faculty enables a person in ever-shifting contexts of change, to grasp that which is strange. In other words, one mimes or copies something—in our case, the colonial hierarchy in French-occupied Niger—to comprehend and master it. Walter Benjamin argued that miming creates a powerful storm of sensations that enable people to understand and master that which is strangely powerful. Following this logic, we can argue that the peoples in Niger copied the colonial French soldiers and administrative officials in order to comprehend and perhaps master them—at least culturally and psychologically.

Just as the Tooru spirits expressed the celestial power of the Songhay kings, so the Hauka sensuously grasped the power of the French: their fiery guns, the ability of their armies to conquer, their seemingly endless supplies of men, weapons, and food, their stern resoluteness, their ability to inflict pain and to regulate. The French had become the epitome of Dongo-like hardness and terror. Might one capture some of that force through mimesis? In place of an officer's bullwhip the Hauka cracked whips fashioned from automobile fan belts. In place of immaculate uniforms, they wore inverted gourds or pith helmets. Hauka spirits walked and talked like soldiers. They held meetings like soldiers at the end of which they made declarations—to refuse to pay taxes in the early years. And when they danced, they invariably asked for fire, which they handled with no ill effect. This handling of fire not only became a demonstration of Hauka invincibility but also a compelling example of embodied celestial firepower, the firepower of Dongo, the spiritual manifestation of hardness. In time spirit possession priests in Niger claimed that the Hauka, those militarily inspired handlers of fire, came from the Red Sea and were, in fact, the offspring of the central deity of fire power and state authority—Dongo.[10] And so the path from the distant past had been followed once again, leading people from myth, to political practice, and finally to spirit possession—all calibrated to make an always already abuse of power a bit more palatable.

French colonialism ended in Niger not with a bang, to borrow from T. S. Eliot, but a whimper. In the regime of the Republic of Niger's first president, Hamani Diori (1960–1974), French officials occupied key positions in the Government of Niger (GON). Indeed, France supplied much of the GON's revenues through generous "contributions" to Niger's gross domestic product. France also maintained a garrison of the French Army in Niamey, the capital city of Niger. Diori had a private understanding with the French government that if his rule were threatened, the garrison would intervene to restore order.[11] Given these financial and military conditions, one could argue that French colonialism had not, in fact, ended with Nigerien independence.

During the Diori years there were no popular uprisings in response to years of massive corruption or even the excessive taxation of rural peasants in years of drought and famine. Following the aforementioned path of the past, Nigeriens submitted to and coexisted with the less than absolute rule of their "powerful" leaders. There are limits, of course, to tolerance of the excessive abuse of power. When famine gripped Niger's countryside in 1974 the Nigerien military obeyed presidential decrees to collect taxes and requisition rural goods—a soldierly act rooted in the precolonial and colonial past. By April 1974 President Diori, however, had passed the limit of the military's tolerance. Led by Lt. Colonel Seyni Kountché, the Nigerien Army toppled Diori from power, killing his wife Aissa, and imprisoning his cronies.

From the very beginning, the Kountché regime stressed its military bearing, its no-nonsense and unflinching style of austere government, and its insistence of "honesty" as opposed to the corruption of the ancient régime—a hard, slimmer's diet. Analysis of the Kountché regime's discourse suggests that Seyni Kountché, himself a Hauka spirit medium, manipulated Hauka sensuousness to consolidate power, design his program for progress, and promote a general state of fear in the population. This fear enabled him to govern Niger with little serious opposition.[12]

In 1974 Kountché's gang, through word and image, constructed an aura of resolute hardness—"sans tendresse." When they appeared in public, Kountché and his military ministers wore battle fatigues, wore sunglasses and assumed menacing postures. These were certainly "military" images but they also implicate Dongo, the tough deity of thunder. They also evoke the great kings of the Nigerien past whose brutal hardness mimicked the dominating behavior of the sky king. In postcolonial Niger the images also evoked Hauka subtexts in which powerful beings control firepower, demand submission, and refuse to retreat in the face of adversity.

One month after taking power, Kountché expelled the French military from Niger. This move, in essence, symbolically ended French colonialism in Niger. The expulsion, in fact, severed an important link between Niger and France, which clearly distinguished the practices of the old and new regimes. Kountché constructed the old regime as tired, uninspired, weak, timid, and corrupt; the new regime was, by contrast, energetic, inspired, strong, bold, and austere. Kountché faced down the French army, the ultimate symbol of power in Nigerien colonial consciousness. Like the courageously cruel kings of the past—and like the Hauka—he did not blink. Kountché had defeated the very institution that had razed and pillaged villages, requisitioned goods, provoked famine, established forced labor gangs, and collected pernicious head taxes. Through victory Kountché demonstrated power and hardness. The Nigerien people submitted to him with the kind of fear and respect that was mythically expressed in Faran Make Boté's capitulation to Dongo. This "hard" mandate enabled him to accumulate quietly enormous wealth.

Members of his own government repeatedly challenged the rule and authority of President Kountché but failed to usurp his power. This tough resilience augmented Kountché's reputation as a fearless and brave man

President Seyni Kountché of Niger, circa 1994. Photographer unknown.

whose connections to the spirit world—his Hauka mediumship—enabled him to have access to both military and celestial firepower. Through his bearing, his words, and his deeds, Kountché triggered cultural memories of past brutalities in order to control the present with fists of stone. In the final *Jeune Afrique* article written about his regime Kountché was asked why his official photo presents a man with a severe expression and menacing eyes. Kountché replied,

Because I am neither tall nor fat, it's a thing with me, to scare Nigeriens . . . You know, Nigeriens are a people who are difficult to govern. That's why I have to beat them from time to time, especially civil servants, students and merchants in order to make them realize that I have my eye on them and they must not play with the state.[13]

Kountché had proved himself to be a man of force, a hard man who held power in a hard place. He had successfully applied the slimmer's diet to Niger and had consumed the spoils.

The end of the Kountché regime led to an ongoing contemporary era of *politique intestin*. From 1987 to the present there have been two military regimes and two democratically elected governments—not to forget a few bloody coups. In their disdainful effort to "consume" Nigerien society, not one of these regimes has been able to consume and redistribute the diminishing store of Nigerien spoils. This recipe has led to ongoing instability, increased repression, and widespread scarcity.

This record of contemporary politics, of course, means little, if anything to the peasant families living in the Nigerien bush. For them the important questions have less to do with a GON-sponsored program than with the presence or absence of rainfall, pestilence, and soldiers. The harsh ecology of the Sahel is so fragile that the slightest disruption can jeopardize the millet harvest and bring on a year of hunger and famine. Gazing at the sky, inspecting the field, or observing the horizon, the farmer calculates if he will produce enough food to feed his family. He wonders if he will avoid the scourge of disease. He hopes that the state and its soldiers will forget about the food he grows and effectively leave him alone to lead his peaceful life in the bush.

When the state makes its presence known in the Nigerien bush, which it has invariably tried to do, a subject, like Faran Maka Boté, has usually submitted to its overwhelming power. He or she then attempts to coexist with it by figuratively disappearing, by providing it with a minimum of his or her labor, by making sense of its madness through the power-ciphering of Hauka spirit possession or, if possible, by migrating to a space beyond the state's trenchant authority. Faced with this sensuous matrix of historical precedent and contemporary possibility, Mounkaila Mayaki chose flight rather than coexistence. He decided to move beyond the hardness of Niger.

———

What, then, is embodied in Mounkaila Mayaki's curious decision to return to Côte d'Ivoire? How can we explain why he would prefer to live in a place where it is possible that he could at any moment be the victim of mob violence—an absurd death? Elsewhere in postcolonial Africa the omnipresence of absurd death is so overwhelming that people have entered a benumbed space in which the present is nebulous and the past is glaringly absent. Writing of the Congo Republic in the wake of longtime ruler of Zaire, Mobutu, Filip De Boeck described a social field reduced to a state of surreal zombification:

In the end, in the postcolonial beyond, certainly during the Mobutu era, we find no pre- or postmortem any longer, no past and no future, no memory and no oblivion, no dead and no living—or rather, only "fake real dead" and "real fake living" (just as there were vrais faux dollars or faux vrais passports). Locked together because of their incapacity both to remember and to forget, they became trapped at the end of history's cobwebs. Beyond the grave there lies no peace, only the shuffling along of severed souls, dead or alive.[14]

Although the Congolese dispossession described by De Boeck and Réné Devisch is hauntingly poignant, it goes without saying that the mosaic of embodied cultural memories can be equally haunting.[15] In Niger the historical and contemporary record is clear. The state, in whatever form, in whatever historical period, has wanted its subjects to remember the unrelenting brutality, hardness, and celestial firepower of the past. In this way the state has attempted to rule its population by, in the words of the late President Seyni Kountché, beating them from time to time.

The cultural memories of Nigerien state power are embedded, as we have already seen, in the recurring performance of myth and spirit possession ceremonies. They are also embodied in the public performance of epic poetry (the epic of Askia Mohammed) and other oral histories.[16] Taking a more sensuous tack, however, we can assume that cultural memories are also infused in familial objects and/or narratives that speak to the lived experience of relatively powerless people like Mounkaila Mayaki, whose story will become a small chapter in a Nigerien history—"from below."[17] In Niger the more individual realm of cultural memory—or sensuous perception—is not usually about bravery or bravado; it is usually about how people learned to coexist with (a) the brutal conditions brought on by the state or (b) the existential uncertainties triggered by guerre intestine, politique intestine, or the harsh Sahelian environment.

For men like Mounkaila Mayaki history seems to conform to Maurice Merleau-Ponty's open-ended phenomenological model. Mounkaila Mayaki's example suggests that for him, history is a matrix of possibilities presented by circumstances of the lived present. From this culturally contoured matrix, his body is infused by those elements that will affect his future. History is therefore internal and external, personal and impersonal, centered and decentered, partial and whole. It charts the rough texture of lived experience along a path that originates in the distant past. It projects a deep-seated cultural imaginary that enables people like Mounkaila Mayaki to make difficult existential decisions.

Does this sensuous knowledge help us to understand ongoing state violence on a continent in which the role of the state has substantially diminished? Does it help us to understand the resilience of people who have suffered from unimaginable loss?[18] Can it help us to explain something as profoundly complex as collective trauma or as disturbingly nuanced as penis shrinking? In the face of multisensorial transnational complexities, can it bring us a dose of intellectual humility? A move toward a more sensuous ethnography, I concluded at the end of the detour that immersed me in the sensuousness of Mounkaila Mayaki's life, may not concretely answer many of the imponderables that give shape to contemporary relations between the state and its subjects in Africa. But it may well enable us to understand better the endless and unstable flows and eddies of the between. It may even enable us to understand more fully that which occurs in the very face of our being.

Mounkaila Mayaki, of course, lives in West Africa, a place where he is immersed in the culture of his ancestors, which means he has the cultural potential to live well, as the French like to say, in his skin. How do West Africans like Issifi Mayaki make their cultural way in a strange place like New York City where the language, culture, and religion are alien and alienating?

Wood

On some afternoons at the Malcolm Shabazz Harlem Market African art merchants would join our informal discussion group. Unlike my friends at the Harlem market, these men were mobile merchants. They would arrive in the United States with containers filled with African art—masks and statues fashioned from wood, iron, or terra-cotta. When they had depleted their inventory, they would return to West Africa, profits in hand, and invest their money in transport, real estate, and, to be sure, more African art.

One afternoon in the fall of 1997, I visited Issifi Mayaki at the Malcolm Shabazz Harlem Market. I relayed to him what I had discovered about "hardness" and the mythic and political history of Niger. He told me that his father was doing well in Abidjan. "He feels safe," Issifi said. "Things are calm in Abidjan. No more rumors of penis-shrinking sorcery."

As we were chatting, El Hadj Harouna Abdou, an African art trader, sat down with us. El Hadj Harouna explained that he had been an African art merchant for almost thirty years. He also wanted to learn more about me. "Where did you learn to speak Songhay?" he asked me, after the traditional series of greetings.

"I lived in Mehanna, Tera, and Tillaberi," I answered.

"I know them well," he answered. He was a tall, angular man with long spindly arms and legs. Etched with lines of long years of travel and toil, his face betrayed his age, which, he told me, was somewhere around sixty. "I'm not certain of the year I was born, but it was around the 'Great Swollen Belly Famine,' which they say took place in 1938." Although his lean features suggested severity, the glint of his eyes, black and clear, suggested a man full of good humor.

"That means you are an elder."

"May God be praised," he said slapping me playfully on the shoulder. "You're not young yourself." He scratched his chin from which sprouted sporadic white beard hair. "You come here often?"

I explained to El Hadj that I was writing a book about the West African traders in New York City. "I think people," I said, "would like to know your stories."

"The people in Harlem?" he asked.

I nodded.

"What about us?" he asked, rhetorically. "We came here years before Issifi and the other traders set foot in Harlem. What about our stories?"

I explained that I heard about African art traders that traveled across the United States, but hadn't met any of them.

"You have now. We are many, but we are not in Harlem. I am here with two of my younger brothers, Yaya and Mamadou. We are all from Belleyara. Do you know it?"

"Yes. It's a large market town on the road to Fillingué."

El Hadj Harouna slapped my shoulder once again. "Iri koy beri. Great God, you know my village." He shifted in his seat. "You must come to the Warehouse and see the *bundu* we have brought to New York."

"You brought *wood* to New York?" I asked incredulously.

El Hadj Harouna flashed me an angular smile. "For us 'wood' is what you call art."

"That makes sense," I said, "most African art is shaped from wood."

"We also sell *botogo.*"

"Mud?"

"We have some very old terra-cotta pieces." El Hadj Harouna shifted in his chair. "What are you doing now?"

I had planned to interview some recently arrived Harlem market traders that afternoon. "I'm at the market today and I return to Philadelphia tomorrow."

"Come with me to the Warehouse."

I dropped my plans for that afternoon and accompanied El Hadj Harouna to the Warehouse, which has been the major storehouse of African "wood" in New York City.

———

El Hadj Harouna and I took the subway to Penn Station and walked west toward the Hudson River in Chelsea. Walking through a patchwork of scrap metal yards, automobile mechanic shops, and taxi garages, compelled me yet again to think about the between. A man like El Hadj Harouna had spent thirty years living between things: between Africa and the Unites States, between the worlds of art and commodity. He seemed to negotiate effortlessly the tangle of cultural and social paths that weave their way through the between, and for that I admired him. Reflecting back on my own difficulties negotiating the anthropological between, I wondered how he was able to draw strength and confidence from both sides of the divide through which he had long traveled. Had I been able to incorporate a small sample of his resolve, I might have been able to return to Niger and continue my study of sorcery.

Our approach to another space between things, the Warehouse, brought me back to the immediate present. The Warehouse is a large six-story facility that comprises one-half of a city block in Manhattan. It stands between 11th Avenue and the Hudson River and as of this writing is still stocked with "African art."

Outside the Warehouse, we saw a line of loading bays—to facilitate shipments—along the north and south sides of the building. When we walked into the Warehouse we left New York and found ourselves in distinctly West African space. Seated in the corridor in front of their stalls, art merchants greeted us warmly in English, French, Songhay, Bamana, and Hausa. The dank air inside the facility smelled like Africa. Acrid scents of wood smoke mixed with the sweet aroma of sandalwood infused the air and brought back memories West African living space.

The corridor led us to a first-floor showroom and meeting center. Bordered by stalls in which individual traders displayed their objects to potential buyers, we came upon a central space outfitted with card tables, frayed junkyard sofas and makeshift chairs. Here clusters of traders, some itinerant, others longstanding immigrants greeted and talked with one another as they ate plates of food prepared by two women in a small room that served as the "African" kitchen. The lighting was dim, making it difficult to see.

Wooden masks and statues—tall, short, delicate, and massive—filled every nook and cranny of space. They were arranged in no particular order. Many of the objects rested on dollies or had been stacked upon one another in dingy corner spaces. Open boxes of beads lay about. Large sacks of fonio, a highly prized West African grain, had been piled on carts. Young men carried art objects inside to be stored or loaded objects into vans to be shipped to North American markets. On that afternoon, like every afternoon, as El Hadj Harouna explained, the Warehouse was a continuous buzz of activity. At midafternoon when the Imam called the Muslim faithful to prayer, though, the blur and din of business stopped. El Hadj Harouna and his brother traders then performed their ritual ablutions and went to pray in the Mosque, a small rectangular room, the concrete floor of which had been covered with oriental rugs. At the Warehouse, I quickly realized, "art," possessing no transcendental qualities, was arranged like any commodity stocked in a storage facility. Here, "art" was nothing more than a piece of "wood" or a molding of "mud" that sometimes might provide a handsome return on investment.

––––––

How and why would West African traders consider African art to be "wood" and "mud?" The answer, I discovered after some research and reflection, devolves from a trading tradition profoundly shaped by Islam and the history of long-distance trading in West Africa. In my book about West African street traders in New York City, *Money Has No Smell,* I described how Islam and the history of long-distance trading in West Africa has shaped the economic and social practices of West African street vendors in Harlem.[1] Although the West African art traders at the Warehouse are quite distinct from the street vendors described in that work, their ideas and expectations about display, trade, and marketing have been no less influenced by religion and history. Like the street vendors, art traders at the Warehouse, I discovered, are usually members of West African ethnic groups—Soninke, Hausa, and Wolof—that have long been the professional traders of West Africa.[2] From the eighteenth century to the present these groups have traded cloth, kola, tobacco, and beads throughout West Africa. Through trade they not only helped to expand the political reach of nascent West African states but also extended the reach of their religion—Islam.[3]

From its beginning Islam and merchant capital have been inextricably linked. Commerce, in fact, has been central to the development and diffusion of Islam.[4] In the Prophet Mohammad's new society, the *Ummah* (community of believers) became a collection of human beings protected by Allah. In theory, allegiance to the Ummah transcended all class divisions and ethnic identification. Mohammad, whose wife Fatima was herself a prosperous merchant, deemed trade an honorable profession. Expansion of trade, in his view, would enable the Ummah to grow, prosper, and expand its power and influence. Trade, according to the Prophet

Muhammad, should be conducted to foster and ensure good social relations; it should be straightforward, reliable and, above all, honest. In various passages of the Koran and the Sunnah, there are many statements about giving false oaths, correct weights, and goodwill in transactions. The Prophet Muhammad stressed that contracts be established clearly and comprehensively. He stood against monopolistic practices and forbade usury because these actions undermined commercial and social relations—which should not be deemed as separate.[5] As pious Muslims, West African art traders at the Warehouse attempt to follow these traditional principles, though some of the dictates, as would be expected, have been refined to fit contemporary economic circumstances.

The economic principles of Islam reinforce familial solidarity generated by the real and fictive kinship ties of West African trading families. As in any kinship system the rites and obligations in West African trading families devolve from three factors: age, gender, and generation. Jean-Loup Amselle has written about these widespread trading families among the Kooroko of southern Mali. Among the Kooroko, the head of a household supplies food, shelter, clothing, and tax money for the people in his compound, who, in turn, give him what they produce. Sometimes the head of household is also a distinguished trader, a *jula-ba,* who manages the activities of a long-distance trading network from the comforts of his compound. Well informed by kinspeople, affines, and friends, the great trader is cognizant of changing market conditions close to and far away from home. When conditions are good, the great trader sends his *jula-ben* (lit. trader-child—younger brothers, children, and his brothers' children) to distant markets to sell kola nuts or buy cattle. In the distant markets (Côte D'Ivoire, Ghana, France, or even New York City) the "children" of the great trader are received, informed, and housed by hosts who usually have blood or marriage ties to the great trader. Following the transaction, the "children" of the trader return home and report to their "father." They receive no remuneration for their economic efforts. In time the paternal kinsmen of the great trader may ask for economic independence, which is granted along with a payment that is used to start a new enterprise.[6]

Sometimes the great trader hasn't a sufficient number of paternal kin to direct his long-distance enterprises. In these cases, the *jula-ba* employs his maternal kin, the children of his sisters, or friends who are not part of his personal kindred. No matter the degree of blood-relatedness, the "children" must all observe the rights and obligations of the great trader's paternal kin. Like the great trader's paternal kin, they receive no remuneration for their initial services. After several successful missions, though, trader "children" in this category can ask their "father" for a loan to buy their own inventory. The "children" continue to perform services for the great trader but have entered into a contractual partnership—albeit an unequal one—with their "father." Indeed, the use of these kin relationships in long-distance trading eases the existential burden of these "strangers in a strange land," traders who are very much between things.

In the early stages of the contractual relationship, "children" must give their "father" two-thirds of earned profits. If "children" manage to regularly earn profits from their loans, the great trader may offer them more credit. If "children" fail to produce profits, which means that they have failed to negotiate the spaces between things, the great trader will continue to employ them but will never grant them another loan. Successful "children" eventually give the great trader 50 percent of the profits. If "children" become prosperous, they take their leave from the great trader and become *jula-ba* themselves, economic masters of being between things.[7]

New World Circuits

During my ethnographic investigations in New York City, I discovered that historic West African trading patterns tend to persist in New York City among West African street vendors in Harlem as well as West African art traders at the Warehouse.[1] Core networks often consisted of paternal and maternal kin ("cousins") linked to a *jula-ba* in West Africa. Other networks linked unrelated traders who came from the same town or region. In New York, though, shared ethnicity seemed to play a greater role than kinship ties in establishing and maintaining networks.[2] Whatever the composition of the art trading network, however, participants, following the dictates of Islam, actively cooperated with one another. They shared market information, divided the costs of transport from New York City to points in the U.S. countryside (called the "bush") and extended credit to one another. Their object was to move as much product ("wood" and "mud") as possible. Funds from the sale of "wood" and "mud" were reinvested collectively in more "wood" but also in precious gems, real estate, and transport vehicles.[3] Money was also sent back to West Africa to support a trader's extended family.

Like the West African street traders in Harlem, West African art traders have had to adjust their commercial practices to North American economic realities They have been acutely sensitive to changing patterns of U.S. consumption. Thirty years ago, when El Hadj Harouna began to trade in "wood," very few traders came to North America. They sold much of their inventory to gallery owners and to small numbers of private clients. In the late 1990s, according to El

Hadj Harouna, the number of traders bringing objects to North America increased exponentially. From El Hadj Harouna's perspective, the North American market for African art had expanded.[4]

There are two possible reasons for the expansion. The excitement surrounding the Museum of Modern Art's (MOMA) 1984 exhibit, Primitivism in Twentieth-Century Art, to consider the first reason, augmented the legitimacy and increased the value of tribal art. This attracted new groups of collectors looking to invest in objects the value of which would quickly increase. The appeal of Afrocentrism, to consider the second reason, triggered much interest in Africa—including interest in African art—in African American communities. In Harlem, African American shoppers have bought the aforementioned Ghanaian "kente" cloth strips and hats from West African vendors. West African beads, incense, amulets, jewelry, and "kente" products, according to West African vendors in Harlem, underscored Afrocentric identification with Africa.[5] Henry Louis Gates suggested that middle-class African Americans often felt the "guilt of the survivor" and bought Afrocentric products as a way of maintaining cultural fidelity with blackness. Kwame Anthony Appiah, author of the much-celebrated *In My Father's House*, wrote:

African American culture is so strongly identified with a culture of poverty and degradation . . . you have a greater investment, as it were, more to prove [if you are middle-class], so Kwanzaa and kente cloth are part of proving that you're not running away from being black, which is what you're likely to be accused of by other blacks.[6]

Understanding this hunger for blackness and Africa, West African art traders realized that by tapping these markets they could make money.

As a result they began to send larger and larger shipments of African objects to North America. Very few of these objects, according to the antiquities dealers with whom I've talked, qualified as "fine art." Some of them, though, qualified as decorative art—high-quality reproductions. The vast majority of the new objects, however, had been marked for quick sales to mass markets. They were mass-produced masks and statues and recently sculpted terra-cotta objects. The mass-produced objects were sold throughout the United States in street markets, well-known flea markets such as those in New Orleans and Santa Fe, and at third world and African American cultural festivals. Decorative objects were sold to wholesalers, to boutiques, to selected galleries, and to private clients.

These markets expanded the networks of West African art traders. Principal traders often remained at the Warehouse to monitor the comings and goings of African objects. Some of the principal traders, I learned, were documented immigrants and remained in New York City; others were older, more-established traders, like El Hadj Harouna and his brothers, who came to New York for short periods of time. They preferred to remain in New York where they sold higher-end objects to local clients or gallery owners. No matter the immigrant status of the principal traders, they were connected to mobile merchants, male and female traders, who came to North America for three to six months. Hauling their own inventory as well as that of older, less mobile traders, they traveled with "chauffeurs," West African men who drove these mobile merchants across the United States. They zigzagged across the country, following circuits of African American and third world Festivals. Well away from the bustle of New York City, they also visited private clients as well as boutiques and African art galleries.

When they traveled, they were received by their North American "hosts," kinspeople or compatriots who had settled in such places as New Orleans, Atlanta, Miami, Chicago, Indianapolis, Houston, Dallas, Minneapolis, Detroit, Denver, Albuquerque, San Francisco, Seattle, and Los Angeles. Hosts often housed their "cousins." They also helped them to store inventory, informed them of potential outlets for their goods, and introduced them to potential clients. In this way, West African art traders increased their client lists. They also knew where to go for restoration—to make "wood" look more like "art"—especially to their high-end clients. In New York, a West African man had a workshop near the Warehouse, where he repaired broken "wood" and "mud." Mobile merchants on the West Coast employed the expert services of art professionals in San Rafael, California, who restored art fashioned from wood, stone, ceramic, ivory, and metals. They also worked on patinas and crafted custom bases. These professionals did restoration of the following types of art: antique, contemporary, ethnographic, Asian, Africa, Oceanic, pre-Columbia, and Indonesian. This restorer said that he did a great deal of work for African traders—especially in wood and the restoration of terra-cotta figures.[7]

Looking to move "wood" and "mud," African mobile merchants traveled from city to city, festival to festival, boutique to boutique, and client to client until they depleted their inventories. When their Econoline vans were empty, they came back to New York, settled their accounts with their "cousins," and returned to West Africa where they settled more accounts—with their "fathers"—reinvested their profits, and looked after their families.[8]

Art

Learning about "wood" and its increasing value placed me in an anthropological between that linked the world of West African commerce to the world of art—galleries, and high-end exhibitions. Rooted in my position between the worldviews of art collectors and African art traders, I tried to understand the conceptual space African art and artists occupied. In time, I learned how and why the valuation of African art had become part of a long process rooted in Western philosophy and the history of European commercial relations.

As became clear in light of my investigation, the space of (African) art has been shaped by an ethos of transcendentalism. In his *Critique of Judgment*, published in 1790, Immanuel Kant first defined the field of rarefied aesthetics by establishing universal criteria of taste in art. In that work, Kant went to great lengths to make vision both the preeminent sense of universal taste and the ontological between separating the observer and the observed. In so doing, he laid the foundation for an objective universal gaze that would elevate so-called high art to an almost sacred plain. This objective, almost quasi-religious in tone, is reinforced tenfold in G. W. F. Hegel's *Esthetics*. Like all the elements in his philosophy, Hegel considered art from a vantage of determinism. Objectively classified, art became part of the more general process of human development, the unfolding of the human spirit. The Hegelian narrative on art is a story that "moves inexorably from the Ancient World, to the Middle Ages, to the Renaissance, and then to the Modern World . . . This story's enabling assumption is that art always already was and that its story always already was there for the telling. No historiography, no social history need intrude on their straightforward and blessedly simple tale."[1] From a Hegelian perspective, the history of art and the objective criteria for its assessment go hand-in-hand with the story of the development of being a human—in the Ancient World, the Middle Ages, the Renaissance and, finally and ultimately in the Modern World. For Hegel, the Modern World means the nation-state built on a foundation of transcendental Christian values.[2] Put another way, the evolution of fine art has been an avenue leading to an evolving set of transcendental experiences—pathways that led to the realization of the human spirit. The story of art is therefore a central theme in the evolutionary march of progress that separated the West from the rest.[3]

The Hegelian take on art compels the tasteful observer to focus on the object rather than the social and economic considerations that led to its production—art for art's sake. "Despite long-standing debates and challenges to the problem and ideal of art's autonomy in the West, for many people engaged with the arts, the category of 'art' remains a resolutely commonsense one, associated with essential value in relation to a generalized human capacity for spirituality and creativity."[4] In the game of artistic judgment, transcendental Hegelianism is very much with us. In his noteworthy book, *High Art Down Home*, Stuart Plattner underscored this very point.

While the specifics of artistic merit are contested by workers in different media, there is agreement that high art should give the knowledgeable viewer a "transcendental" aesthetic experience that can change the way the viewer looks at reality. This sort of art is often challenging to the average viewer, difficult to interpret, and sometimes ugly, confusing, or otherwise upsetting. For the connoisseur, high art can stimulate intense emotional and intellectual responses.[5]

Connoisseurs have been collecting "art" for a very long time indeed. With the growth of the nation-state, however, private collections of transcendental objects became increasingly housed in various kinds of state-sponsored museums. Many scholars have linked the growth of "art" to colonial exploitation and the processes that legitimized imperial expansion—the civilizing mission of European nation-states. Despite the pull and power of ongoing discussion of transcendental art, as Shelly Errington pointed out in her insightful book, *The Death of Authentic Primitive Art and Other Tales of Progress*, "art" did not come into existence without a market. The great art auction houses, Sotheby's and Christie's, were both founded in the eighteenth century. Markets for high art expanded considerably in the nineteenth century—especially toward the end of that epoch. Impressionism, which was an artistic revolt against the aesthetic power of French academicism, was central to the development of modern art. Rather than exhibiting their art through "academic" channels, the impressionists displayed their painting at private exhibits. These exhibits, which culminated in their last group show in 1886, established the impressionists as practitioners of the avant-garde. Their art also generated incomes that enabled many impressionist artists to pursue their art full time.

The impressionists showed that financial success for artists was possible through the activities of key dealers and friendly critics, independent of state of official patronage. Moulin points out that Pissarro, Degas, Monet, Renoir and other impressionists earned incomes commensurate with those earned by civil servants (1987). Their "outrageous" art, when sold to discriminating, adventurous collectors, produced middle-class incomes for the artists.[6]

Plattner went on to describe how impressionism established a new network among avant-garde artists, dealers, critics, and collector-connoisseurs. This network provided both the cultural and economic foundation for such various twentieth-century avant-garde movements as futurism, cubism, abstract expressionism, minimalism, conceptual art, and so on. The recognition of economic incentive and the production of value, of course, did not diminish the importance of an art object's transcendental power—one source of its economic allure. Sensing perhaps the allure and power of transcendentalism, dealers adopted an ethos of display that mimicked that of the great museums—high ceilings, white walls, dim lighting, and minimal presentation. This aesthetic is still with us as any visitor to a high-end art gallery in Manhattan can attest. Plattner described a photo of an avant-garde art gallery in St. Louis. "The huge spaces, high ceilings, and dramatic exhibition style are designed to impress the viewer with the museum quality of the work."[7] Beyond its transcendental allure, of course, "museum quality" also means "high prices."

The tack of linking transcendentalism, economic incentive, and visual display has been very much evident in the development of taste in and the market for so-called "primitive art."[8] Following Errington's succinct chronology, we must go back to the 1913 Armory show, which introduced modern art to North America. The impact of the show eventually compelled rich patrons, including Abby Aldrich Rockefeller, to create the aforementioned Museum of Modern Art (MOMA) in 1929. Through exhibitions and its growing renown, curators at MOMA gave avant-garde art a profound legitimacy, which, of course, increased its value.

Meanwhile, Nelson Rockefeller began to collect "tribal" art from Africa, Oceania, and the Americas. When Rockefeller became MOMA's director in 1950, the museum paid serious attention to so-called "tribal" art. Just as MOMA's attention to modern art gave it a widespread aesthetic legitimacy and economic appeal, so its exhibitions of "tribal" art increased the desire for and the economic value of objects produced by nameless artists in Africa, Oceania, and the Americas. Critics wrote about these objects with new appreciation. Sensing the economic opportunity presented by "tribal" art, dealers purchased these kinds of objects from faraway worlds.

In 1957 the Museum of Primitive Art opened in New York City. Because the Rockefeller collection comprised its core, it became the focus of "primitive art" in North America. It remained open for two decades.

[The] two decades mark the golden age of primitive art's legitimacy. The existence of so many wonderful objects, beautifully exhibited and celebrated in fine arts museums as art, attested to the unproblematic nature of the category of authentic primitive art. During the period liberal and right-thinking people admired and celebrated it. Art historians and anthropologists discovered primitive art as a worthy subject of study, and an increasing number of books and articles appeared on the topic. A few art history departments hired specialists in primitive art, and several Ph.D. programs in non-Western art were established and produced their first graduates; a number of major museums established departments and curatorial positions of primitive art. As an essential category, primitive was almost unchallenged.[9]

The Museum of Primitive Art closed to make way for the Michael Rockefeller wing of the Metropolitan Museum of Art. When that opened in 1982, primitive art had found a place in one of the most legitimate and prestigious spaces of art. The display reproduced the aesthetic qualities valorized by the thought of Kant and Hegel—high ceilings, open spaces, and minimal presentation—a display that impelled close examination of the object's "transcendental qualities." Freed from the conditions of their production, the museum context gave these objects a timeless quality.[10]

In 1984 the MOMA's aforementioned Primitivism in Twentieth-Century Art exhibit extended the legitimacy of "tribal" art. The exhibition attempted to demonstrate how so-called primitive art had inspired the great practitioners of modern art. Georges Braque and Pablo Picasso, both of whom collected "tribal" art, kept many of the pieces in their studios. By juxtaposing those objects to various modern works, the exhibit curators wanted the viewer to see unmistakable parallels in form. In this way, "primitive" art was not simply a legitimate category, but had

African art for sale down the street from MOMA on 53rd Street in
Manhattan. Photograph by Jasmin Tahmaseb McConatha.

become—at least in the eyes of some scholars, connoisseurs, and dealers—the inspiration for cubist and surrealist art. How wonderful it would
be to own an object that had inspired Picasso! In this way the Primitivism
in Twentieth-Century Art exhibit generated enormous interest in primitive art. Several new museums opened—including the revamped and re-
housed Smithsonian National Museum of African Art as well as the Museum for African Art in New York City. For their part, critics and scholars
wrote much-appreciated books and articles about primitive art. Journals
like *African Arts* gave increased scholarly legitimacy to objects from the
third world.[11]

This series of events helped to reinforce a set of criteria for taste in "primitive" art. The objects needed provenance to establish their authenticity. Since the identity of the makers of most primitive objects remained unknown, provenance was linked to an object's history of collection, sale, and exhibition. Objects collected and/or owned by well-known connoisseurs, artists, or dealers would be highly valued—an important piece. The value would increase, moreover, if the object's plastic qualities conformed to the formal simplicity of modernist aesthetics.[12]

In the 1930s James Johnson Sweeney, who as curator of MOMA from 1935 to 1946 and then director of the Guggenheim Museum from 1952 to 1960, was one of the most prominent art historians of his era, wrote:

In the end, it is not the tribal characteristics of Negro art nor its strangeness that are interesting. It is its plastic qualities. Picturesque or exotic features as well as historical and ethnographic consideration have a tendency to blind us to its true worth . . . It is the vitality of forms of Negro art that should speak to us, the simplification without impoverishment, the unnerving emphasis on the essential, the consistent, three-dimensional organization of structural planes in architectonic sequences, the uncompromising truth to material with seemingly intuitive adaptation of it, and the tension achieved between the idea or emotion to be expressed through representation and the abstract principle of sculpture.[13]

Although Sweeney's ideas represent the intellectual ethos of the 1930s, they continue to reverberate today, for they underscore the timeless, transcendental contours of the object rather than the economic and sociocultural contexts of its production. They underscore how "tribal objects" continue to gain the aesthetic legitimacy and economic value of high art. Sweeney's aesthetic continues to shape the way dealers display "tribal art." Those displays may well provide the museumlike context that triggers the transcendental moments that compel collectors to frequent galleries and art exhibitions to find and perhaps buy an "important" piece.

14

Intersections

From the late 1990s to the spring of 2001 the detour that had led me to New York—and away from sorcery and Niger—gently twisted and turned me in new and fascinating directions. Although I continued to visit my friends at the Malcolm Shabazz Harlem Market, I spent more and more of my New York City time at the Warehouse observing and, to some extent, taking part in the commercial activity that moved "tribal" pieces from Africa to Manhattan and then west, south, and north to Los Angeles, Chicago, Atlanta, New Orleans, Denver, and Santa Fe, New Mexico. Sometimes, I would help my friends unpack a container that had arrived at Port Elizabeth in New Jersey. Sometimes we'd go out to JFK Airport to clear a shipment through customs. Sometimes, I would spend an entire day sitting with Bubul, the "wood" doctor, who worked in a dank, dim, windowless vault tucked away in the bowels of the Warehouse. Bubul, who lived in Brooklyn, came from a small town in Burkina Faso called Gorom Gorom, which was not that far from the Nigerien border and from Wanzerbé, the aforementioned village of Songhay sorcerers. He had also spent quite a bit of time in Mehanna, the site of my earliest fieldwork in Niger. Now he worked in a stuffy vault in Chelsea, Manhattan, surrounded by broken masks, a variety of woodworking tools, and an array of Minwax cans. I watched him work, fetched him a tool or a can of glue, and talked with him about Niger, Burkina Faso, and the strange ways of Americans.

"Why is it," he once asked me, "that Americans make appointments to see one another? I don't understand it. At home," he continued, "we just walk over to someone's house or village—no appointments—and we talk, sip tea, and eat. For you, your relationships are like business."

More often than not, however, I would spend my time sitting on a bench in front of El Hadj Harouna's stall, which was located along a small musty corridor that led to the bathroom, which, in addition to its obvious uses, was also used for prayer ablutions. El Hadj Harouna held court, to say the least, in a very busy corridor. He was one of the oldest of the African art dealers in New York. Younger dealers, some of whom were passing through, others of whom had already spent years in North America, routinely came by to pay their respects. They would never sit down next to El Hadj Harouna. Those spaces were usually reserved for guests like me or for his peers, elders all, many of whom had been in the art trade for more thirty years. Every day, we'd talk about changes in the art trade, about difficulties in getting quality pieces, about how the low-quality pieces that had flooded the market had often undermined the trust they had established with longstanding clients and gallery owners, who now demanded "papers" (or provenance) for more "expensive" objects.

These men, I gradually realized, knew a great deal about art. From their perspective the art they traded was "wood," a mere commodity, and yet, having internalized Western conceptions of art for art's sake, they knew exactly how to market their wares to North American buyers. Almost every African art trader I met in New York or on my travels to Atlanta, New Orleans, Chicago, and Santa Fe, carried copies of the journal *African Arts,* exhibition catalogs or reference books like Frank Willet's classic work, *African Art.* These publications usually contained photos of "important" pieces in their possession.

One day in the early spring of 2001, as El Hadj Harouna went off to recite his midafternoon prayers, a middle-aged trader, Ousmane Gado, a short, thick-bodied man, sat down next to me. On that day he was dressed formally in a *boubou,* a baby-blue damask robe the collar of which was stitched with swirling patterns of gold embroidery. The robe covered a matching shirt with gold embroidered cuffs and a matching pair of trousers.

When I first encountered Ousmane Gado at the Warehouse, I spoke to him in French, assuming that he, like most of his colleagues, came from a Francophone West African country.

"I do not speak French," he said in the lilt that defined a West African version of English. "I am Gambian."

Unlike El Hadj Harouna, Ousmane Gado had been based in New York City for more than six years but spent much of his time as a mobile merchant selling his objects at art trade shows and flea markets. He liked to talk about his travels to South Carolina, Florida, Texas, New Mexico, and California. On the day that he and I sat alone on the bench in front of El Hadj Harouna's stall, he asked me how I had liked my visit Santa Fe the previous week.

"How did you know I had been there?"

"I saw you on the plaza."

"And you didn't stop to say hello?"

He shrugged. "We were in our van and we on our way back to the highway." He paused a moment. "I apologize. We should have stopped. We are too long in America."

Ousmane Gado changed the subject. "Do you know about the New York International Show?"

"No."

"It's a big exhibit," he informed me, "and it's coming to town on May 21 and May 22. You should go. You will see the big dealers and their high-priced pieces."

———

I took up Ousmane Gado's suggestion enthusiastically and went to Tribal Antiquities: The New York International Show, which was held at the Seventh Regiment Armory. Situated at Park Avenue at 67th Street on the Upper East Side of Manhattan, the Seventh Regiment Armory had long been the locale of high-end art exhibitions in New York City. It has also been, in fact, the site of an annual world-renowned tribal antiquities exhibition. Given its fame and its opportunity for profitable exchange, the 2001 event drew an impressive array of well-known "tribal" antiquities dealers, who displayed their treasures with great panache. These professionals presented their jewelry, textiles, masks, and statuary with proper mounting and proper lighting—a presentation that not only augmented desire for an object's "allure" but also increased its perceived value.

In 2001, fifty-two dealers paid substantial fees to present their antiquities in New York. Of the fifty-two dealers represented at the Tribal Antiquities show, seventeen offered works of African art. Some of the dealers showcased West African masks and statuary, including some old terracotta figures; others featured Central African pieces: masks and statuary fashioned from wood, old carved ivory, and iron weapons. One dealer displayed Neolithic projectile points from West Africa.

Propelled by various agendas, five groups of visitors streamed through the dimly lit corridors. Several dealers, who decided for various reasons not to display their pieces, trickled through the crowd. Perhaps they would find a bargain. Maybe they would size up the market. A swell of collectors moved through the aisles, hoping to add "important" pieces to their private fine arts collections. A strong current of curiosity seekers coursed through the aisles, intending to look and learn rather than study and buy. Along with a few students of the art market in New York I meandered through the crowd, hoping to arrange future interviews or gather pertinent information.

On the first day of my visit a group of collectors gathered around a particularly compelling display of Central African masks and statuary. At these antiquities shows collectors are often distinguishable by age and manner of dress. They are usually middle-aged people often dressed in dark suits. This particular group of collectors talked in hushed tones. One collector asked the dealer about patina and provenance.

After several moments of informed exchanges I noticed Ousmane Gado walking up to our group. He had discarded his damask boubou for a stylish tweed sport coat and black dress slacks. He gave me a complicit wink as he approached a tall silver-haired gentleman dressed in a navy blue suit.

"Sir," he said in distinctive West African lilt, "I notice that you are admiring the Fang pieces," referring to rare reliquary statues that had been long ago carved in Gabon.

"They're magnificent, aren't they?" the gentleman answered.

"Yes, they are," Ousmane Gado agreed. "Beautiful lines. They speak to me."

The gentleman smiled. "They have collected some fine ones here."

"Sir," Ousmane Gado said, "if you like what you see here, I have some very similar pieces." He paused a moment. "Much better prices."

"Really," the gentleman said.

"Here is my card," he said. "Contact me if you wish. I will be in New York City for three more weeks." He looked again at the Fang pieces. "If you like, I have a few of these pieces in my van, which is parked around the corner. We could go and take a look?"

Moments later Ousmane Gado and the tall silver-haired gentleman left the Seventh Regiment Armory to look at art "displayed" in a van. In the process they were about to negotiate a new space—of African art.

———

That new space of African art, I realized, was one of many examples of people empowering themselves from within the between. Ousmane Gado knew very well how to negotiate the sinuous path of the between.

He found himself an empowered player between the worlds of "art" and "wood." His spatial position didn't immobilize him. His orientation didn't compel him to deny the existence of either "art" or "wood." Instead, he sought a new space between the two worlds from which he might creatively expand his operations. The same can be said for the genteel collector. Sometimes, though, the intersection of two worlds that you find in the between can lead to misunderstanding.

In June 2001, I went to the Warehouse to visit several Nigerien art traders who had recently come to New York City. As usual there were several vans backed up to loading docks. Young men loaded "wood" into the vehicles or took "wood" from them and stacked it on dollies. I also noticed a black Mercedes sedan parked in front of the Warehouse's front door. Because a Mercedes sedan was not an unusual sight on Manhattan streets, I gave it little thought. When I entered the Warehouse, though, I came upon a crowd of African traders gathered around three visitors. I immediately recognized one of the visitors—Richard Holbrook, who at that time was outgoing U.S. ambassador to the United Nations. In his company there was a man and a woman who, unlike Ambassador Holbrook, were dressed informally.

"What's going on?" I asked several traders.

"Important people have come to visit us," one trader said in French.

A female trader grabbed my arm. "Look at them," she said, also in French. "Important people. The ambassador to the UN and the American ambassador to Nigeria."

"And the woman?"

"Mrs. American Ambassador to Nigeria."

"I see."

"Do you want me to introduce you to them?"

I demurred.

"That's okay. They have so much money, but they won't buy anything here," she said, shaking her head. "You wait and see if I'm right."

The president of the African Art Traders Association led the trio on a tour of the Warehouse. Africans in New York City had created this voluntary organization to defend their economic and social interests in the United States. The president was a prosperous man from Mali who that day was dressed in a gold-embroidered white damask robe. They poked around the trader stalls on the ground floor, inspected the African kitchen, where two women were making ground nut stew, looked at the mosque, and took the freight elevator upstairs to inspect the storage facilities.

I met the Nigerien trader I had been looking for and we went up to the fifth floor to see his new inventory. He opened his storage bin to reveal a small room filled with old and new pots from Ghana, Nigeria, and Niger. He also had brought sacks of dried medicinal herbs, some old farming tools, a few weapons, and a collection of old brass and copper rings. We used a flashlight to look more closely at the objects. Many of the pots had broken during transport. We talked about medicinal herbs. Even though I didn't want to purchase anything, I bought a few copper and brass rings out of respect for our trading relationship. Having known many traders over the years, I knew it would be insulting to inspect a trader's goods and then refuse to buy something. Satisfied, the trader then closed his storage bin and we got on the freight elevator, which serendipitously stopped on the third floor. The group of dignitaries got on and we all descended—very slowly—to the ground floor. Talking animatedly about the Warehouse, they looked as though they had thoroughly enjoyed their visit. My friend and I followed them to their car where a driver waited. A crowd of traders flocked around them. Some offered them "wood." Others offered business cards. One trader promised to find a rare object. Standing beside his car, Ambassador Holbrook collected a pile of business cards. I noticed that he treated everyone respectfully. I heard him invite the president of the African Art Traders Association to lunch, and they got into the sedan and left.

Back in the Warehouse the visit had generated a great deal of discussion. My friend, the Nigerien trader, had talked briefly to Ambassador Holbrook. He said that the dignitaries had behaved respectfully and that their visit had honored the African community. On a more practical level, he noticed that they hadn't bought anything. I encountered the woman who had offered to introduce me to the dignitaries.

"Did they buy anything?" she asked.

"I don't think so."

She shook her head. "See what I told you," she said.

Among people who "know" about African Art in New York City, the Warehouse was considered an interesting place to visit but not a place to buy "authentic" African art. Curators and gallery owners often told me that the stalls and storage bins were filled with tourist art. One person who collects West African art said, "The place is great, but it's filled with fakes. If you look very carefully, you might find a real gem."[1] Put another way, the Warehouse was a cultural curiosity. Who would think that a six-story storage facility in Chelsea, Manhattan, would be filled with West African traders who had fully stocked it with "African art?"

And so, from within the space of African art, which is, in part, framed by Kantian and Hegelian notions of taste and authenticity, the Warehouse is a fascinating place to see but not a good place to purchase art.

This notion may well have shaped the observations and behaviors of the ambassadorial visitors. From within the space of West African "wood" (and "mud"), which is framed both by the history and traditions of Islam and long-distance trade and by a history of fleeting cross-cultural encounters, the Warehouse is a place where one engages in commerce, the sale of "wood and "mud." For West African traders, commerce, following the dictates of Islam, is usually not deemed separate from social relations. When people visit an African vendor at a market or an art trader at the Warehouse, they should buy something even if it is a small purchase. In this way, social relations are established and mutual face is maintained. Here, we have a classic case of a mismatch of intentions that generates misunderstandings and disrespect. "They came to visit, but they didn't buy anything."[2]

And yet, in the space between "wood" and African "art" things are not always what they seem to be. Art doctors like Bubul and experts in restoration can manipulate objects and transform them into "fine art." Skilled artisans can play with patina. They can also quickly age "wood" to make it look like an antique.[3] Old broken pieces of terra-cotta are easy to come by in West Africa. These can be recombined to mold figurines that resemble thousand-year-old excavated objects. These pieces are then presented to buyers as "old" and of "museum quality" when they are, in fact, decorative objects. Museum curators, in fact, spend an increasing portion of their time talking to investors who want to know the value of the piece of (African) art they have purchased. Given the flood of "wood" floating in the African art market, vetting objects has become serious business. Before a Sotheby's tribal art auction, experts are called in to authenticate pieces. In some cases objects have to be removed from the auction list.[4]

When you collect African art in the contemporary market, the intersection of spaces—of meaning—becomes a rather complex affair. From the standpoint of curators, connoisseurs, and high-end gallery owners, you want to collect fine African art from reputable dealers—men and women who have established reputations based upon the "authenticity" of their objects. High-end dealers and connoisseurs buy from other high-end dealers or from reputable collectors who choose to sell their objects. This group attends such auctions as Sotheby's annual tribal arts auction in New York City, where bidding can sometimes increase the price of an object. They also flock to the annual New York tribal antiquities show. They may also buy objects at special auctions like the one in Paris in June 2001 that sold the famed Hubert Goldet collection.[5] On increasingly rare occasions, they buy objects from African traders, hoping to find a diamond in the rough, which is a conceit, as Steiner suggests, that African art traders, like Ousmane Gado, fully understand and manipulate.[6] The collector's orientation to the objects has been shaped, in part, by the aforementioned Kantian-Hegelian aesthetic that focuses upon the age-less, transcendental nature of the object—qualities that imbue the object with legitimacy and value. For this group, value is important, but it is not the solitary force that drives buying and selling.

There is a second group of collectors for whom investment value is the solitary force that compels buying and selling. Like all people interested in fine arts, these collectors pay great attention to prices paid for works of (African) art. They would know, for example, that the May 2001 Sotheby's tribal art auction generated $6.8 million in sales. They, too, buy objects at Sotheby's auctions, estate sales, and at high-end galleries. They may also be on the client lists of West African traders. These collectors look to buy low and sell high. Sometimes they buy "art," which is, in fact, "wood" or "mud," in which case, they have bought high and, if they so choose, will have to sell low. Experience, ideology, and identity politics drives a third group of African Art collectors to buy objects. These people may in-clude African Americans inspired by some variety or version of Afrocen-trism.[7] A carved object from Africa becomes more than a work of plastic art; it is an emblem of pride. This group of collectors pays a wide variety of prices for African objects ranging from finely crafted decorative pieces to mass-produced tourist art. Some of the mass-produced objects can even be found in such discount stores as Marshalls and T.J. Maxx. Each group, then, brings a different set of aesthetic, economic, and ideological expec-tations and meaning into an encounter with an African trader. Even so, they are all seeking, in one way or another, an enriching authenticity.

The fourth group, of course, is composed of "kinship"-based networks of African traders. This group is highly diverse. Long-term traders are quite knowledgeable. They take their better pieces to reputable art restorers. They may take their "important pieces" to well-known African art experts to seek their endorsement.[8] These traders reserve their best objects for customers willing to pay good prices for "quality" objects. Even so, many of them believe, to paraphrase Errington, that "authentic" primitive art has died.[9] Accordingly, the bulk of what they offer is decorative—mass-produced objects ("wood" and "mud") that can be bought easily and cheaply for quick, profitable sales. Sales bring in much-needed cash. They use some of this cash to pay off debts to "brother" traders or to reinvest in inventory. Much of the cash is sent home to support large families that have become dependant upon a steady flow of foreign exchange. Using this foreign income, elders and children can remain in the rural areas of West Africa where food has become expensive and jobs remain scarce.[10]

African art at Marshalls, Rehoboth Beach, Delaware, summer 2002.
Photograph by the author.

The income also empowers other family members to establish small rural or urban enterprises.[11] Put another way, selling "wood" and "mud" enables West African art traders to meet many of their social and cultural obligations, which means that their kinspeople honor them—especially when they return home.[12] The crossroads of African art are, then, a series of places where space and meaning are continuously negotiated and renegotiated in the between. Given the nature of these ephemeral "nonspaces," is it any wonder that the people who fleetingly inhabit them are filled with transitory misunderstandings and residual antipathies?[13]

Sitting in the dank dim light that descends like a fine mist upon the bench in front of El Hadj Harouna's African art stall, I came to several realizations. Given my own set of experiences between theory and practice, between Africa and America, between rationality and emotion, I knew full well that the between is an unavoidable space that creates creative and intellectual tension. Sometimes these tensions could immobilize you. Sometime they could be extremely diverting. The tension of the between, after all, had diverted me from the path of sorcery and had led me to the complex social arenas of New York City. And yet, as I sat on El Hadj Harouna's bench, I understood that the between was much more complex than I had ever imagined. In New York, I discovered that the multiple layers of ever-shifting social relations and sinuous strands of cultural interpretation had seeped into contemporary urban life. This expansion presented significant challenges to doing anthropology.

Where might anthropologists fit, I wondered as the Warehouse muezzin called the faithful to late afternoon prayer, into these ever-changing spaces that lie between things? Like any curiosity seeker, we anthropologists could easily dive into the transnational currents of a place like the annual New York tribal antiquities show. Engaging in participant observation, we would be well positioned to study the blending of people and the interpenetration of universes of meaning that constitutes a transnational space. We could conduct informal and formal interviews and gather economic, demographic, and sociological data. And yet these simple and straightforward methods would be confounded, would they not, by a man like Ousmane Gado, who went to the annual tribal antiquities show at the Seventh Regiment Armory on Park Avenue and 67th Street and convinced a seemingly well-heeled investor to look at the "wood" stacked in his van.

For me, this small slice of interaction compelled much intellectual rumination about issues central to our comprehension of contemporary social life in North America. It triggered a reflection about how "art" had been constituted and how global flows, which have brought to North America "wood" and "mud," had undermined the "authenticity" of "art." This observation prompted further thoughts about of Jean Baudrillard's notion of the hyper-real in which the power of copies seems to overwhelm that of the original. In the world of the hyper-real, the fast, high-octane world of copies—of the mimetic faculty—fuels the double-barreled engines of mobile, informal economies.[14]

In these fast-paced contemporary worlds, I concluded, it becomes increasing difficult to "read" objects. Can "wood" or "mud" become art? These considerations, of course, triggered reflections about the changing world of aesthetic legitimacy and the volatility of markets.[15] They also touched upon the sociology of art in contemporary worlds. Connoisseurs, curators, and high-end gallery owners may have aesthetic as well as economic motives for maintaining an ethos of art for art's sake, based in part upon deep-seated notions of sublimity and transcendentalism. Investors, mid- to low-level collectors and boutique owners, may have economic and ideological motives for entering African art markets. As for the African art traders, many of them, as I've already stated, have a sophisticated comprehension of the aesthetic, economic, and political forces that drive the markets they attempt—often with great success—to exploit. In the end, the art that they sell has only a fleeting value. It has been a material investment that has enabled many of them to meet considerable economic and social obligations that have evolved from Islam and from the history of long-distance trading in West Africa.

It is fair to say that the anthropological path through the between is one filled with stimulating complexities. As I have previously mentioned, anthropological spaces have always been complex—perhaps more complex—than we have been willing to admit or express.[16] As readers of Erving Goffman's work would know, even the most miniscule of everyday interactions are laced with nuanced social negotiations and multilaminated cultural innuendoes. Social scientists have gleefully isolated rules for linguistic and social behavior to make sense of interactional chaos, and yet, as Goffman demonstrated in his later work, especially, *Forms of Talk* (1981), actors regularly violate rule-governed behavior. Goffman's work celebrated the complexities of the between within a relatively homogeneous cultural frame. His books analyzed the private and public microbehaviors of mostly mainstream Americans.

Almost thirty years after the publication of *Forms of Talk,* the United States, as the most recent U.S. Census has indicated, is a much more diverse nation. Some 11 percent of Americans are foreign-born; 20 percent of Americans speak a foreign language at home. In some urban areas, like New York City, these percentages are significantly higher, which means that cultural hybridity—the intercourse of universes of meaning and intent that fills the spaces of the between—increasingly characterizes our public encounters. This hybridity, in turn, makes the ethnographic enterprise exceedingly difficult. As I stated above, it renders the narrowly focused anthropological study an anachronistic illusion. These thoughts prompted worry about my ethnographic project in New York. How could I represent the complex social patterns that comprise the social world of West African immigrants in New York City?

One possible path through the thicket was suggested in a recent book, *Global Ethnography,* in which a group of Berkeley sociologists presented a series of case studies that underscore the importance of empirically grounded ethnographic research in contemporary social worlds. They argued that social theorists have been so far removed from ground-level social reality that they often overlook important dimensions of global processes. The lead author, Michael Burawoy, made an important point: to understand contemporary worlds scholars must opt for dwelling rather than travel, for theory shaped by data rather than vignette. Considering how global and local forces interact to effect immigration, informal economies, transnational trade networks, and local-level politics, scholars, as George Marcus underscored in his book *Ethnography through Thick and Thin,* have already begun to take up this challenge.

———

Having completed their late-afternoon religious obligations, the faithful walked by me as I sat on the bench in front of El Hadj Harouna's art stall, pondering the whys and wherefores of a life in anthropology. Some walked and prayed; others, fingering their worry beads, greeted me in English, French, Songhay, or Hausa. Then an unexpected moment of quiet slipped into the corridor, which rifled me back to my inner conversation. Yes, dwelling rather than travel and theory shaped by data rather than by vignette seemed like necessary conditions for doing contemporary ethnography. But were they also sufficient conditions? Could these principles enable me—or any anthropologist—to become comfortable in my skin, as the French like to say, in the ambiguous spaces of the between?

15

Weaving the World

As spring slipped into summer and the heavy humidity of a New York July pushed itself deeper and deeper into spaces like the Warehouse, I wondered how I might ever write about the fascinatingly complex networks of West African merchants, be they the street traders of the Malcolm Shabazz Harlem Market or art specialists like El Hadj Harouna, who worked out of the Warehouse. The information they had provided me was circuitous and multilayered. How would I ever be able to make sense of it, let alone transform this utter tangle of data into a coherent anthropological text? In previous work the writing techniques I used had been relatively straight-forward. When writing about sorcery, I used the memoir as a way to try to represent the rich nuances of Songhay esoteric practices.[1] The description of Songhay spirit possession required a text, laced with passive voice constructions that more or less resembled the academic essay: theoretical parameters were set at the onset, data were then presented, and in the last chapter, concluding statements were made.[2] In biographical or theoretical works the textual options I faced also seemed clear-cut.[3] With the New York work, however, no textual strategy seemed to present itself.

I spent more and more time in the dim, dank space in front of El Hadj Harouna's stall at the Warehouse, fretting about my textual quandaries. One day, though, I curiously began to think about Songhay weavers. Like Songhay sorcerers, weavers are people who are comfortable in their skin. In Songhay weavers are called *cakey*, and they pass their skill and knowledge across the generations from father to son. Knowledge of weaving came to Songhay from across the

Sahara sometime in the twelfth century. Since that time, Songhay weavers have produced blankets, woven in strips, of incomparable beauty, blankets that are highly coveted throughout West Africa for their bright colors and their intricate geometric designs. Weavers are full of knowledge about the historical tradition of their craft. They know the intricacies of the loom and of warp and weft.

One old weaver I knew liked to talk to me about the history and philosophy of weaving. He told me how young weavers eat a magical substance that enhances their skill and enables them to see patterns. He talked about how weaving connects people to the world. As the sun was setting one afternoon, creating a bright red rim on the barren horizon, he told me a wonderful story about weaving and weavers.

————

A long time ago three men sat down at their looms to weave. The first man said, "Would it not be wonderful if the world was like a blanket—warp and weft combining in patterns that create beauty?"

The second man said, "That would be wonderful. We could weave the world and there would be no conflict, no jealousy, and no betrayals."

The third and oldest weaver said, "A blanket, my brothers, cannot change the world. It cannot rid the world of conflict, jealousies, and betrayals. We can weave the world, and that act brings to it the great beauty that our color and patterns provide. That beauty protects us, if only a little, from conflict, jealousy, and betrayal."

"But how can we be sure that our threads will protect people?" the first man asked.

"Why weave, if weaving cannot set the world straight?" the second weaver asked.

"We weave," the third weaver said, "because it was the passion of our ancestors. It is also our passion. We must make sure that that passion, which connects past and present, is woven into our textiles. It's the passion that protects, that makes the world a little bit more like a blanket."

"But we weave and weave," the first weaver argued, "and it makes no difference in the world."

"How do we live in the world?" the second weaver asked.

"With patience," the third weaver said. "If you are patient and vigilant, you will find what you're looking for. Your path will open. You will bring beauty to the world."

————

As I was thinking about the old weaver's story, Yaya Harouna, who was El Hadj Harouna's younger brother, sat down next to me.

"Paul," he said, "why are you smiling?"

I explained my dilemma. I had already told him and his brothers that I wanted to write a book about the West African traders in New York. I had also explained that I hadn't yet figured out how to proceed.

"But we have seen your other books. They look good."

I had shown him and his brothers my books. Jean Rouch used to argue that Songhay and Hausa people, many of whom are illiterate, found books to be meaningless. By contrast, these mostly rural West Africans took immediately, he argued, to the language of film. That was and is incontestably true, but I have also found that the Songhay and Hausa people I had met, being Muslim, had a profound respect for scribes—people who could write letters, poems, or history. In my experience, they graciously extended that respect to me, especially in my role as the *anasaara alfaggah* of 125th Street in Harlem. "You have my thanks, Yaya, but this work is very different."

"But we see you here, smiling. What are you thinking about?'

"Weavers," I said, a bit sheepishly.

"Yes! They are great artists," Yaya said. He was a large man with a round face, a flat nose, and widely spaced clear eyes that expressed both concern and curiosity about the world. "We say that their blankets weave the world."

"That's what I've heard," I said.

"If you don't know what to do," he suggested, "maybe you should think about your book the way a weaver thinks about a blanket. Can you not weave the world with words?"

———

Exactly! It is a usually unacknowledged fact in anthropology that our "informants" are often the source of our inspiration. Jean Rouch was no stranger to innovation. He spent his career as filmic iconoclast. And yet, he willingly acknowledged that many of the ideas for his most creative films came from his Nigerien collaborators—Damouré Zika, Lam Ibrahim, and Tallou Mouzourane. The storyline for Rouch's incomparable *Jaguar* came from Damouré. Many of the scene innovations in that film emerged from the creative fun generated when Rouch hung out with his gang.

Yaya Harouna provided the innovative spark that enabled me to write *Money Has No Smell* as if it were a Songhay blanket. I produced a text in patterned strips and once those strips had been crafted, I tried to weave them together. The warp and weft of the strips foregrounded the stories of three West African traders, whose compelling tales of creative adaptation to the alienating quandaries of transnational New York, I hoped, would give the text a humanistic texture. Here were stories of men who walked on a path of cultural adventure that cut through a strange and complex landscape. How did they make their way from rural Niger to New York City? How did they construct multinational trading networks? What was the role that Islam played in their way of trading? How did they respond to U.S. racism? How did they adapt to the alienating aspects of contemporary U.S. culture, especially as it orchestrates itself in urban New York? Those strips revealed a complex pattern, and yet the strips had to be connected in order to weave a complete blanket—to weave the world. And so, I used social analysis—of transnationalism, of the West African culture of trade, of contemporary immigration, of U.S. state power in its local, regional, and national aspects, of the social alienation of Muslim West Africans in the secular United States. The result was a book in which I tried, like the Songhay weaver, to connect the individual to the group, the neighborhood to the world, and the narrative to its larger context. That, as Yaya Hamidou would argue, was my attempt to rearrange a tangle of ethnographic data in order to weave the world and explore the interstices of the between.

In time, though, the threads of any blanket eventually wear down. In that circumstance, you can try to mend the blanket, which means you use new threads to produce the same pattern. Placed in a scholarly context, you may find yourself using slightly different words, but you end up saying the same thing—an occupational hazard for scholars!! Sometimes, though, you find yourself once again caught between patterns that have lost their power to bind the story. That's when you can no longer mend the blanket. That's when you begin to weave a new work and tell a new story.

16

Immunology and the Village of the Healthy

My new story began in 2001 when I discovered that I had cancer. On a cold February afternoon on my way to Philadelphia to see a play, I went to see my physician for an annual physical. Usually these checkups were routine exercises during which we talked more about hiking, traveling, and cuisine than my medical issues, which, in my case, had been minimal. When my doctor examined my abdomen, he discovered a mass.

"Wait a minute," he said. "That shouldn't be there."

Fear rifled through my body. "What shouldn't be there?"

He put my fingers on the spot and pressed down. "Feel that?"

"Yes," I said. "It feels hard."

"It should be spongy," he said. "It's probably nothing, but we'll need to check it out."

Through a series of diagnostic misadventures in the sinuous maze that constitutes the world of U.S. medicine, I eventually learned that I had non-Hodgkin lymphoma (NHL). The "mass" turned out to be a rather large abdominal tumor filled with indolent follicular lymphoma cells. Indolent follicular lymphoma, I was told, which is the most common type of NHL, can be "managed" for long periods of time. Even so, in whatever of the twenty forms it takes, NHL remains, for now, an incurable disease.

Learning that I had an incurable disease came both as a surprise and a shock. I felt great, exercised regularly, and had been practicing yoga for almost thirty years. How could

I have cancer? How much would I have to suffer? How long would I live? Like most people, the menacing presence of malignant cells in my body ignited fires of fear. In a flash, cancer had abruptly taken control of my life and forced me onto a dreadful new path that promised pain and suffering. The prospect of a slow and painful death made me tremble. These troubling thoughts transformed me into a powerless person. I longed for my old life. But in my dazed and confused state, I felt incapable of recapturing any part of it. My days in the village of the healthy had come to an abrupt and irrevocable end.

For most of us, illness is a sudden nuisance that requires a quick fix. This fix enables us to reenter our usual space in which we have some sense of control over our lives. In an orderly universe, categories are pure and separate—the antithesis of the between in which nothing is clear and separate. In an ordered reality, health is separate and distinct from illness. In my book, *Stranger in the Village of Sick,* I called this ordered place of physiological normality, the village of the healthy. Those fortunate to live in this village rarely think about illness. Illness, after all, is a momentary phenomenon. With proper treatment, we can return to the warm and secure space of the village of the healthy and return to our "normal" way of being in the world. In the village of the healthy, thoughts of illness recede into the background of our consciousness. Illness remains distinctly other. Like the plague, the thought of cancer becomes remote in time and space.

The idea of "living with an illness" usually runs counter to major themes in U.S. culture. No one wants to live with an illness. If we contract an illness, we want to conquer it. Illness and medical discourse are metaphorically framed in terms of war. We are at war with disease. We fight infection. Bacteria invade our bodies and colonize our cells. Our immune systems produce natural killer cells that ambush the invaders so that we can win our battle with illness.

It is not uncommon for most people, including cancer patients, to think of malignant cells as alien invaders that are completely separate from our bodies. Despite this widespread notion, cancer *is* something that the body—your body—produces. Most people refuse to accept this fact. Arthur Frank writes, "Cancer is not some entity separate from yourself . . . Most people opt for the tumor-as-alien. At the extreme is Ronald Reagan's well-known statement about his cancer, 'I don't have cancer. I have something inside of me that had cancer in it, and it was removed.'"[1] This statement summarizes an immunological attitude—an unwillingness to accept that cancer is self rather than other.

In his ground-breaking work *The Age of Immunology*, David Napier underscored the central importance of metaphor in the categorization of knowledge and the delimitation of practice. More specifically, he demonstrated how immunological thinking, in which the self (the body) maintains its health by destroying not-selves (others/foreign bodies) triggers specific sets of practices not only in medicine but also in ecology and foreign affairs. In *The Age of Immunology* selves eclipse others and uniformity triumphs over difference.

It is difficult to categorize *The Age of Immunology*. Although Napier described and critiqued a variety of literatures that contribute both to medicine (immunology) and anthropology, this book is an anthropological contribution to epistemology. Therein lies its importance. It is a text in which the author is not afraid to discuss big questions. For me, *The Age of Immunology* is not an exercise in medical anthropology or science studies; rather, it is a substantial extension of Michel Foucault's project to understand the organization of knowledge.[2] One of the cornerstone's of Foucault's earlier "archaeological" work is the notion of the episteme. Developed in both *The Archaeology of Knowledge* and *The Order of Things,* Foucault saw the episteme as a kind of frame in which knowledge is organized. These frames shifted with history and the advancement of knowledge. At the end of *The Order of Things,* Foucault introduced the modern episteme within which scholars in the newly developed human sciences grappled with the finitude of human being. The contingency of that finitude has brought uneasiness to scholars in the human sciences. Indeed, some of the great thinkers in intellectual history—Marx, Lévi-Strauss, and, of course, Foucault himself—constructed intellectual projects that sought to transform human finitude and contingency into complex abstract systems through which they attempted to "explain" and "order" human being. This epistemological tack has been at the heart of modernist anti-humanism. As Napier would argue, this epistemological orientation has compelled scholars to preserve the abstract, purified, and homogeneous center at the expense of the concrete, polluted, and diverse periphery. None of this modernist theorizing, of course, took on the vexing contingencies of real selves confronted by real others. As Jean-Paul Sartre wrote in *No Exit:* "L'enfer, c'est les autres." Even though "Hell is other people," Sartre argued, we need those pesky and troublesome others to affirm our existence.

In *The Age of Immunology* Napier focused squarely on the links of self to other, on the confrontation of center and periphery. His scope, however, was not limited to strictly immunological topics. Beyond his discussion of the metaphoric organization of immunological knowledge and his critical assessment of the curious rationalism of oncology or his description of the logic-defying eruptions of auto-immune disorders, Napier employed immunological metaphors to probe critically a wide variety of topics. He considered, for example, the auto-immune dimensions of international development—"Foreign Aids"—as well as the shallow and distant engagement of multiculturalism. In these cases, Napier demonstrated powerfully how foreign debt and politically correct discourse are used to (a) make marginal others "more like us," or to (b) maintain polluting others as dependant and distant. These "liberal" tactics, Napier suggested, preserve the homogeneity of the center, a homogeneity that leads eventually to implosion and entropy.

The Age of Immunology is certainly a devastating epistemological critique of medicine and the human sciences. And yet, its theme carries us beyond medicine and social science. Napier demonstrated, in fact, how the knowledge and practices of non-Western peoples—the domain of anthropological description—offers a way to bridge the gap between self and other, between center and periphery. In so doing, he argued that we can create a kind of inventiveness—as opposed to innovation—that ultimately reinforces the homogeneity of the center—that enables us to grow. Through his description of Balinese ritual practices Napier showed how the Balinese take on the considerable risk of injecting into their being the potential dangers of otherness. Although this incorporation may cause some degree of pain and suffering, it empowers the Balinese to strengthen ultimately themselves as well as their communities.

Toward the end of *The Age of Immunology* Napier advocated embryological thinking as a path toward a future of medical humanism, social invention, and cultural growth. In the immunological age, the self/not-self opposition is foundational. In this fundamental confrontation selves become immune—safe—if and only if the dangerous not-self—bacteria, viruses, tumors, or radically different others—is either marginalized or destroyed. The human embryo, of course is the fundamental exception to immunological thinking. Here, the self—mothers—routinely accept the presence of the fetus—not-self—into their wombs. The result of this primary incorporation is growth, eventual birth, and the reproduction of the species. Napier extended embryological metaphors to sociocultural practices. What does it mean for human beings to embrace immunological metaphors? It means, he argued, that we will eventually destroy biological and cultural diversity. In the absence of diversity and the presence of immunity, we become increasingly dimmer and dimmer copies of our homogeneous selves until we fade away into entropy's all-encompassing ether. In the end, Napier suggested, our future depends in large measure upon our willingness to embrace the wisdom of non-Western peoples, those dangerous others, who have long understood the critical importance of more fully incorporating biological and sociocultural diversity into their social lives.

———

Immunological metaphors, of course, play a central role in how we organize our thinking about cancer, how we use immunology to distinguish the village of the healthy from the village of the sick. Cancer, as we have already seen, is conceptualized as war—an ongoing battle between our selves and the invading "not-selves," which we must destroy if we are to survive. In this metaphorical space, diagnostic tests become reconnaissance missions to detect foreign invaders. Once the invaders are located, specialists gather intelligence on them. What type of invader has been identified and how advanced is its invasion? Once this intelligence has been analyzed, the medical command center meets and decides on the best battle plan, which, more often than not includes precision incineration (radiation), strategic removal (surgery), and systemic poisoning (chemotherapy). Viewed from this metaphoric vantage chemotherapy treatments, for example, become search-and-destroy missions, to resuscitate a military term of the Vietnam era, that are designed to annihilate as many invading cancer cells as possible.

Just before the battle begins, the command center supplies you with information about the battle plan. Using information from chemical weapons suppliers, they tell you what to expect in combat. Yes, the weapons do kill the enemy—cancer cells. But "friendly fire" also kills some good cells, which brings on a wide array of physical symptoms—battle fatigue.

When I began chemotherapy in 2001, oncology nurses gave me several documents to read so I knew what to expect.[3] One document described the usual side-effects of chemotherapy treatments: hair loss, mouth sores, nausea, and infection. The nameless writers of this document counseled readers to get a buzz cut to reduce the psychological shock of being suddenly bald. We were advised to use mild shampoos, soft hairbrushes, and a low heat setting on hair dryers. Somehow, the anonymous writers thought that these tactics would delay the inevitable loss of hair. Because the "fire power" of anticancer drugs not only destroys fast-dividing malignant cells but also equally speedy mucosal cells, we could expect mucositis. Here the writers recommended a soft, bland diet. You wash down these field rations with plenty of fluids and make sure to brush your teeth frequently with mild toothpaste and a soft toothbrush. Nausea is perhaps the most widely known side-effect of chemically induced search-and-destroy missions. When chemotherapy drugs kill healthy cells, substances that make you sick to you stomach are released into the blood. Drugs and dietary adjustment, according to the document, can minimize nausea. The most serious side-effect of chemotherapy, according to the document, is infection. Chemotherapy drugs reduce the number of infection-fighting white blood cells. Accordingly, cancer patients are highly prone to a variety of infections. In battle it is therefore recommended to take your temperature every day, wash yours hands frequently, take daily baths or showers, use electric razors, and handle food properly. The writers also suggest that you avoid crowds, immunization shots, fever-reducing aspirin, and pimple popping.

After reading this document which, to say the least, was sobering, the nurses handed me drug company specifications on the toxins they were about to drip into my bloodstream: Cytoxan, Vincristine, prednisone, and Rituxin. Here are the specifications on Cytoxan. It provokes bone marrow suppression, which depletes white blood cells as well as platelets. This suppression can produce the following side-effects: fever, chills, red skin sores, severe cough, sore throat, increased bruising, blood in the urine or stool, bleeding gums, nose bleeds, hair loss, bladder irritations, and nausea. The manual on Vincristine was similar. Like Cytoxan, Vincristine suppressed white blood cell production but also suppressed red blood cells, which might bring on (battle) fatigue, as well as hair loss and nausea. If Vincristine leaked out from the IV site, it would ulcerate the surrounding tissue. Its neurological side-effects were the most serious, for Vincristine could cause numbness, tingling, and cramping in the extremities. In time Vincristine's cumulative effects might produce peripheral neuropathy, the loss of sensation in the feet and hands. Other symptoms included shortness of breath, double vision, severe jaw, and back or leg pain. Seven years after my last dose of Vincristine, I still experience frequent hand and foot cramps. Prednisone, the widely prescribed queen of steroids, also had a plethora of side-effects including, but not limited to nausea, anorexia, increased appetite, rash, acne, poor wound healing, insomnia, muscle weakness, euphoria, psychosis, depression, headache, dizziness, seizures, fluid retention, hypertension, blood clots, increased blood sugar, osteoporosis, back pain, herpes, and fungal infection. My dose, the aforementioned 180 mg per day, made me a prime candidate for any number of these conditions. Unlike the other anticancer drugs in my personal arsenal, Rituxan, the monoclonal antibody that attaches to the surface and then destroys lymphoma cells, has relatively mild side-effects.

The most striking feature of this battle manual discourse is the complete lack of attention to the delicate psychological state of the patient who is encouraged to soldier on, to grin and bear it, and to maintain a stiff upper lip. Imagine what it's like to receive a diagnosis of cancer, which most people take as a death sentence, and then be given the grim details of the battle plan. The shock of diagnosis is often so psychologically devastating that many cancer patients receive their battle instructions in a kind of haze. This numb reaction speaks to the resignation of people who feel caught in a room, to evoke Sartre once again, with "no exit."

Even so, cancer remains a "war" between selves and "not-selves." This metaphorical fact, in turn, evokes themes more appropriate to military culture. In military culture, one is taught to follow orders. Cancer patients are supposed to maintain a positive and winning attitude as they avoid crowds, brush their teeth with soft toothbrushes, and confront the pain and suffering of toxic treatments. Lack of obedience and a state of disorder create inefficiency and weakness. Health is orderly; illness is disorderly. Disease is disorder. There are neurological disorders, gastrointestinal disorders, and, of course, psychological disorders. As in the military, disorders are culturally unacceptable in mainstream U.S. culture. Through frontal attack, we therefore engage in monumental efforts to order our disorders. We are encouraged to change our diets and moderate our drinking and smoking. We pay billions of dollars annually to ingest millions of over-the-counter and prescription drugs. We sometimes agree to cosmetic, minor or major surgery. Following this military logic, if we are somehow disorderly and eat too much meat, drink too much alcohol, or smoke too many cigarettes, then we have only ourselves to blame for our serious illnesses. In immunological culture disorderly behavior results not only in social disorder but also life-threatening physical disorder. Orderly behavior, by contrast, is what we expect in the village of the healthy where, despite occasional disruptions, everything fits into its rightful place.

17

Entering the Village
of the Sick

When you enter the village of sick you leave what seems an orderly life and find yourself mired in the between. You have a disease with no cure. You are between health and illness. As the French philosopher Maurice Merleau-Ponty once said, in the village of the sick you discover a space that is between "everywhere and nowhere." When you first enter this village the light is dim and the thin air makes you gasp for breathe.

No matter your orientation to the world, the path to a diagnosis of cancer, which is a path that leads you to the village of the sick, presents severe challenges to immunological thinking. For one thing, the path toward diagnosis erases certainty from life. Just the possibility of developing a serious illness like cancer throws you into a fast-moving stream the current of which takes you to an unknown destination. In fact, diagnosis is a patchwork of contradictions that forces you to admit that life is full of ambiguities, full of uncertainties. When you are told that you have cancer, you find yourself rooted to a point on an existential crossroad. You suddenly realize that your life has been forever altered. You look back wistfully to your past life in the village of the healthy but ruefully understand that there is no way back to your old life. You gaze upon the path that leads to the village of the sick, the space of your new life in which illness becomes your constant companion, in which uncertainty establishes itself in the forefront of your consciousness, in which the once clear distinctions between health and illness

CHAPTER SEVENTEEN

and self and not-self melt into the air. Illness is no longer a nuisance that is brought to a quick end through pharmacological or medical intervention. Illness, rather, consumes your physical and emotional life with pain, uncertainty, and chaos. You are on a bridge, or what al-'Arabi called the *barzakh*, that spans the two sides of the between. Thus situated in the between, the clarity of the immunological world that constitutes the village of the healthy fades away. As you cross the threshold to the village of the sick, clear skies give way to rolling fog. You ask yourself: will the fog lift?

—————

When I learned definitively that I had non-Hodgkin lymphoma, nothing could keep me from thinking about what was happening to me. I worried about my future. I spent hours reading about the side-effects of chemotherapy, information that filled me with fear and anxiety. I geared myself for body-wrenching nausea, bone-weary fatigue, and hair loss. I bought an electric razor to avoid excessive bleeding—chemotherapy, as previously mentioned, can reduce blood-clotting platelet levels—from a shaving cut and a soft toothbrush to guard against painful mouth sores. I also read the literature about Rituxan, an antibody cloned from mice that could be dripped into my bloodstream to kill lymphoma cells. Although this drug had fewer side-effects than the chemotherapy medicines, it, too, could cause serious problems—fever, chills, and heart irregularities—especially the first time it was administered. I also didn't know if my medical insurance would cover its cost—more than $5,000 per dose.

I had suffered through hardships in the past. Professional struggles, family concerns. I had managed to resolve most of these problems. I also thought that the ordeals I had faced as a young apprentice sorcerer had strengthened my emotional and physical resolve. But I wondered if I was tough enough for cancer. As much as possible, I made practical as well as emotional preparations for chemotherapy. But was I ready to face the physical and emotional trauma?

The atmosphere at any cancer treatment center is difficult to bear. No degree of architectural planning or interior decoration can alter the heavy reality of a room filled with cancer patients. My brother Mitchell wanted to accompany me to my first treatment. Conversation was muted in the waiting room. There was no laughter. A mother and her teenaged daughter, the color drained from their expressionless faces, sat stiffly and silently in their seats. A skeletal man, sporting perhaps a three-day growth of beard stubble, fidgeted in his chair. Parked next to him was a portable

128

oxygen machine, marking him a lung cancer patient. A slender woman wearing a headscarf stared at the ceiling. One of her arms had swollen to the size one would expect in a woman three times her weight. Removal of her lymph nodes had caused the backup of lymph fluid that made her arm swell to elephantine proportions.

As a veteran of many diagnostic trials as well as a previous visit to the cancer center, I felt some distant kinship with these people. I still had my hair and felt myself to be physically fit, and yet, we all shared the burden of cancer. Cancer always makes you confront death—you are on a bridge that connects life and death. This unwelcome and unexpected positioning quickly erodes the gender, ethnic, and class differences that divide U.S. society. At the cancer center social differences among university professors, construction workers, and sales clerks quickly fade away. Cancer makes us involuntary kin in the village of the sick. This realization sank me further into silence.

Mitchell and I were led to a sterile examination room, where we sat down. I shivered. Attempting to add a touch of "warmth" to the setting, someone had hung a painting—a house at the beach backgrounded by blue sky, puffy cumulus clouds, and soft surf. After a few moments of stressful anticipation, Joel Rubin, my oncologist, walked into this surreal setting. "Hello," he said brightly.

Joel, who preferred first-name exchanges, sat down on the swivel stool and looked at my chart and swiveled toward me. "Your blood work is perfect," he said looking at the numbers. "I'll monitor your weight and pressure over the course of the treatments."

I sat silently in my chair. "How long will the treatments last?"

Joel shrugged. "That depends on how you respond. It could be as short as six months or as long as one year." He rolled the swivel chair closer to us and cleared his throat. "Have you thought about treatment options?" he asked.

On the previous visit to the cancer center, Joel had suggested three possible treatment alternatives for my NHL. The first was watch and wait. NHL is a disease that can develop slowly. One may have lymphoma cells swelling lymph nodes or building bulky tumors, but not present any symptoms—weight loss, low-grade fevers, and night sweats. One treatment alternative, as Joel explained, was to delay treatment until the onset of symptoms.

Standard chemotherapy would be the second treatment alternative. I would receive three drugs, Cytoxan, Vincristine, and prednisone. Nurses would administer the Cytoxan and Vincristine through an intravenous drip. I would take 180 milligrams of prednisone a day, a massive amount, for seven days. At the end of three weeks, I'd come back for another treatment, and so on. Joel had said that this treatment was usually effective for NHL patients like me.

The third treatment alternative would combine chemotherapy with Rituxan, the immunological medicine that contains antibodies that attach to specific antigens, molecules found on most lymphoma cells. The intercourse of antibody to antigen brings on the death of the malignant cell presumably without killing healthy cells—an advance over standard chemotherapy agents that destroy healthy as well as cancerous cells. Although it had been approved by the U.S. Drug Administration for several years, Rituxan had been used only to treat lymphoma patients for whom chemotherapy had not worked or for previously treated patients whose cancer had returned. Very few people had received Rituxan as initial therapy. Fewer still had received it in tandem with chemotherapy.

"I've read the clinical studies," I began, struggling to sound professional, "and I'm impressed with Rituxan. The side-effects are few and seem limited to the first infusion. It also seems very effective against the kind of NHL that I have." I paused. "What kind of impact do you think Rituxan will have on patients like me?" I asked Joel.

He shrugged. "I don't know. There are a few clinical trials that suggest that Rituxan makes chemotherapy drugs more effective. But we really don't know."

Another of those troubling answers that quickly increased my anxiety—a typical response to many of the treatment options offered to cancer patients. There had been so many new clinical developments—with only preliminary clinical results—in the treatment of lymphoma that physicians like Joel Rubin simply didn't know the medical repercussions of every new therapy. In clinical trials, researchers use cancer patients—as volunteers—to test the effectiveness of new cancer drugs, but it takes years for specialists to obtain conclusive results. Despite the inconclusiveness of Joel's response, I appreciated his expression of uncertainty. "I'm also concerned about the cost," I added.

"It's very expensive," he said. "I've got several patients like you and their insurance has covered it. If yours doesn't, I can offer it to you at cost."

"I'd like to try Rituxan."

Mitchell also thought it a good idea.

"If one of my family members had NHL," Joel added, "I'd recommend this combination therapy." He wrote down some notations on his chart and stood up. "Excuse me a moment, I need to do some calculations." He left.

Faced with an incurable disease, I decided I'd take risks that I might otherwise forego. But I was still uncertain about my decision.

A few moments later Joel came back. "We are just about ready. This is how your treatment will work. First, you'll get some steroids to prevent nausea. Then you'll get a small dose of Vincristine followed by Cytoxan. That will take about ninety minutes. We'll follow the Cytoxan, with some Benadryl and Tagament, which prepares you for Rituxan, which has to be given very slowly. The whole treatment process will take about five hours."

At that moment the disruptive seriousness of my state hit me like a Nigerien dust storm. Even if the chemotherapy treatments were successful, they would still change my life dramatically. I was at the portal of the village of the sick. Faced with these overwhelming circumstances, I struggled for strength. Slowly, I sensed a familiar tingling in my stomach—a sorcerous tingling. Blood surged through my veins. My senses finally began to wake up to the world in which I now found myself. I heard the soft voice of Adamu Jenitongo, my teacher and mentor: "You've found your way back to the path," he said. "Step onto it and walk forward. Let sorcery help you."

Adamu Jenitongo had helped me once again. Because this moment was a crucial one in my life I now knew what to do—reconnect with what has given me strength in the past. I turned to Joel Rubin. "Could I hold your hand?" He looked at me with some skepticism. I turned toward my brother and took his hand.

"There are different paths of treatment," I said softly to Joel. "You have your way of treating illness. I learned another way from my African teacher that I would like to use now." I paused. "This treatment will bring physical and emotional disorder, pain and suffering to my life. Disorder deepens illness. If I am going to get well I also need to follow the old ways of the sorcerers. I will try to harmonize the world in the way my teacher taught me. This will help me."

I held their hands. Joel patiently looked at me as I began to recite the genji how, the text that Adamu Jenitongo had taught me many years before. "In the name of the High God. In the name of the High God. I speak to east. I speak to the west. I speak to the north. I speak to the south. I speak to the seven heavens. I speak to the seven hells. I am speaking to N'debbi and my words must travel until, until, until they are known. . . ."

I finally loosened my grip on their hands. Falling back in my chair, I took a deep breath. The words had comforted me. They made me feel more able to face what was ahead.

"What was that?" Joel asked.

The author in the infusion room, spring, 2001. Photograph by Jasmin Tahmaseb McConatha.

"That's the genji how. It's an incantation that harmonizes the forces of the bush. The bush, here," I added, "is disharmonious. The words are in Songhay," I said. "It's the language of three million people in West Africa. I learned it when I lived there as a young man." Joel had known that I was an anthropologist. "I studied with a sorcerer for seventeen years. Like you," I told him, "I learned to be a healer—a different kind of healer. My teacher always said that there are many paths to well-being. I now understand more fully what he meant."

"I'd like to learn more about this," Joel stated.

I wondered what he really thought. I appreciated his willingness to participate in a healing ritual that was so alien to his own training.

Shifting from the spiritual back to the practical, Joel stood up and gave me my file. "Are you ready?" he asked.

I nodded.

"Follow me." We came to the end of the corridor and walked toward the front of the building to a nurse's station set off from the "infusion room" by a wood counter. Joel approached one the oncology nurses, a tall and very attractive blond woman named Jennifer. If anyone were to drip poison into my body, I thought, let it be Jennifer.

Joel introduced us and handed Jennifer my file.

"It's good to meet you, Paul," she said with a smile. "I'll take very good care of you."

I turned to Joel. "You see, the magic is already beginning to work!"

Jennifer took us to the "infusion room," a square space separated into four alcoves by dividers. Each treatment alcove held several medical recliners, flanked by upholstered chairs and swivel stools. Gold-plated art deco light fixtures attached to the cream-colored walls softened the effects of the florescent lighting. The linoleum tile looked cold and uninviting.

"Find a seat," Jennifer said. "I'll go and mix your medicines."

She disappeared behind the nurse's station. My brother went outside to make some phone calls. I picked a chair closest to the nurses and the bathroom. Several patients, surrounded by family members or friends, were undergoing treatment. As chemotherapy medicines slowly dripped through plastic tubes and entered their bloodstreams, they slept, talked quietly, read, or, simply stared at the ceiling. My anxiety returned. I felt butterflies in my stomach. Perhaps I had been too quick to acknowledge the power of the genji how. Confronted by sobering circumstance, I again whispered the genji how, and followed that with an incantation for protection, which, like the genji how, I had learned many years before. The incantation is recited to Harakoy Dikko, goddess of the Niger River and mother-protector of human beings.

She gave birth to Suntunga. She gave birth to Muntanga. The Sah Tree. The Dugu Tree. The Wali Belin Tree. The Kasa Tobe Tree [sacred trees of Harakoy Dikko's domain under the Niger River]. The master of the small festival, Dikko; the master of the big festival, Dikko . . .

The words again brought me a degree of comfort. To complete the ritual, I spat very slightly on the linoleum floor. I hoped no one noticed. Songhay sorcerers spit after reciting an incantation so that their words carry to the east, the west, the north, and the south. Several minutes later, Jennifer returned.[1]

That was my first day in the village of the sick. In the days that followed I discovered a whole series of twists and turns on the path that connects the two sides of the between.

Sorcery in the World

In 1990 I fled the space of Songhay sorcery, concluding that it was a brutal world. At that point, I had no desire to walk a path through a space of deep existential uncertainty. So-and-so glanced at me the wrong way, should I seek magical protection? So-and-so offered me food, should I trust it? I have a sharp pain in my leg, has so-and-so sent sickness to me? When I precipitously left Niger more than eighteen years ago, my study of Songhay esoterica suggested that in worlds of sorcery there are "top guns," men and women who are feared and respected for their sorcerous power. Every day other men and women, who seek to replace them, challenge their standing and prestige. Having been the target of one of these sorcerous challenges, I realized that they are serious acts that sometimes carry lethal consequences. Yes, I had learned sorcery from one of the great practitioners, Adamu Jenitongo of Tillaberi, Niger. Despite the power of the weapons (potions, power objects, and the genji how) he had passed on to me, I concluded that I would never possess the proper belief and stamina to pursue sorcerous power. For me, the genji how became little more than a sequence of poetic words.

Many years later, though, when I sat in Joel Rubin's examination room the words of the genji how surged like a current into my consciousness. They had become central weapons in my "fight" against lymphoma. I finally realized that I had misunderstood the deep meaning of the incantation. It was a sorcerous weapon that could divert death. It was a sequence of words that could reestablish harmony in chaotic circumstances. What I hadn't realized was that the power of the incantation comes from the combination of two components: disharmony and peace. By creating harmonious peace in the "infusion room," the genji how primed me to confront the devastation of cancer and the indeterminacies of life in the village of the sick.

———

Twenty-five years after Adamu Jenitongo first introduced me to the world of sorcery, the specter of cancer in my life compelled me to revisit that strange universe. My knowledge of sorcery provided me with comfort in the village of the sick. My own religious background, Judaism, gave me a set of abstract principles about the world in which I lived but provided no concrete formulas for dealing with an unexpected and incurable disease. From my new vantage as a person living in the village of the sick, sorcery, by contrast, provided a reassuring set of principles about how to live in the world. And yet, how many cancer patients, as one of my friends put it, have "sorcery in their pocket"? Before I became a cancer patient, I would have said that very few people have "sorcery in their pocket." I would have also said that to have "sorcery in your pocket" is a mixed blessing. Although it can make you strong, it also makes you vulnerable.

Time and experience have taught me that everyone, especially cancer patients, can have "sorcery in their pocket." As I now understand it from the vantage of sorcery in the world, sorcery is a set of embodied principles. It is more than a set of esoteric practices; it is a way to carry oneself in the world. The genji how, for example, is an intrinsic part of sorcerous ritual. Its powerful words prepare a setting for sorcerous actions. Songhay sorcerers always begin their work with ritual texts like the genji how. Sometimes, they use it to divert death or sickness. Above and beyond its specific uses, the genji how is a ritual incantation, something that is said the same way and in the same context day in and day out, year in and year out. Through the recitation of the genji how the sorcerer attempts to maintain a semblance of order in the world.

Like the genji how, rituals set the world straight. Scholars often associate rituals with religious life and suggest that they constitute that which is considered sacred. Religious services, for example, are a collection of ritual incantations (prayers, hymns, and invocations) that bring to worshippers a sense of calm and peace. In search of calm and peace, people seek solace in churches, synagogues, and mosques—especially when they must confront trying personal experiences or troubling public events.

Rituals, however, also work their magic in the routine world of everyday life. Each of us has her or his personal rituals. Doing certain things when we wake up or go to sleep may help to "set the world straight" and bring us a sense of calm. Some people may run or stretch every morning before going to work; other people may take a soothing bath at night before going to bed. I like to wake early, brew coffee, and write. When we are able to perform these personal rituals, they give us a good feeling. They make us feel, if only for a little while, that we can generate and maintain a measure of control over our lives.

When you learn that you have cancer, things spin out of control. You are thrown into a world of medical procedures and inconclusive diagnoses. What's more, you have to interact with technicians and medical professionals, many of whom can be insensitive. Beyond that, the texture of your social relationships shifts. Your friends and family may shower you with too much attention and concern; they may talk too much about your disease. Some of your friends and family may seek comfort in denial; they avoid the subjects of illness and death. Meanwhile, you find yourself in the vortex of a whirlwind. No matter what kind of support you have from friends, family, and professionals—and the importance of this support cannot be overestimated—the cancer cells have appeared in your body, which means that ultimately you, like the African sorcerer, must face your fate alone.

Confronting cancer is a frighteningly lonely proposition. How do you confront your isolation? How do you face your fate? As Adamu Jenitongo had taught me twenty-five years earlier, Songhay sorcerers have one suggestion. They say that you should diligently perform personal rituals. Throughout my treatments for lymphoma, I tried to follow this principle. Seated in the medical recliner in the "infusion room" of the cancer center, I'd recite the genji how and follow it with an incantation for protection. Once I had spit lightly into the air so that my words would infuse the "infusion room" with old and powerful sounds, I'd spread a piece of Malian *bokolanfani* fabric—black geometric patterns on brown homespun cloth—over the drab brown table next to my chair. I would take my jazz tapes—Coltrane, Gillespie, Mingus, and Hamilton—and put them on the cloth next to my Walkman and several Ironman energy bars. When Jennifer, my oncology nurse, came in to connect me to the intravenous line, I would put on my earphones and fly away to some distant spot in John Coltrane's musical universe. Throughout the treatments, I never varied my ritualistic routine: genji how, incantation for protection, cloth, jazz, and Ironman energy bars. The routine helped me to endure five- to six-hour treatment sessions. In my social and physical isolation, they helped me to confront the physical and emotional pain that I was experiencing. They gave me a degree of control over an uncontrollable situation. I am also convinced that they primed the immune system to purge my body of lymphoma cells. After three treatments, the combination of chemotherapy and Rituxan had shrunk my abdominal tumor by 50 percent. What's more, I hadn't lost my hair and had retained enough energy to teach, write, and even travel a bit.

Engaging in personal rituals, of course, cannot guarantee a successful course of chemotherapy, but it can assure, I think, a certain sense of personal control, which goes a long way toward maintaining the quality of life. Any cancer patient can engage in this kind of ritual. Before treatment, you might recite a certain prayer or poem, like the genji how, that gives you comfort. You might wear clothing that makes you feel confident. You might bring food that fuels your energy. You might bring music that sends you on a soothing dreamlike journey. These personal rituals transform a clinical encounter into a meaningful personal odyssey. They bring you peace, following the wisdom of the genji how, so that you can be ready for what life has presented on your path.

———

When I fled Niger and the world of sorcery in 1990, the challenge that Sorko Djibo presented to me in 1977 faded into the background. He had wondered if I would ever learn how to "see," "hear," and "feel." It had been many years since I pondered the possibility of seeing something that was invisible, of hearing something that made no sound, and of feeling something that had no tangible surface. It did indeed take me many years to understand that Djibo's comments encapsulated the central tenants of Songhay sorcery. It takes a lifetime, I realized from my vantage in the village of the sick, to learn how to "see," "hear," and "feel" the world.

During the many hours I sat in the infusion room as chemotherapy drugs dripped into my bloodstream, I had a great deal of time to think about my education in sorcery. Among the first steps of my education was learning how to "see." For sorcerers, to "see" is to look deeply into the past, present, and future—the art of divination. Songhay sorcerers use one of two methods to "see"—geomancy and divining shells. The geomancer traces lines in the sand and uses a complex numerology to read past, present, and future. Although this technique is rarely used in Niger, variations of the practice are widely employed throughout west and central Africa.

Divining shells are more commonly used in Niger. Before Adamu Jenitongo taught me how to "see," I observed scores of divining sessions. The sorcerer typically throws small white shells—the cowry shells that had once been used as currency in precolonial Niger—to assess a person's situation or to discover the source of his or her misfortune or illness. After the sorcerer has read the shell configurations, he or she prescribes a course of action—a series of animal sacrifices, an offering to the blind, or a course of herbal medicines. Anthropologists have written extensively about divination. For the most part they see it as a complex mathematical system that uses sophisticated scales of probability to deliver results.[1] I relied on this anthropological literature to try to make sense of the divination sessions I had witnessed. Despite the insights that this anthropological knowledge provided, I failed to grasp the relationship between the shell patterns and the sorcerer's observations. I did learn that if the small opening of the shell faces up, it is "female." Conversely, if the large opening faces up, the shell is "male." Beyond this primary distinction, I made little sense of how the infinite combinations of "male" and "female" indicated betrayal, jealousy, illness, or death.

After a session with Adamu Jenitongo, I asked my mentor about how he read shells.

"That," he said, "I cannot tell you. You must learn for yourself. You must receive 'sight' from Wambata."

Wambata was the headstrong Songhay spirit that lived near cemeteries. "What does Wambata have to do with 'seeing'"? I asked.

"I will try to give you sight," Adamu Jenitongo said, "and then you can better understand Wambata."

He invited me into the conical spirit hut and asked me to sit down on a palm frond mat. He took out three large red kola nuts that had been stored in water in a small clay pot for three days.

"Put these over your eyes," he ordered.

He then began to recite a series of incantations. Sitting there with the cool kola nuts pressed against my closed eyes, I wondered how this ritual might give me "sight." Listening to these incantations impelled me to think about what Adamu Jenitongo had already taught me about the Songhay view of divination. The world, according to Songhay belief, is a dangerous place filled with potential misfortune. You expect to confront all sorts of trouble—betrayal, loss, and illness—along your path. Although you cannot expect to evade misfortune, which is the norm rather than the exception in life, you can try to be prepared for it. One way to do so is divination. A diviner can throw shells to pinpoint where and when you will confront misfortune on life's path. Forewarned in this manner, you might be able to take preemptive measures—offerings, a course of fortifying medicines—to confront better the trouble that fate invariably brings your way.

This viewpoint did not seem terribly exotic to me. It made me think of my grandmother's considerable fear of the evil eye. Like many Songhay people she saw misfortune in every nook and cranny of the world. Thinking that the evil eye would punish self-assurance, ostentation, and beauty, she, like many other Eastern European Jews, Greeks, and Italians, stressed modest self-presentation and avoided making positive statements.

Hearing the praise names of Wambata, spirit of death and goddess of divination, jolted me from my reveries. Adamu Jenitongo recited her praise poem with emphasis and deliberation. It is a poem that describes the clairvoyant powers of a willful female spirit, the mother of death.

From listening I understood clearly Wambata's capacity to see clarity—the past, present, and future—in "the brightness of the sun," in "the glow of the moon," in "a bowl of milk," or in "a pool of blood." I wondered, though, how Wambata's capacities might be extended to me.

"You now have vision," Adamu Jenitongo stated when he had finished.

"You mean that if I throw shells I'll see the past, present, and future?"

The old man chuckled. "I have given you the potential for vision. You must find you own way to sight. Be patient, your path will open in front of you." He put some grated kola under his lip. "When it opens depends upon you and Wambata." He pulled a leather pouch from one of the pockets in his tunic. He counted thirteen cowry shells and put them into a cloth satchel, which he tied shut.

"Take these. They will help you to see."

I thanked him and took the shells and put them into the pocket of my tunic.

"These are Wambata's shells. She will not speak through other shells."

Late that afternoon I returned to a friend's house and eagerly attempted to throw the shells to divine his future. The configurations did not reveal anything about my friend's past, present, or future. I did not hear Wambata's voice.

One year later I returned to Niger to continue my studies with Adamu Jenitongo in Tillaberi. He taught me sorcerous incantations and allowed me to observe sorcerous rites but had nothing to say about divination. After several weeks at his compound, I asked him to again teach me about the cowry shells.

"Maybe it's time for you to visit your friends in Mehanna."

I followed his advice, not knowing how my friends in Mehanna, the town where I conducted my early field research, could help me to learn how to "see." As it turned out, my trip to Mehanna enabled me to learn more about divination than I had anticipated. At the market I saw a friend,

Fatouma Seyni, who asked me to visit her house late one afternoon. After we drank tea and chatted, Fatouma told me that she was a diviner.

"The shells say that I should teach you about divination," she informed me.

The path of divination had opened for me—at least partially. I took lessons from her. She taught me configurations that indicated sickness, death. She showed me how to detect the presence of a witch, the loss of money, and the arrival of good fortune—either money or good health—after a bout of sickness. She taught me how to see a "path that was blocked" and to divine what might be blocking the path. She pointed out how to "see" trouble on a person's path. After helping me to learn a little bit about reading shells, she abruptly dismissed me. "You've learned enough for now. You'll be back. I've seen it in the shells. When you return, we'll continue."

Reluctantly I did as she asked and returned to Tillaberi to say my farewells to Adamu Jenitongo. Before leaving Niger that year, I threw shells for several associates in Niamey, Niger's capital city. I now could see sickness and good fortune but didn't know how to attribute them to a particular person. I had yet to hear Wambata's voice.[2]

⸻

The development of "my vision" has been a slow process. As the years have progressed I have learned more about a seemingly infinite array of shell configurations. Ten years after first studying with Adamu Jenitongo, I began to sense Wambata's voice during divination sessions for friends and family. That gentle breeze of a voice would give me a point of reference in shell configurations, which enabled me to make better sense of the patterns. I gained some ability to see/hear the past, present, and future. My path, as Adamu Jenitongo would have said, had opened. This development encouraged me to throw shells more regularly. My enthusiasm, though, exacted a price, for, like my teacher Fatouma Seyni, this turn of events also gave me severe headaches. When I became more circumspect about throwing shells, the headaches disappeared. The experience reminded me once again that one should learn about sorcery in a deliberate and respectful way.

The shells have taught me a number of important lessons about living life in the contemporary world. Sorcerers cannot master shells, as the Songhay would phrase it, unless they have mastered themselves. Such mastery means that sorcerers need to know themselves, to evoke the ideas of Antonin Artaud, with a "cruel" honesty. As this emotionally painful self-vision ripens with age, so does the capacity to read the past, present, and future. Following this path, the sorcerer learns to see as well as look, to hear as well as listen.

Twenty-five years ago, Djibo Mounmouni said to me, "You look but you don't see. You listen but you don't hear. You touch but you don't feel." Although my abilities cannot be compared to Adamu Jenitongo's or Fatouma Seyni's, I slowly and deliberately tried to develop my sensuous capacities. When my path unexpectedly led me into the village of the sick, these sensibilities deepened. When I stepped into the world of cancer and experienced blood tests, CT scans, PET scans, bone-marrow biopsies, and the cool surge of chemotherapy drugs in my blood, I understood more fully what it meant to see, to hear, and to feel.

———

Among many African peoples specialized knowledge, as previously mentioned, is a precious commodity. It is not something that an individual owns; rather, it is something that one masters, refines, and passes along. Sorcerers fit into this category. They attempt to heal the sick, but their orientation to knowledge reflects more of a group orientation that usually leads to a humble and respectful approach to illness and healing. Sorcerers are considered the embodiment of power. They are the masters of incantations, plants, and magic. And yet, sorcerers do not "own" this power; the power "owns" them. It is said that in the process of eating power, in the form of millet paste mixed with powdered tree barks, sorcerers are consumed by power. Some sorcerers may become accomplished practitioners who attract clients from far and wide, but no matter their renown, the collective power of "those who came before" restrains their sense of self. In this way the sorcerer is part of a larger tradition of sorcery. Traditions of the past constrain an individual's will in the present. The precedents of the past set the parameters within which sorcerers learn, practice, and refine their power. By the same token, these precedents underscore the limits of an individual sorcerer's power as well as his or her obligation to pass power on to the next generation. Sorcery, then, is far more powerful than any sorcerer is. These time-honored principles chart a sorcerous course that slowly leads from youthful arrogance to seasoned humility.

Like sorcery, cancer, I came to understand through my experience in the village of the sick, charts a course toward humility. Cancer propels you down a difficult path on which it was important to be humble. If you are arrogant about life and believe that you can master illness, a disease, like cancer, can force you into a needlessly desperate corner. The onset of many cancers is sometimes sudden and without symptoms. A healthy, active person, who exhibits few, if any, symptoms, is suddenly told that she or he has cancer, a pronouncement that, in the minds of many people, is usually the equivalent of a death sentence. Optimism fades and feelings of control over one's life dissipate. Fear and helplessness fill the void created by this unexpected confrontation with death. Fear and helplessness can trigger depression, which often follows a cancer diagnosis.[3] Life spins even more out of control as we worry about a painful and premature death.

No formula can wash away the pain and suffering that comes with the diagnosis and treatment of cancer. For many people, denial can have short-term effectiveness. For others, faith, spirituality, and/or religious ritual can provide solace. Support groups can decrease the cancer patient's isolation. In a support group you are more likely to say what you feel and take comfort through commiseration with others who more or less share your fate. Even so, can participation in support groups deflect powerful themes that culturally disadvantage cancer patients? Perhaps they can to some extent. But can they alter the general perception that cancer is evil, that cancer changes social relationships? As I indicated earlier, no matter the degree of support you have, cancer patients, like the African sorcerer, must confront their illness alone.

Such a lonely assessment is by no means a prescription for hopeless pain and suffering. On the contrary, a sense of humility, a central theme in Songhay sorcery, can put pain and suffering into a context larger than the personal. This view is the one that most Songhay people hold. Illness is always lurking. Like the High God and the spirits, the force of illness is greater than any individual is. Illness is part of life; it lies within us and waits for the right moment to appear. The ideal for Songhay, especially Songhay sorcerers, is to live "well" within the parameters set by an illness. Songhay sorcerers believe that if you learn to live with illness, your being becomes stronger and stronger.

———

In Niger sorcerers are usually solitary figures. They usually live at the edge of town and serve as physical intermediaries between the relative tranquility of the village and the chaotic danger of the bush. Situated at the edge of reality, the sorcerer is utterly alone. Although sorcerers are, like other people, members of families and networks of friends, these loved ones and friends cannot help them to confront the underside of the world. Sorcerers are the solitary spiritual guardians of their communities. Through ritual incantations and offerings, they attempt to balance the disruptive forces of the bush, which, in turn, creates harmony in the world. In a harmonious context, sorcerers attempt to develop their vision. They throw cowry shells to "see" bits of the past, present, and future. The shells chart a course on which sorcerers are eventually able to cut through life's haze and see things clearly. After years of concentrated effort the capacity to see things more clearly than others develops into a seasoned humility. Elder sorcerers come to understand that they are a relatively small part of a great tradition—a trickle in the flow of history. They realize that the knowledge they have acquired is borrowed and that their responsibility is to refine what they have learned and pass it on to the next generation. Ideally, this realization enables them to be more comfortable in their skins and gives them the courage to confront the world with a degree of strength and dignity. This awareness can enable them to live well in the world.

Like Songhay sorcerers, cancer patients are also solitary figures who are continuously in the between. The disease makes you the intermediary between the tranquility of family life and the disruption of illness. You live at the edge of the village of the sick. You see your friends and family in the village of the healthy. Although you can visit them frequently, your place is elsewhere. Your life on the edge makes you a lonely figure in the world. Like the Songhay sorcerer, you, too, can use ritual, both spiritual and pragmatic, to establish harmony in your world. Like the Songhay sorcerer, you, too, can try to see things clearly and develop a strong-willed humility. Like the sorcerer, you can realize that time on earth is borrowed and must be eventually paid back. This realization can make you more comfortable and give you the courage to confront the existential imponderables of being diagnosed with and treated for cancer.[4] That is the central lesson of sorcery in the world.

19

Remission

From my vantage inside the gates of the village of the sick, I learned, however reluctantly, that many, if not most, cancers are incurable, which meant that when I completed a successful course of treatment I, like millions of other cancer patients, entered the curious world of remission. The term *remission* comes from the verb *to remit,* which can refer to, among other things, states of relief, abatement, hiatus, interruption, respite, stoppage, and subsidence. Except for "stoppage," none of the meanings associated with "remission" signify a permanent condition. Words like *relief, abatement, interruption, respite,* and *subsidence* suggest a return to a previous state. *Hiatus,* the classic position in the between, suggests a temporary place between what was and what will be. In the end remission means that you have to spend years "sitting on your hands," as my internist told me after a nine-month course of chemotherapy," or "being on hold," or "waiting for the other shoe to drop."

When you enter the zone of remission, you are very much in the between. You find yourself in a foggy space between the once comfortable assumptions of your old life and the sudden uncomfortable expectations of your new life. Once you enter the village of the sick, as I have previously stated, you can never fully return to the village of the healthy. During chemotherapy, you reside deep within the village of the sick. The routine of treatments and side-effects consumes your thoughts and takes up your time. When you reach the calm waters of remission, however, the physical impact of side-effects diminishes and your strength slowly returns.

You have the energy, in fact, to walk to the gate of your new village. From there you see the open gate to the village of the healthy. In your state of "respite," you can leave the space of sickness and walk the short distance to the zone of health. People there know you and greet you. Even so, you realize that you have changed. People there talk to you and wish you well, but you quickly understand that your time in the village of the sick has set you apart. You know that you can mingle among the healthy and even though you desperately want to resettle in that village, you sense that your place is elsewhere. In the village of the healthy you are surrounded by family and friends but often feel alone. In the village of the sick you are surrounded by strangers but are silently bonded to them. They know what you know.

There are, of course, many people today who live in village of the sick, all of whom are continuously between things, continuously in states of "remission." Arthur Frank refers to these villagers as members of the re-mission society. They are people, who

are effectively, but could never be considered cured . . . Members of the remission society include those who have had almost any cancer, those living in cardiac recov-ery programs, diabetics, those whose allergies and environmental sensitivities require dietary and other self-monitoring, those with prostheses and mechanical body regula-tors, the chronically ill, the disabled, those "recovering': from abuses and addictions, and for those people, the families that share the worries and the triumph of staying well.

Put another way, remission is an indeterminate state par excellence. You are neither sick nor healthy. Seen in this light, remission is an example of what the late Victor Turner called liminality. "Liminal entities," Turner wrote in his classic work, *The Ritual Process*, "are neither here nor there; they are betwixt and between the positions assigned and arrayed by cus-tom, convention and ceremonial."[1] Turner went on to describe the char-acteristics of people who find themselves in liminal states. They tend to be humble and follow instructions without complaint—the cancer patient following the advice for combating the side-effects of chemotherapy drugs. They tend to accept regimes of pain—the cancer patient authorizing a course of chemotherapy, surgery, or radiation. They are reduced to a com-mon denominator, "the cancer patient," so they might be reconstructed. These processes, Turner suggested, trigger an intense camaraderie, which undermines previously recognized differences in age, social status, and ethnicity. In the infusion room, as we have seen, there can be a powerfully unstated camaraderie. University professors, sales clerks, attorneys, and sanitation workers get the same "treatment." This recognition creates a sense of solidarity. Turner called this camaraderie "communitas."

As Turner has variously noted, liminality is a common phenomenon in human experience. It is a central component of rites of passage, ceremonies that mark the most important events in the life cycle: birth, initiation, marriage, and death. Many anthropologists have written about initiation rites. Before their initiation, boys and girls in many African societies are considered children. During the initiation period, boys, for example, often learn about hunting, farming, sexuality, and religion. During this period of liminal training, groups of boys, who are considered neither children nor adults, are isolated in sacred spaces. At the end of this initiatory training, ceremonies are performed that symbolically mark the transition from childhood to adulthood. In some societies the transition is marked by circumcision or scarification. In a few societies, neophytes are literally buried. They leave their childhood in mock graves and arise from them as adults.

Like the West African initiates-in-training, cancer patients are liminal figures in society. Like neophytes, cancer patients are often symbolically set apart by stereotypical images: a pasty skin, a hairless head, a shuffling walk, a skeletal body. These are images of impending death. Considering the intense fear of death in U.S. society, these images sometimes make us shudder and promote avoidance. Like many neophytes, cancer patients submit to regimens of pain—chemotherapy, which they usually receive in specially outfitted rooms. Infusion rooms, as previously described, are often arranged to encourage informal talk and camaraderie. Communitas may or may not surface in the infusion room, but cancer patients who are in or who have completed treatment—"survivors"—are encouraged to participate in support groups. Bonded by the cancer experience, strangers feel comfortable enough to openly express their fear—of pain and death—to one another, confessions that would make an "outsider" uncomfortable. From a liminal vantage, these encounters are part of "survival" training, a way of making treatment and remission easier to bear.[2]

The liminality of cancer patients, though, has a curious twist. For most initiates, liminality is a transitional state. Having learned the secrets of the hunt and having been circumcised, West African boys leave the isolated sacred space of their training and return to the village as young men. No longer betwixt and between, they are reintegrated into society. As for cancer patients, they, too, can look forward to the end of their isolation, to the end of chemotherapy and its debilitating side-effects. At that point they are in remission, which continues rather than ends their liminality. The twist, then, is that the liminality of the cancer patients may subside but it rarely ends. Even though remission brings on a relatively healthy state, there is, for all intents and purposes, no full-fledged return to the village of the healthy. This path marks a course of continuous liminality.

Cancer patients are not the only people who walk the path of continuous liminality. Many immigrants never quite feel at home in the host country. Among the Songhay, sorcerers find themselves in a state of continuous liminality. They wander amid the shadows of social life where life is more than what it seems. They walk in the nebulous place—the between—where the social and spirit words intersect, a place where one false move can result in blindness, paralysis, or sometimes, the premature death of a child.

Like remission, continuous liminality is hard to bear. You feel marked as an outsider. You may think that people are trying to avoid you. When you do interact with other people, you often sense that they avoid bringing up certain subjects. Beyond these social limitations, continuous liminality offers no conclusions, only more treacherous terrain to negotiate.

Remission is especially difficult for a person whose worldview is shaped by the immunological thinking so characteristic of the village of healthy. At the end of treatment, the side-effects of chemotherapy finally fade away. The aches and pains dissipate. The mouth sores disappear. Your throat clears. The fevers subside and your appetite returns. Once again, energy courses through your body. Even though you feel "normal," you think about cancer every day. You realize that cancer is a wanderer who may knock on your door at any moment. This uncertainty is difficult to confront. In remission, some cancer patients become bitter and resentful. Following the path of immunological thinking, others try to conquer their adversary. Like a powerful football team, they try to pummel their opponent into submission, forcing the enemy into the background of their consciousness. Indeed, this tactic enables some people to lead full and "normal" lives in remission—at least until remission ends.

But there is another way, I've learned, of confronting the imponderables of remission. Instead of denying the presence of cancer in your life, why not incorporate it into your being. This tack, which conforms to what David Napier called "embryological thinking," has been long employed by many non-Western peoples. The Songhay people are a case in point. Swept up in the strong current of life, many Songhay people think that life is a loan that can never fully be repaid. On the due date, you can make a payment, but you'll never be able to pay off the principle. You would like to think that your payments, though never complete, make lasting contributions to family, friends, and community.

Adamu Jenitongo in Tillaberi, Niger 1987. Photograph by the author.

This orientation to the world engenders considerable respect for the forces of the universe, including the ongoing presence of illness in the body. Illness is not the enemy, but rather an ongoing part of life. Following the prescriptions of Songhay healers, when illness appears, it presents you with limitations; but if you can accept these limitations and work within their parameters, you can create a degree of comfort in uncomfortable circumstances. By incorporating cancer into your being, you can, like the cyclist Lance Armstrong, use it to build strength and endurance. Armstrong has written that were it not for his cancer diagnosis and treatment, he would not have ever won the Tour de France.[3]

The voice of my Songhay teacher, Adamu Jenitongo, sometimes comes to me in my dreams. He reminds me to accept my limitations and to purge resentment from my being. He urges me to be patient in an impatient world. He asks me to be humble and to refine my knowledge, so that others might learn from it. And yet the wisdom of sages like Adamu Jenitongo, I've concluded, is no quick fix for people with cancer. Even so, his wisdom is instructive. Remission is stressful. It is not easy being continuously betwixt and between orderly health and disorderly illness, between the fragility of life and the certitude of death. When I get a virus or an ingrown hair, I wonder if my cancer has returned. My being is filled with anxiety, when I undergo a yearly CAT scan. As I await the results, like a defendant waiting to hear the jury's verdict, I wonder what it would be like to go through another round of treatment. And yet, remission's stressful junctures are few and far between.

Following the path of Adamu Jenitongo, which puts you in an indeterminate space where you are everywhere and nowhere in the between, it may help to accept remission's limitations and seize the moment. In so doing, you can acknowledge that our time on earth is short and that a central mission in life is to contribute knowledge—whatever that may be or entail—to our families, friends, colleagues, and communities.

20

Reconfiguration

The specter of cancer in my life compelled me to reconsider what it meant to live anthropology. In the human sciences, we are still very much mired in immunological thinking that is deeply rooted in the village of the healthy. In immunological thinking we may find ourselves in the between, but we tend to gravitate toward one pole of the chasm to the exclusion of the other. Thinking immunologically, we strive to transform the chaos of social relations into some semblance of order. Michael Taussig expresses this point with eloquence:

We strip the unknown of all that is strange. We show it who's boss, the basic rule of a university seminar. We tolerate neither ambiguity nor that which won't conform. The second and even greater misfortune here is that we thereby forget how strange is the known. This is why I have not sought masterful explanations but for estrangement, the gift of ethnography no less than of literature.[1]

In taking "control" of things, we attempt to stop the continuous flux of experience and create works that divide the world into discrete categories. We break down wholes into their constituent parts, dismantling the vibrant bridges that connect the two poles of the between. And yet, as the late Jacques Derrida liked to say, the language we use to project our immunological ideas is subversive; it continuously undermines our penchant for clear categorical thought.[2] Consider what Maurice Merleau-Ponty had to say about painters, writers and representation.

We usually say that the painter reaches us across the silent world of lines and colors, and that he addresses himself to an unformulated power of deciphering within us that we control only after we have blindly used it—only after we have enjoyed the work. The writer is said, on the contrary, to dwell in already elaborated signs and in an already speaking world, and to require nothing more of us than the power to reorganize our significations according to the indications of the signs he proposes to us. But what if language expresses as much by what is between words as by the words themselves? By that which it does not "say" as by what it "says." And what if, hidden in empirical language, there is a second order language in which signs once again lead the vague life of colors, and in which significations never free themselves from the intercourse of signs.[3]

Can we ever get past, Merleau-Ponty wondered, the pervasive and ongoing interpenetration of elements—signs, bodies, and beings—in the world? For Merleau-Ponty, then, immunological thinking would project a powerful set of metaphors into the world. Although metaphors like "cancer as war" have their pragmatic uses, in the end they turn out to be illusions of reality that lull us into a false sense of control.

Surrealists, like André Breton, long ago realized that the world cannot be transformed into a machine that generates a perfect matrix of right angles all of which fit together seamlessly.[4] They suggested that such right-angled perfection lulls us into a deep sleep from which only a few people will emerge. For social scientists this sleep, to which Taussig alludes in his recent book, *Walter Benjamin's Grave,* is called "the dead hand of competence." The "dead hand" guides us into space in which institutions and an established set of prescriptions sets us onto a path that leads to the construction of conventional knowledge. In the end, the dead hand kills the world, reducing it to a set of rules, a collection of formulae, or, better yet, to a perfect language. That language, of course, is a discourse of mastery.

And yet the social world repels such disembodied description. It is far more complex and wondrous than our who's-the-boss descriptions would indicate. It refuses to be reduced to its constituent parts. We don't capture it in our representations, following the aforementioned logic of Songhay elders; rather, it captures us.

When I confronted the indeterminate reality of cancer diagnosis, treatment, and remission, my perception of the anthropological odyssey shifted. Why had I spent so much time and effort attempting to write about "how things work"? I had tried very hard to understand the mysteries of spirit possession and sorcery. I had grappled with the issue of how to write about social life. Despite my efforts, the results of my research, like the irreducible quandaries of social life, had been inconclusive. Considering these inconclusive results, why did I persist? Like most writers, I wanted my ideas discussed and debated. Like most anthropologists, I wanted collegial affirmation. Like most scholars, I wanted to make contributions to knowledge.

Faced with a disease that can be "managed" but not "cured," I wondered about my obligations as an anthropologist. Should I continue to write "thickly" described stories? Should I continue to attempt to refine social theory? I now believe that one of our most important obligations is to use our skills to bear witness. In so doing we are compelled to tell stories about kinship as well as cancer that shed light on social realties. As participants in and witnesses to social life, we are obliged to choose any number of genres—essays, ethnography, film, photography, poetry, fiction, and art—that make our stories accessible to a wide range of audiences. This shift may bring harmony to a cancer center, infuse an infusion room with a touch of warmth, or make the emotional instabilities of remission a bit easier to bear.

Getting to this point of reconfiguration demands that we take epistemological risks to meet the complex and ever-shifting challenges of the contemporary world. If you are in a state of remission, risks are perhaps easier to take. In remission circumstances force you to live in ambiguous states of uncertainty, to live in continuous liminality. Because we all are, in a sense, in remission, anyone can choose to follow this uncertain path. As the surrealists knew long ago, if we embrace the indeterminacies of the world we soon find ourselves in a place of unimaginable growth and power. In such a place, our reconfigured thinking is empowered to confront the complexities of contemporary social worlds with creative verve. By embracing the world, we ensure that it will not deposit us in its wake. In the end, reconfiguring anthropology—or any other pursuit of knowledge—in this indeterminate way may propel us to the path long followed by Songhay sorcerers and classical scholars, the path that leads to an embodied enlightenment.

Ethnography

More than twenty years ago I had a conversation with Adamu Jenitongo that would have considerable bearing on my life in the world. It was a hazy late afternoon in Tillaberi, Niger. From our vantage atop a wind-carved sand dune, we could see the Niger River snaking southward, its waters glistening in the golden afternoon light. The clang of bells announced the arrival of a long line of cows and sheep, returning from a day in the bush. Clouds of dust formed in their wake. The rhythmic thump of pestles pounding mortars echoed in the dry air as women transformed millet seeds to millet flour, which would soon be boiled into a nutritious paste that would be topped with a spicy peanut sauce. Shaded from the soon-to-set afternoon sun, which was still hot, Adamu Jenitongo sat on a palm frond mat on the east side of his grass spirit hut, a small dome with a diameter of no more than fifteen feet. He had wrapped a black turban around his small head and wore baggy pants and a tunic both of which had once been white. Time, dirt, and dust, however, had transformed the fabric into a color that looked more like the washed-out beige of a dried millet stalk. With his back resting against the thatch of the spirit hut, he rubbed a kola nut on a metal grater and then took a handful of grated kola and put it under his lip.

Earlier, when Adamu Jenitongo had seen me walking by, he motioned for me to approach. "Come and sit, my son," he said.

We sat in silence, like two cats on a perch, for what seemed a long time.

Eventually, Adamu Jenitongo spat out some kola and said, "What are you doing?"

"Sitting here with you," I responded, confused by the question.

Dissatisfied with my response, he posed the question again.

"I'm not sure what I'm doing," I admitted.

He nodded. "That's a better answer. Can we ever be sure about what we are doing?"

Another long silence settled between us and I thought about his comment. "I guess not," I admitted.

"Yes. The most important thing is to do things that are worth doing."

"But how do you know what is worth doing?" I asked. "Can you avoid taking the wrong path?"

"No, you cannot, my son. It is very easy to take the wrong path and waste your time and energy. We all do that. But if you are patient, life will teach you what is important and you can concentrate on that."

———

I have long struggled to determine some sense of what is important—at least for me. One thing I've realized is that you cannot say that "this" is important and "that" is not. You can say that there are a range of things that are important and a range of things that are not. There are things that are important in your personal life that may well be distinct from things that are important in your professional life. And to confound matters even more, there are things that are important in your personal life—my experience with cancer—that can have a profound impact on things that are important in your professional life. In anthropology, perhaps the most personal of the human sciences, the personal usually has a deep impact on the professional. For me, living anthropology has been profoundly personal.

Anthropology has long been a highly specialized discipline in the human sciences. We have always had geographical areas of expertise, but now we have so many specialized pursuits that it is hard to know what living and doing anthropology might entail. In addition to the more traditional pursuits of kinship, economic exchange, religion, and social change, colleagues today pursue research on immigration, globalization, poverty, and its relation to health and well-being, aging, citizenship, violence, political advocacy, and human rights discourses. This scholarship has produced a rich literature filled with complex insights about the human condition. This knowledge, I am confident, will enable present and future anthropologists to confront the social issues that will challenge our adaptation to social life in the twenty-first century.

When asked what anthropologists do, the late Clifford Geertz quipped, "We write."[1] Over the years our writing has built a deep and varied anthropological record that has documented the diversity and vitality of human social life. And yet, beyond functionalism, beyond structuralism, beyond poststructuralism, beyond postmodernism, global ethnoscapes and the latest twist on human rights discourses, there lies the bedrock of anthropology—ethnography, our enduring gift to the world, a gift that sometimes enables readers to understand the wisdom of others, which, in turn, can open their being to an increasingly complex and interconnected world. Ethnography is something that is important to me.

The idea of ethnography, of course, is a slippery one. Some people consider ethnography more like a method of doing social research than a distinct literary genre.

I have also subscribed to this notion. When Adamu Jenitongo asked me about my "work," I would sometimes answer with the Songhay equivalent to "ethnographic research." When I list scholarly activities for a departmental annual report, I always include "engaged in ongoing ethnographic research."

The methods of "ethnographic research" include the fabled notion of participant observation, informally and formally structured interviews, surveys, and archival study. These methods usually generate data that result in the publication of theoretically informed essays that refine our capacities to understand social and cultural processes. These same methods sometime produce results that are transformed into book-length studies that we call ethnographies.

During the last twenty-five years there has been much debate about ethnography. Anthropologists and literary theorists have discussed the conventions of ethnographic representation.[2] These debates led to critiques of ethnographic realism, a textual convention in which ethnographers attempt to use their specifically circumscribed data to represent a totality.[3] Drawing upon these critiques, anthropologists began to experiment with ethnographic form, writing works that did not conform to the tried and true realist structure of theoretical introduction, presentation of data, and conclusion. Instead, they wrote dialogical ethnographies or texts that foregrounded narratives in which the presence of the ethnographer, the empowered person who controlled the construction of the text, was reflexively acknowledged.[4] If truth be known, many of these "experimental texts" have been less than noteworthy and, like more classically structured ethnographies, are now closed to the world as they gather dust on library shelves.

From my vantage as an ethnographer, the central question is, how can an ethnographic work, based on long-term research, remain open to the world? What is it about certain ethnographic texts that, year after year, continue to attract readers? It is clear to me that there is no one way to write an ethnographic text. Each body of ethnographic material is unique and therefore requires a specifically contoured textual strategy. Beyond that textual specificity, as in my attempt to weave a blanket that depicts the world of West African immigrants in New York City, there are key elements that must be present in the text if ethnographers want their works to be read by a wide range of readers over a long period of time.

One element is a sense of locality. When you read a memorable ethnography, the spaces/places of that book become etched in your memory. After finishing the work, you might say, "I felt like I was there. I felt the pulse of the sun and the itch of dust in my eyes." Another element involves the construction of character. Who are the people in the ethnography? How distinctive is their talk? What traits and behaviors determine their particular character? What motivates their behavior? Are they memorable? When you read about them, can you say, "I got to know this man or woman."

Even if you sensuously describe the physical attributes of the ethnographic locale and sensitively construct the character of the people who live there, you have only met the necessary, but not the sufficient, conditions of memorable ethnography. For the latter, ethnographers as well as their characters need to grapple with the things that are most fundamentally human—love and loss, fear and courage, fate and compassion—deep issues that connect readers to the people they encounter in ethnographic texts. "Yes," you might say, "I can identify with the author and the friends he describes."

There are a number of ethnographic works that artistically combine the elements outlined above. One such work is Piers Vitebsky's *The Reindeer People,* published to much critical acclaim in 2005. Vitebsky is an ethnographer's ethnographer. All of his works have evolved from long and intense field study during which he mastered multiple languages and built extensive and deep friendships with the peoples he has attempted—with great success, in my opinion—to describe. Such is the case with the Eveny, a Siberian people that Vitebsky masterfully describes in *The Reindeer People.* Through his linguistic mastery and his long participation in things Eveny, Vitebsky quite willingly describes how his life has become—

CHAPTER TWENTY-ONE

Piers Vitebsky. Courtesy Piers Vitebsky.

over time—entwined with those of his Siberian friends. By following a winding, time-tested path of social and emotional implication, Vitebsky produces a profoundly human portrait of the Eveny. Such humanism is, I think, the central ingredient in the recipe for producing great ethnography. As Adamu Jenitongo liked to say to me, "You may write a good deal about us, but to understand us, you must grow old with us."

The Reindeer People showcases Vitebsky's historical, political, and ecological erudition. It also demonstrates his enviable capacity to describe vividly the breathtaking sweep of the Siberian landscape. The book, however, is not centrally an analysis of historical, political, or ecological events, but of how the Eveny, who are also noted for their shamanistic practices, have struggled to adapt—over time—to an ever-challenging and ever-shifting complex of change. With the skill of a seasoned novelist, Vitebsky paints portraits of a cast of characters whose strengths take charge of the story, giving to this work the power that evolves when an ethnographer is able to combine engaging narrative with insightful analysis.

When you near the end of Vitebsky's deeply human portrait of the Eveny, you don't want the text to end. You have immersed yourself in an ethnography that reaffirms the common threads of our humanity, which, in turn, deepens your sensitivities to the human condition. Considered in this light, ethnography can sometimes be a bridge that connects two worlds, binding two universes of meaning. It can be a path that entwines the distant lives of others to our more familiar being—a place in the between that is a gift to the world.

22

Memoir

During my last visit to Adamu Jenitongo in 1987, we spent afternoons lounging on pillows arranged on straw mats rolled out over the sand under the spirit possession canopy. The canopy consisted of thatch that had been tied down on wooden beams that fit snugly into fork-ended poles that had been anchored in the sand. During possession ceremonies, the spirit possession musicians, a monochord violinist and three gourd drummers, would situate themselves and their instruments under the front-center of the canopy. When the rhythmic music flowed into the air, a crowd would gather behind the musicians, taking advantage of a shady spot to listen to the music and watch the graceful dancing of spirit mediums.

Most afternoons, though, the spirit possession canopy served as a place to relax and talk. One day during my visit, I joined Adamu Jenitongo under the canopy. It was midday and intensely hot, which slowed considerably the pace of life. No visitors had appeared and most of the family could be found inside their mud-brick houses awaiting the slow descent of the sun, which by midday had blanched the sky. Adamu Jenitongo sat on a small stool and wove strips of palm frond into the rope. His granddaughter, Jamilla, sat near him. Jamilla's father, Moru, lay on his back, his head resting on a leather pillow.

After the customary afternoon greetings and some commentary on the heat, I asked Adamu Jenitongo why he was weaving rope.

"It's something I do to pass the time during the heat. We can use it to tether the sheep and the goats." He asked after me and my work. I had been reading to him the page proofs of my book about Songhay sorcery, much of which was about his life and work. I had also shown him the book's cover, a picture of him, dressed in robes and a turban. He stood tall and proud and held his special wooden stick, which he called "*korom genji*," that which heats up the bush. During our readings, he listened intently so that he could correct my errors. The whole process had taken over a month because I had to translate as we proceeded. "When will people see the book?" he asked eagerly when we had finished.

"In several months, Baba," I answered.

"You've told my story, my son, and I am grateful."

"Thank you, Baba." I was very pleased with his praise.

"But to tell my story," he said, "you have had to tell your story as well. It takes two hands," he said, using a well-known Songhay proverb, "to secure a friendship."

"Or to tell a story," I said.

Adamu Jenitongo nodded and went back to his weaving. Moru wondered if the rains would soon come to break the latest wave of heat. Jamilla's mother came and carried her daughter off to Moru's mud-brick house. Donkeys brayed and a dog barked.

Baba had once again taught me a lesson—this time about writing a memoir.

Although it is a very slippery slope, writing a memoir is something that many anthropologists may want to pursue at some point in their careers. Memoir is important because as a genre, it can extend substantially the readership for things ethnographic. When you write a memoir, you attempt, however selectively, to open your being to an invisible audience of readers, and that is one of the great appeals of the genre. Like living anthropology, the memoir is personal, which can make readers feel like they are getting a "real" story presented in accessible prose.

That said, the memoir is a very tricky enterprise. In far too many cases, the author is so focused on recounting, sometimes in excruciating detail, the intricacies of her or his life that the text can become a tedious exercise in solipsism. In describing the details of life, it is very easy to slip over the line and write narratives of limited interest. In the end, the lives of most of us are not as interesting as we think they are.

Illness narratives are among the most popular memoirs. When illness sends you into the turmoil of uncertainty, you feel the need to tell your story. For some reason, telling the story of your illness brings on a sense of clarity and calm. The medical sociologist Arthur Frank called this practice "wounded storytelling."[1] These stories give voice to the pain, suffering, frustration, and fear that shadow the pathways in the village of the sick. Their telling undoubtedly has a psychologically therapeutic effect, for it makes a person feel that she or he is not alone in an alien space. They connect you to other people who "really know what you know." The positive power of narrative, especially for people who live in the village of the sick, may well be the reason why so many cancer patients participate in support groups or join on-line discussion groups. These are places where patients can tell their stories to highly receptive and existentially comprehending audiences who give them supportive feedback and advice. There are countless Web sites, like that of Lance Armstrong Foundation, where patients can log on to read illness narratives, participate in on-line discussion forums, or retrieve information on the latest advances in the treatment of their particular disease.

Illness narratives are usually short, poignant, and intimate. Cancer narratives, for example, usually start with the existential insecurities that are associated with diagnosis, followed by the utter despair one feels when he or she is told, "You have cancer," followed by the trials and tribulations of chemotherapy treatments and their side-effects, followed by an eventual emergence into a state of remission. Looking back on their experiences, most of these mini-memoirists report a sense of renewal and a reordering of personal priorities. Their confrontation with adversity, they usually report, makes them more resilient, more insightful. Like my late mentor Adamu Jenitongo, "wounded storytellers" say illness has given them a fresh and more appreciative perspective on life. They often speak of being able to sense what is truly important in life.

There are, of course, few things more intimate in life than illness. And so it stands to reason that illness narratives are widespread. Within the context of support groups and on-line illness/wellness discussion communities, these intimacies are articulated in a well-defined context. Here, narrative intimacy provides emotional support to your socially circumscribed audience. But do these intimate narratives work for larger, more diverse groups? Can the circumscribed intimacy of illness narratives be extended to a wider audience? Should they?

There is no shortage of full-length illness memoirs, most of which describe in great detail the courage, resolve, and resilience of the author-patient. Many of these works have merit, for they connect the experience of the author to thousands of people in relatively similar circumstances. The greatest strength of these memoirs is their penchant for storytelling.

Their great weakness is a paucity of insight. Consider Joni Rodgers's humorous but bittersweet tale, *Bald in the Land of Big Hair*.[2] Rodgers, the author of two previous novels whose crazy characters underscored the contingencies of life, skillfully injected humor into the serious tale of the diagnosis and treatment of lymphoma. Consider also Fran Drescher's *Cancer Schmancer*, the television actress's memoir of her battle with breast cancer. In her book Drescher described how she used her mental robustness—some might say stubbornness—to will her cancer into submission.[3]

The best cancer memoirs, however, are those in which authors use their illness experience as a framework for broader discussion. In her classic *Illness as Metaphor* Susan Sontag used "cancer" as a framework for a historical and literary discussion of the social categorization of illness. Stuart Alsop's memorable *Stay of Execution* was a riveting account of the author's confrontation with an aggressive form of leukemia. In addition to providing a memorable description of what it felt like to be afflicted with leukemia, he used his experience to reflect on such broadly based issues as courage, sacrifice, patriotism, World War II, and the demise of the East Coast WASP establishment. In *At the Will of the Body*, Arthur Frank recounts his experiences with heart disease and cancer to suggest ways that people can make sense of illness. He also used his memoir to argue for more aggressive patient advocacy. No matter the subject, the best illness memoirs are those that use narrative, like those of Sontag, Alsop, and Frank, to contribute to a broader sense of well-being in the world.[4]

The same can be said for memoirs of travel, like Rory Stewart's incomparable book, *The Places in Between*. On one level, Stewart's tale was one of travel adventure, the story of his walk, with friends and his dog, across war-torn Afghanistan in the cold and snow of winter. But Stewart told his story in order to explore the history and culture of Afghan peoples, demonstrating the real costs of sectarian (Shia against Sunni) prejudice as well as interethnic strife. Beyond that, his story described people, who despite their struggles with war, poverty, and much loss, still managed to extend themselves to strangers like Stewart, who suddenly and unexpectedly showed up in their isolated villages. The villagers, no matter the despair of their circumstances, provided Stewart whatever food and comfort they could manage. By the end of the memoir, Stewart has used his improbable adventure as a way of introducing readers to the texture of social life in contemporary Afghanistan.

Two of the best writers in anthropology, Ruth Behar and Kirin Narayan, have followed this prescription in their ethnographic memoirs. In *The Vulnerable Observer*, Behar demonstrated quite powerfully how elements

CHAPTER TWENTY-TWO

Kirin Narayan. Courtesy Brent Nicastro.

of personal experience affected her creative approach to the central issues of anthropological practice, ethics, and representation. In *My Family and Other Saints,* Narayan told the story of her family to reflect upon the existential and spiritual quandaries of life in a globally integrated world.

As in ethnography, the memorable memoir is usually a text like those of Behar, Narayan, Stewart, Sontag, or Alsop in which the author constructs the personal as a bridge, a *barzakh,* to make once again reference to al-'Arabi, that connects outer realities to inner impression, others to selves, and readers to writers. In this way, these memoirs bring together disparate worlds and construct a deeper awareness of our common humanity.

Like the most memorable ethnographies, memoirs are also remarkable works of the imagination.

23

Imagination

In March 1990 I arranged to meet Jean Rouch for breakfast at 8:30 at a small café close to his apartment. Even though Rouch, in his own words, was a person who was always "punctually late" (*punctualement en retard*), I arrived on time at the L'Observatoire, one of Rouch's favorite cafés, which is situated on the corner of the boulevard Montparnasse and rue de L'Observatoire in the 14th arrondissement of Paris. I was pleasantly surprised when he showed up just a few minutes late. As always, he was dressed in blue: a dark blue blazer, a baby-blue dress shirt, and a blue silk ascot, all of which complemented his khaki trousers.

We greeted one another. Jean smiled and slapped me on the shoulder. "The croissants at this café are special," he said. "This is one of two cafés in Paris in which croissants are not shaped like crescents. Let's order some and you can tell me whether or not they are indeed the best you have ever tasted."

We ordered a basket of non-crescent-shaped croissants and two café au laits, which turned out to be two bowls of steamed milk flavored with dark-roast coffee. As we began to eat, a tall, slender young woman whose skin was the same color as café au lait, approached our table, clutching to her chest what appeared to be a manuscript.

Looking at Rouch, she said: "You are Monsieur Rouch?"

"Yes?"

"We have an 8:30 appointment."

Rouch hit his forehead with the palm of his hand. "Indeed," he said looking at me.

"I've come all the way from Martinique to meet with you about my doctoral thesis," she said, looking at Rouch.

"I've made two appointments for the same time," Rouch said. "Where are you sitting, Madame?"

She pointed to the other side of the café. "Paul, enjoy the croissants. I'll be back soon and we can begin our conversation."

Forty-five minutes later, Rouch returned to our table. "That charming woman is a teacher in Martinique and she's written a very good thesis."

"She came a long way to see you, Jean."

He winked at me. Looking at his cold bowl of coffee and the empty basket of croissants, he said: "Let's order more café au lait and croissants.

When the café au lait and new basket of croissants arrived, I asked Rouch if he would talk to me about his early days in Wanzerbé, the famous village of Songhay sorcerers. I told him that I was writing a biography of him, called *The Cinematic Griot,* and I needed background information on his early film, *Les magiciens de Wanzerbé.*

"What do you want to know about?"

"I want to know about the time you went there with the French administrators who wanted to verify if the sorcerers of Wanzerbé actually carried small metal chains in their stomachs." In the film, there is a scene of a sorcerer who, in trance, brings up one such chain, which dangles for a few moments between his lips.

"Oh, the French administrators who wanted to uncover the secrets of Wanzerbé."

"Yes. Can you tell me about that?"

Rouch sipped his coffee and buttered a croissant. "Get your tape-recorder ready. We must make sure you get down all the details."

Just then a young man, also holding a manuscript, approached the table.

"Monsieur Rouch," he announced, "we have an appointment for 10:00 a.m., do we not?"

"You are?"

The man, a German doctoral student living in Paris, had written a dissertation on ethnographic film practice and wanted to give his thesis to Rouch.

Rouch stood up and winked at me. "He's worked very hard on this, Paul. I'll be back soon."

He returned to our table around noon, looking a bit tired. "Shall we see what's for lunch?"

"That's a good idea." Having known Rouch for many years, I realized that this was his way. I always appreciated the time he gave me even if we had to endure many interruptions.

We ordered *blanquet de veau,* one of the best dishes at the café, and after lunch Rouch talked to me about sorcery in Wanzerbé.

———

That afternoon we talked a great deal about one of his early films, *Les magiciens de Wanzerbé.* When people saw the incredible footage of a sorcerer throwing up a small metal chain, which in non-trance states resided in the sorcerer's stomach, several French administrators wanted to learn more about the secrets of Wanzerbé. In the first case, the French administrator for Tera, the district in western Niger in which Wanzerbé is situated, traveled to Wanzerbé to learn about sorcery. Stepping across the threshold of a world beyond his comprehension, he suffered a mental breakdown soon after his arrival. French doctors evacuated him to a hospital in Niamey, Niger's capital city, where Rouch saw him in "a state of disorientation." He was soon taken back to France and by the time he set foot on French soil, he had regained his lucidity. He did not return to Niger.[1]

The administrator's replacement also wanted to "master" Wanzerbé. He invited Rouch to participate in an experiment. Like most people with scant experience in West Africa, he did not believe it possible for a person to live with a metal chain in her or his stomach. One way to test the veracity of this sorcerous claim would be, he reasoned, to X-ray one of the old sorcerers. Traveling with a portable X-ray machine and a generator, Rouch and the man arrived in Wanzerbé late one afternoon. They set up camp in Zongo, the neighborhood of strangers—anyone not born in the village. As dusk settled over the village, they sat in canvas director's chairs and sipped whiskey. In the distance, Djajé, the chief sorcerer of Wanzerbé, looked at them as he strolled by. Just thereafter the French administrator fainted. Like the first administrator, he, too, was evacuated. He did not return to Wanzerbé. No one returned to conduct a similar experiment.

A third administrator in Tera, a judge, also traveled to Wanzerbé to learn about sorcery. When he began to interfere in village politics, he became paralyzed from the waist down. The judge was evacuated to Niamey, where physicians treated him. His condition did not improve. Colonial officials ordered the judge's evacuation to France. When he reached France, he regained the ability to walk. He did not return to Niger.[2]

———

CHAPTER TWENTY-THREE

"Sorcery," Rouch went on, "is no game, is it?"

"If you've been to Wanzerbé, you know it's no game," I stated in agreement.

"It is an extraordinary place," Rouch admitted.

Our conversation continued on through the afternoon. We drank white wine spritzers and discussed Marcel Griaule, Lévi-Strauss, Luc de Heursch, Jean Cocteau, François Truffaut and Jean-Luc Godard—people that Rouch knew well. Rouch also recounted his adventures with his longstanding African friends and collaborators, Damouré Zika, Lam Ibrahim, and Tallou Mouzourane. Toward dusk, Rouch looked at the fading light outside.

"I would love to have dinner, Paul," he said, "but I've already missed several appointments and, as it is, I'll be late for another meeting."

"I understand," I said. "It has been a lovely day."

Rouch smiled. "It has been a good one. There's one thing I need to say."

"Yes?" I wondered what he was going say.

"Those men who went to Wanzerbé, they all lacked imagination," Rouch said. "Their vision was closed to the world. You need to be open to the world, Paul," he said. "Play with your imagination."

In Jean Rouch's universe there were few if any limits placed upon the imagination. In Rouch's world of "deep play" dreams became films; films became dreams. Feeling was fused with thought and action. Fusing poetry and science, Jean Rouch guided us into a wondrous world of the imagination, where we not only openly link ourselves to others but also experience the deep connection between outer self and inner being.

At that moment, Rouch, of course, used the complex notion of imagination as a gloss for (artistic) creativity. Philosophers have long contested the whys and wherefores of imagination. In his *de Anima,* Aristotle likened the imagination to something that we would today call a mental image. He and his followers considered it from what we would today call a cognitive perspective. With the rise of British empiricism in the seventeenth century, imagination was seen in terms of common sense. The creative associations of imagination, like those articulated by Jean Rouch, had their origins in eighteenth-century Romanticism. In the twentieth century, some philosophers, especially those of the analytic persuasion, wondered if human beings did, in fact, possess an imagination. More recently, philosophers have pondered the relation of imagination to subjectivity and, of course, the link between image and imagination.[3]

Here is not the place to delve into the details of this contested arena of philosophical debate. Getting back to Jean Rouch's view on imagination, what role does the imagination play in the creative arts? N. J. T. Thomas suggests that

the principal reason that imagination is thought to be particularly relevant to the arts arises from the ability of artists to see and to induce the rest of us to see aspects of reality differently or more fully than is ordinary—to see things as—we otherwise might not.[4]

From this vantage imagination leads us to religious sensibilities, to an appreciation of what William James called "radical empiricism," to the apprehension of the unseen. Referring to the centrality of the imagination in religious thought, William C. Chittick wrote, "In putting complete faith in reason, the West forgot that imagination opens the soul to certain possibilities of perceiving and understanding not available to the rational mind."[5] In Islam, Chittick argues, the imagination is particularly important. "By granting an independent ontological status to imagination and seeing the visionary realm as the self-revelation of God, Islamic philosophy has gone against the mainstream of Western thought."[6] These notions once again lead us back to the ideas of Ibn al-'Arabi and his notion of the *barzakh*—as imagination. Following this path, Vincent Crapanzano says that

[i]f we take the imagination, as Sartre and in his own way Ibn al-'Arabi do, as presenting that which is absent or nonexistent, we have to conclude that it is through an activity, which rests on the nonbeing of its object—the image—that we uncover those gaps, those disjunctive moments of nonbeing, that punctuate our social and cultural life. The imagination also provides us with the glosses, the rhetorical devices, the narrative maneuvers, and the ritual strategies to conceal those gaps. We uncover, as it were, nonbeing through an act that postulates nonbeing, as we conceal that nonbeing through a nonbeing we declare, in ritual at least, to have full being—plenitude. What is more "real" than objects of ritual? . . . Is it this paradox that leads to the continual (if repetitive) elaborations in ritual and drama, in literature and art, especially and most purely in music, of the asymptotic moment of crossing, that renders imaginative frontiers so menacing as they fascinate and enchant us? Such subterfuge, if one may call it so, is a source of our unending social and cultural creativity—or its cessation—through repetition and the declaration of that repetition as ultimate truth.[7]

In other words, the imagination, in all of its artistic permutations, enables us to approach the world afresh. Inspired by the imagination, art enables us to weave the world, to design a new blanket. As Jean Rouch would say, the imagination enables us to tell stories, which give birth to new stories, which generate, in their turn, more stories. In the end, the imagination always brings us back to the story.

Stories

In ethnographies, memoirs, novels, and films, anthropologists tell other people's stories. In so doing, we tell our own stories as well. Many scholars may object to this assertion. How can we reduce all of our efforts, our participant observations, structured and unstructured interviews, our excursions into the dusty byways of archives, to the telling of stories? How can we suggest that our reasoned discourse so boldly and confidently expressed in essays and scholarly monographs are no more than stories? Can there be reconciliation between stories and science?

The separation of science and story is perhaps another instance of the disturbing turbulence of the between that compels us to focus on one side of "being" to the exclusion of the other. Scholars may favor science over story, determinacy over indeterminacy, and thereby refuse to accept the messiness of social relations—something well expressed in stories. Following Taussig, you can "lay bare what goes on in anthropological fieldwork as a prolonged encounter with others fraught with misunderstandings that actually open up the world more than do understandings."[1]

In his classic essay "The Storyteller," Walter Benjamin sadly asserted that the productive forces of modernity have triggered the decline of storytelling.

. . . The art of storytelling is reaching its end because the epic side of truth, wisdom, is dying out. This, however, is a process that has been going on for a long time. And nothing would be more fatuous than to want to see in it merely a "symptom of decay," let alone a "modern" symptom. It is, rather, only a concomitant that has quite gradually removed narrative from the realm of living speech and at the same time is making it possible to see a new beauty in what is vanishing.[2]

Benjamin went on to suggest that the rise of the novel brought on the decline of storytelling. Novels are written in isolation from others. There is no direct contact between novelist and reader. Through its narration, the storyteller's experience, by contrast, created a bridge between story-teller and audience, a bridge on which the experience of the storyteller was transformed into the experience of those who listen to her or his tale. Storytellers

reach back to a whole lifetime (a life, incidentally, that comprises not only his own experience but no little of the experience of others; what the storyteller knows from hearsay is added to his own). His gift is the ability to relate his life; his distinction, to be able to tell his entire life. The storyteller: he is the man who could let the wick of his life be consumed completely by the gentle flame of his story. This is the basis of the incomparable aura of the storyteller.[3]

Extending Benjamin's insights on how stories have mediated bourgeois and peasant, civilized and primitive, Taussig reflected critically on the importance of stories in anthropology.

This mediation between bourgeois and peasant has of course been crucial to the stories that anthropologists have built all their work on since E. B. Tylor published the path-breaking *Primitive Culture* in 1872, if only because in the field (that sonorous term) it is always by means of stories (occasionally termed "cases") that "informa-tion," whether on "kinship" or on "mythology" or "economics" or whatever is in fact transmitted to the investigator . . . whose job it is to further mediate to the bourgeois readers. Anthropology is blind to how much its practice relies on the art of telling other people's stories—badly. What happens is that those stories are elaborated as scientific observations gleaned not from storytellers but from "informants."[4]

Like the art of conversation, which, in gloriously unhurried form, is practiced every day at the Malcolm Shabazz Harlem Market, storytelling has doubtlessly declined in modern and postmodern times. And yet, the stories that ethnographers, memoirists, novelists, and playwrights weave into tapestries sometimes create bridges between writer and reader, bridges that transform the experience of the writer-storyteller into that of the reader. Taussig's critique was fundamentally correct but perhaps a tad too cynical. After all, he doesn't mention memorable ethnographies like Vitebsky's *The Reindeer People,* or films like Rouch's *Jaguar,* or memoirs like Narayan's *My Family and Other Saints,* works consisting of ingeniously woven stories that speak to the issues that define the human condition. These are works that celebrate the indeterminate wonders found in the between.

At this point on my anthropological path, it is clear to me that the dynamics of the between propels us inexorably toward the story. Beyond the theory of the moment, is there not always a story to tell? The great contemporary novelist Tim O'Brien, like Jean Rouch, understood this central truth of the human condition. "Stories are for those late hours in the night when you can't remember how you got from where you were to where you are. Stories are for eternity, when memory is erased, when there is nothing to remember except the story."[5]

Whatever form they take, stories are indeed for an eternity. Like the stories of Adamu Jenitongo, they wind their way through our villages and in their telling and retelling, they link the past, present, and future. To tell these stories is to take off on the wings of the wind, a wind that carries us ever closer to the elusive end of wisdom. In the end it is the texture of the story that marks our contribution to the world, the contour of our stories that etches our traces in the world.

Epilogue: Flying on the Wings of the Wind

The example of the late Jean Rouch may well provide a model of how to live in the indeterminate betweeness of the imagination. The greatest issues of Rouch's time—war, colonialism, and racism—fired his imagination. They inspired him to seek new ways to understand and represent the complex forms of his social world—new ways to sweeten life in the world. No matter the challenge he faced, Rouch was unafraid to take risks, to try something new, or to bear the consequences of his choices. When he found himself, as was often the case, on an intellectual, artistic, or cultural crossroads, Rouch would often choose the less traveled path and ask, "Pourquoi pas?" Why not try something different? This playfully deep creativity met the challenges of the complex social forms he attempted to describe and understand

Consider how Rouch confronted the philosophical complexities of the Dogon people. The late Germaine Dieterlen once called the Dogon, who live along the Bandiagara cliffs in northeastern Mali, the philosophers of West Africa. Indeed, if you read the transcriptions of Dogon songs and sayings, it becomes evident that they have long pondered the mysteries of life and death. But it is through the *Sigui* ceremonies, held every sixty years, that the Dogon dramatize their most profound thoughts about the imponderables of life and the nature of death. Although anthropologists like Marcel Griaule had written authoritatively about the Sigui, no anthropologist had ever witnessed a Sigui ceremony. Given the prospect of a new sequence of Sigui ceremonies that would begin in 1967, how should anthropologists approach this complex ceremony? Rouch thought that film, rather than a more "acceptable" textual evocation, might be the medium to probe the deep philosophical mysteries of the ceremonies.

Overcoming a variety of obstacles, Jean Rouch and Germaine Dieterlen filmed the entire sequence of Sigui ceremonies between 1967 and 1973. In 1967 Rouch, Dieterlen, ethnomusicologist Gilbert Rouget, and sound technician Guindo Ibrahim traveled to Yougou to film the first of the seven yearly ceremonies. Shaded by a giant baobab tree, the Sigui initiates, all men naked to the waist, danced in a serpentine procession. Rouch wrote:

I will always remember this sequenced pan . . . of several minutes, where I discovered the Tai square overrun little by little by a serpentine line of men, classed strictly by age ranks, all dressed in indigo cotton trousers, bare-chested, wearing on their necks and ears and arms their wives' or sisters' adornments, their heads covered by white embroidered bonnets . . . carrying in their right hand a fly whisk, and in their left hand the *dunno*, the T-shaped chair, and singing to the rhythm of the drums: "The *Sigui* takes off on the wings of the wind."[1]

Like the Sigui, Rouch and camera took off on the "wings of the wind" and flew for seven years.

Prior to the film, the Dogon had a particularistic view of the Sigui. They knew how to stage the Sigui ceremonies celebrated in their own villages. Using the filmed images of the entire ceremonial sequence, which included symbolically distinct footage from seven villages along the Bandiagara cliffs, Rouch and Dieterlen could interpret the Sigui from a broader perspective. From this vantage, they discovered that the Sigui was fundamentally about life, death, and rebirth. During the first three years of the cycle, the ceremonies, performed in Yougou, Tyougou, and Bongo, evoked the whys and wherefores of death in the world. The final four ceremonies, performed in Amani, Ideyli, Yami, and Songo, evoked themes of life in the world. The sixty years between ceremonial cycles represented the sixty-year life span of the first human being, Diounou Serou. The Sigui, in fact, is the seven-year celebration of Diounou Serou's immortal reincarnation as a great serpent. The serpent, symbolized by the serpentine line of dancers described above, flies on the wings of wind. The Sigui takes off in Yougou. After a seven-year journey that winds like a snake through the major Dogon villages, the Sigui returns from Songo to the place of his death and rebirth, Yougou, where, after another sixty years, the cycle will repeat itself and the world will be reborn—in 2027.

Like the Dogon who live between the sixty-year cycles of the Sigui, between death and rebirth, Rouch tapped the unstated tensions of the between to confront the complex issues of power and race. He did so by making provocatively imaginative films of what he called "ethno-fiction." These included *Jaguar* (1957–67), *Les maitres fous* (1955), *Moi, un noir* (1958), *La pyramid humaine* (1959), *Chronique d'un été* (1960), and the wonderfully humorous *Petit à petit* (1969).[2] In all of these films, Rouch collaborated significantly with African friends and colleagues. By situating himself in the indeterminacy of active collaboration, which involved all aspects of shooting and production, Rouch used the camera—an instrument between the filmmaker and the filmed—to participate fully in the lives of the people he filmed. This collaboration in the between resulted in a new kind of film that provoked a wide range of audiences into imagining new dimensions of sociocultural experience. Many of the films of this period cut to the flesh and blood of European colonialism, compelling us to reflect on our latent racism, our repressed sexuality, and the taken-for-granted assumptions of our intellectual heritage.

Through his provocative films, Jean Rouch unveiled how relations of power shape our dreams, thoughts, and actions. He used film as a medium to bridge the spaces between things, spaces that empowered him to take risks in order to tell his stories, stories that enabled the dead to live again, stories that empowered the young to connect with their past and imagine their future. Such is the work of ethnography. Such is the legacy of storytelling. Such is the anthropologist's gift to the world.

———

For the epigraph to my first book, *In Sorcery's Shadow,* I chose a favorite aphorism from Wittgenstein's *Philosophical Investigations*: "We see the straight highway before us, but of course we cannot use it, because it is permanently closed." The straight highway is a tempting path. You make good time traveling to your destination and there are few, if any, surprises along the way. Although our experiences "in the field" may take us on a "being-there" detour, our "being-here" institutions lead us back to the tried and true highway which often bypasses the wonders of the inexplicable.

And yet, there is something irreducibly powerful about the social worlds we confront on the anthropological path. Despite my best efforts at systematic explanation, the Songhay worlds of sorcery and spirit possession have resisted the reductive force of theorization. The complex social forms constructed by West African immigrants in New York City have also defied theoretical reduction. Although the power of these fundamental social phenomena pushed me toward the side roads of experience, my intellectual socialization always lured me back toward the straight highway, the place where disciplinary contributions—and reputations—are made. Even though I tried to represent my ethnographic experiences in various ways—fiction, essays, ethnography, and memoir—I, like most scholars, still wanted to produce a theoretical treatise that colleagues would cite in their disciplinary debates.

When cancer came into my life, forcing an unavoidable confrontation with mortality, my orientation to the world changed. I finally understood the existential implications of taking detours. Richard Rorty eloquently captured the philosophical nature of these implications in his groundbreaking work, *Philosophy and the Mirror of Nature.*

Great systematic philosophers are constructive and offer arguments. Great edifying philosophers are reactive and offer satires, parodies, aphorisms. They know their work loses its point when the period they were reacting to is over. They are intentionally peripheral. Great systematic philosophers, like great scientists, build for eternity. Great edifying philosophers destroy for the sake of their own generation. Systematic philosophers want to put their subject on the secure path of a science. Edifying philosophers want to keep space open for the sense of wonder which poets can sometimes cause—wonder that there is something new under the sun, something which is *not* an accurate representation of what was already there, something which (at least for the moment) cannot be explained and can barely be described.[3]

In retrospect, taking the detour to an edifying approach to life in which things sometimes "cannot be explained and can be barely described" enables us to let go, to open our being to the wonders of living in the world. It also brings us back to al-'Arabi's conception of the between, a place in which we acknowledge the fleeting wonder of a blazing sunset, the short-lived but unforgettable tang of a spicy West African sauce, the quickly dissipating sounds of a lullaby, or the brief but powerful shock of being touched by Hauka spirit.

More than three decades ago the Hauka thrust me fully into the indeterminate fluidities of the between. For many years I ignored the unnerving nebulousness of being between by seeking concrete answers to the quandaries of the human condition. In the end, the sinuous path I have described in these pages has led me not to some grandiose conclusion about the nature of human being but rather to accept the ultimate impermanence of things. It has led me not to semiconscious travel on the straight highway but to passionate flight on the wings of the wind.

Like so many before me I am forever between things. I am between Africa and America, between Songhay and English, between "being there" and "being here," between self and other, between health and illness. Flying higher and higher on the wings of the wind, I am between sky and earth. Below me, I have left traces of my knowledge for the next generation of anthropologists. Above me, the ancestors patiently await my arrival.

Notes

PROLOGUE

1. See MacDougall (2006), 8.
2. See McIntosh (2004).
3. See Crapanzano (2003), 57. As Jean Rouch would have said, I stumbled upon Sufi thought "comme ça." In the 1990s I read several collections of Sufi stories but never applied Sufi ideas to my thinking about anthropology. As I thought through an earlier version of this book, I happened to read Crapanzano's *Imaginative Horizons*. His passages on al-'Arabi struck a chord, which compelled me to read more about Sufism and to plunge into al-'Arabi's fluid world in which the imagination is at the forefront of consciousness.
4. Ibid., 57–58; see also Chittick (1989).
5. Crapanzano (2003), 58.
6. Ibid., 64. Inspired by Arnold Van Gennep's early twentieth-century analysis of rites of passage, Victor Turner in *The Forest of Symbols* introduced to a broad audience of anthropologists the notion of liminality, the state of being betwixt and between things. Here he also discusses the notion of "communitas," the social bonding that occurs when initiates experience liminality as a group. Like most anthropologists, I have long admired Turner's analysis of the liminal, but in the past had an admittedly narrow appreciation of its existential importance. Recent events in my life—being in remission after having been diagnosed with and treated for cancer, have provided me a fuller, more philosophical take on the liminal. Al-'Arabi's complex and perhaps more nuanced notions of the liminal, embodied through the mystical image of *barzakh*, the bridge, precede those of Van Gennep and Turner by almost eight hundred years.
7. See Stoller (1989b; 1995).

CHAPTER ONE

1.   This summary of research trends is purposefully streamlined. The issues that I gloss over are, of course, highly complex and have been and will continue to be debated. My purpose here is not to thoroughly debate the epistemological issues of the 1960s and 1970s but rather to describe, albeit briefly, the intellectual climate of my years as a graduate student.
2.   This group included Chomsky and his *Aspects of a Theory of Syntax* (1965) but also a group of his students who were doing analyses of generative semantics.
3.   See Malinowski, *Argonauts of the Western Pacific* (1922); Radcliffe-Brown, *The Andaman Islanders* (1922); and Firth, *We, the Tikopia* (1936).
4.   Tambiah (1994), 117.
5.   Ibid., 115–16.
6.   Horton (1970), 159.
7.   Ibid., 160.
8.   Sperber (1985).
9.   Ibid., 49.
10. Lévi-Strauss (1967), 206.
11. Ibid., 227.
12. Ibid.

CHAPTER TWO

1.   See Goodman (1978); Wittgenstein (1953). As in chapter 1, these reflections on relativism, a subject of long and complex debate in anthropology and philosophy, have been truncated to maintain the flow of narrative.
2.   Tambiah (1994), 129.
3.   Ibid., 129.
4.   Ibid., 130.
5.   Geertz (1984), 274.
6.   Ibid., 276.
7.   Ibid., 276.
8.   Evens (1996), 29.
9.   Ibid., 30.
10. Stoller (1989a; 1997).

CHAPTER THREE

1.   Stoller and Olkes (1987), 24.
2.   Ibid., 70.
3.   Ihde (1976), 19.
4.   Husserl (1970), 12.
5.   Jackson (1996), 2.
6.   See Schutz (1962).

7. Evens (1996), 30.
8. See Bourdieu (1990).
9. Jackson (1996), 22.
10. Ibid., 26.
11. Merleau-Ponty (1962), 137.
12. Jackson (1996), 3.
13. Stoller (1997).
14. Calvino (1996).
15. Adapted from Shah (1993).

CHAPTER FOUR

1. See Stoller and Olkes (1987), 98–102; see also Stoller (2004a), 83–89. I should point out that given the Islamic nature of Songhay society, most of my experience in Niger was in the public and private worlds of men. Being "adopted" into Adamu Jenitongo's family afforded me some degree of contact with women, but even that was limited. I should also add that some of the most important insights about Songhay sorcery came from female practitioners like Kassey of Wanzerbé and Adamu Jenitongo's sister, Witili, who lived in Niger's capital city, Niamey. Indeed, it is said that if a woman, like Kassey, becomes a master of sorcery, she is more powerful than her male colleagues.
2. Stoller and Olkes (1987). Adamu Jenitongo had no objections to the publication of this incantation as long as it was printed in translation. He thought it wrong to publish it in Songhay, for the sound of the words embodies their power.
3. Stoller and Olkes (1987), 101; Stoller (2004a), 81–81.
4. Merleau-Ponty (1962).
5. There are many books on anthropological methods that cover a wide range of qualitative and quantitative methods. There are also annual field schools during which students learn both qualitative and quantitative methods.
6. Geertz (1983).

CHAPTER FIVE

1. See Stoller (1999), chapter 1.
2. Lévi-Strauss (1967).
3. Stoller (1997).
4. Merleau-Ponty (1964).
5. Charbonnier (1959) as cited in Merleau-Ponty (1964), 31.
6. There is a vast literature on the crisis of representation in anthropology that spans two decades of academic debate. Among the most important theoretical works along these lines are Marcus and Fischer's *Anthropology as Cultural Critique* (1985); Clifford and Marcus's edited volume *Writing Culture*

(1986); Clifford's *The Predicament of Culture* (1988); and Rosaldo's *Culture and Truth* (1989).

7.   There were also many attempts to put into ethnographic practice the theoretical principles that emerged from the "crisis of representation." Some of earliest of these works include Paul Rabinow's *Reflections on Fieldwork in Morocco* (1985); Dumont's *The Headman and I* (1987); two works by Crapanzano, *Tuhami* (1981) and *Waiting* (1985); Allen's *The Hold Life Has* (1988); and Narayan's *Storytellers Saints and Sinners* (1989).

CHAPTER SIX

1.   There is an extensive literature on processes of globalization. Included among the early key texts, one should cite the myriad works of Saskia Sassen, including her important book, *The Global City* (1991) and Harvey's *The Postmodern Condition* 1989. Later works include Appadurai's *Modernity at Large* (1996) and Burawoy's *Global Ethnography* 2000, not to forget scores of other books and essays that have appeared both in the scholar and popular publications.
2.   See Stoller (1989a, 1989b, 1992, 1995, 1997a); Stoller and Olkes (1987).
3.   See Stoller (1997b, 2002).

CHAPTER SEVEN

1.   Social complexity, of course, is nothing new to anthropologists; it has always been a fundamental challenge to anthropological description. Marilyn Strathern underscores the centrality of complexity to the anthropological enterprise.

> Complexity is intrinsic to both the ethnographic and comparative enterprise. Anthropologists are concerned to demonstrate the social and cultural entailments of phenomena, though they must simplify the complexity enough to make it visible. What appears to be the object of description—demonstrating complex linkages between elements—also makes description less easy. (Strathern 2005, xiii)

In his book *The Moment of Complexity,* Mark Taylor states that the world is undergoing a signal set of economic, social, and cultural changes (Taylor 2002; see also Stoller 1998; Castells 1996, 1997, 1998; Harvey 1989). Underscoring the disruptive as well as creative impact of technological innovation throughout history, Taylor writes:

> We are currently living in a moment of extraordinary complexity when systems and structures that have long organized life are changing at an unprecedented rate. Such rapid and pervasive change creates the need to develop new ways of understanding the world and of interpreting our experience. (Taylor 2002, 65)

The world has long been organized on an industrial production/modernist axis. The contours of industrial production that are underscored in

modernism, in fact, have had an impact on how we manage space, how
we organize time, and how we make sense of our experience. Inspired by
the textures and lines of the machine, modernists have tried to craft order
from chaos. This symbolic and/or concrete order has often taken the form
of the grid. Cities have consisted of straight-angled blocks; philosophical
theories have been clean, crisp and uniform. Language is derived from
unencumbered speaker-hearer relationships.

Focusing on Jacques Derrida's famous penchant for deconstruction, Taylor
writes:

> While exposing systems and structures as incomplete and perhaps repressive,
> deconstruction inevitably leaves them in place. This is not merely because
> deconstruction involves theoretical analysis instead of practical action but also
> because of the specific conclusions reached by the theoretical critique. Instead
> of showing how totalizing structures can actually be changed, deconstruction
> demonstrates that the tendency to totalize can never be overcome and, thus, that
> repressive structures are inescapable. For Derrida and his followers, all we can do is
> join in the Sisyphean struggle to undo what cannot be undone. (71)

There are even traces of grid-like modernism in Baudrillard's hyperactive,
hyperreal world of simulations. The real, which has been forever lost,
is juxtaposed to the hyperreal (Stoller 1998). Put another way, Jean
Baudrillard's theory of simulation is, like Derrida, an attempt to undo what
cannot be undone.

Taylor's critique is intellectually stimulating but provides no concrete
solution to the problem of representing complex social forms. Other
scholars, of course, have attempted to provide a different set of metaphors
that ethnographers, among others, might use to represent complexity.
Consider Gilles Deleuze and Félix Guattari's famously difficult work, *A
Thousand Plateaus,* an attempt to break through the restrictions of linear
thinking. A key concept in this work is the rhizome.

> A rhizome has no beginning or end: it is always in the middle, between things,
> interbeing, *intermezzo.* The tree is filiation, but the rhizome is alliance, uniquely
> alliance. The tree imposes the verb "to be," but the fabric of the rhizome is the
> conjunction, "and . . . and . . . and . . ." This conjunction carries enough force to
> shake and uproot the verb "to be." Where are you going? Where are you coming
> from? What are you heading for? These are totally useless questions. Making a
> clean slate, starting or beginning again from ground zero, seeking a beginning or a
> foundation—all imply a false conception of voyage and movement (a conception
> that is methodical, pedagogical, initiatory, symbolic . . .) (Deleuze and Guattari
> 1987, 25)

Deleuze and Guattari suggest that scholars proceed from the middle rather
than from the beginning or end, that scholars learn how "to move between
things, establish a logic of the AND, overthrow ontology, do away with

foundations, nullify endings and beginnings" (25). The notion of the rhizome clearly provides a model for thinking about the dizzying array of complex assemblages that constitute contemporary social worlds. Following Deleuze and Guattari, the challenge of cultural description is to imagine new categories of interpretation that reflect more accurately the creatively unstable dynamics of contemporary social and intellectual life (see Taylor 2002; Deleuze and Guattari 1987; Latour 1993).

2. See Stoller (2002).
3. Ibid.
4. Ibid.
5. Ibid.

CHAPTER EIGHT

1. Stoller (2002), 178–79.
2. Ibid., 4–5.
3. Reuters, March 7, 1997.
4. Ibid.
5. See Jackson (1998), 49.
6. Ibid., 53.
7. Ibid., 54.

CHAPTER NINE

1. See Lévi-Strauss (1973); Bourdieu (1990).
2. Merleau-Ponty (1962).
3. Jackson (1998), 3.
4. Merleau-Ponty (1964), 204.
5. Merleau-Ponty (1970), 29. See also Shaw (2002).
6. Merleau-Ponty (1970), 44.
7. Bayart (1993), 37.
8. Ibid., 235.
9. See Stoller (1989, 1997); Masquelier (2001).
10. See Chernoff (1979); Friedson (1996); and Comaroff and Comaroff (1997).
11. Comaroff and Comaroff (1997), 271.
12. Bayart (1993), 238.
13. Ibid., 243.
14. Bayart (1993), 268. There is a growing literature on the declining influence of the state in Africa. Some of the best essays can be found in Werbner and Ranger, *Postcolonial Identities in Africa* (1996) and Werbner, *Memory and the Postcolony* (1998). Other important essays in this domain include Devisch (1995), Mbembe (1992); Mbembe and Roitman (1995); and Bayart (1993).

CHAPTER TEN

1. See Rouch (1953, 1989); see also Konaré Ba (1977).
2. Charlick (1991), 34.
3. William Ponty, Archives de Afrique Occidental Francais (AAOF), Afrique III, dossier 26, 38 bis.
4. Olivier de Sardan (1984), 151.
5. Stoller (1995).
6. Bastide (1978).
7. Echard (1992), 97.
8. See Stoller (1992, 1995); Rouch (1955, 1956).
9. See Taussig (1993).
10. See Rouch (1978, 1009); Stoller (1995).
11. See Charlick (1991); Stoller (1995).
12. See Stoller (1995).
13. *Jeune Afrique* (1987), 67.
14. See De Boeck (1998), 51.
15. See Devisch (1995); Shaw (2002).
16. See Hale (1990, 1999); Stoller (1997).
17. See Olivier de Sardan (1976).
18. See Nordstrom (1997).

CHAPTER ELEVEN

1. See Stoller (2002); see also Steiner (1994).
2. See Hopkins (1975).
3. See Curtin (1975); Meillassoux (1991).
4. See Mennan (1986).
5. Ibid.
6. See Amselle (1971).
7. See Amselle (1971); Stoller (2002).

CHAPTER TWELVE

1. See Stoller (2002, 2003).
2. See Stoller (2003).
3. Ibid.
4. Ibid.
5. See Stoller (2002). Napier makes a similar argument in the first two chapters of his *Foreign Bodies* (1996).
6. Gates as cited in Wilde (1995); Appiah in Wilde (1995); see also Early (1997).
7. Interview with an art restorer at the New York Tribal Antiquities Show, May 21, 2001.

8. See Stoller (2002; 2003). Dealers and collectors, of course, have their own networks, a subject ably discussed in Price (1989) and Marcus and Myers (1995).

1. Errington (1998), 51.
2. Morris (1987).
3. Current trends in philosophical thinking have greatly questioned the "universal" gaze constructed by the likes of Kant and Hegel. Beyond various works in social constructionism, deconstruction, and theories of simulacra, recent studies have highlighted the heterogeneous nature of contemporary complex systems (see Foucault 1970; Derrida 1987; Baudrillard 1981; and Taylor 2002). Despite these recent philosophical insights, the resilience of static universalism seems surprisingly strong.
4. Marcus and Myers (1995), 7.
5. Plattner (1996), 6–7.
6. Ibid., 30.
7. Ibid., 126.
8. See Marcus and Myers (1995); Price (1989).
9. Errington (1998), 68.
10. See Clifford (1988); Torgovnick (1990); Steiner (1995); Marcus and Myers (1995); and Price (1989).
11. The National Museum of African Art and the Center for African Art have both flourished during the past fifteen years. Early in their histories, the museums were housed in rather small spaces. The National Museum's collection was first housed in Frederick Douglass's Capitol Hill townhouse. In the late 1980s the museum moved to its current underground digs on the Mall. Its scope and importance have expanded significantly. In New York City, the Center for African Art first opened in 1984 on 68th Street in midtown Manhattan. In 1992 it became the Museum for African Art to reflect the expanded focus of its activities. After moving to an address on Broadway in SoHo, the museum moved to a temporary location in Long Island City until its permanent come on Central Park South will open in 2009.
12. Recent works about African systems of aesthetics have challenged the reigning modernist aesthetic. In that work scholars have set new criteria, including African theories of form and aesthetics, to judge the quality and set the value of a work of African Art. See Armstrong (1971); Blier (1994, 1996); Vogel (1997): and Ravenhill (1996). Even so, one wonders how much this finely tuned scholarship, which wisely considers African art from the vantage of African aesthetics, challenges the modernist aesthetic and its influence on "taste" and "value"?
13. Sweeney (1935), 11, cited in Errington (1997), 92–93.

CHAPTER FOURTEEN

1. Discussion with a well-known anthropologist who did extensive fieldwork in Mali, April 6, 2000.

2. In my experience among Muslim traders, including art traders, it is very important that transactions reinforce social relations, which, it could be argued, extend from what the Prophet Mohammad had to say about the social contours of economic practices (see Mennan 1986).

3. Interview with an art restorer at the New York tribal antiquities show, May 21, 2001; see also Steiner (1994), 159–62.

4. Personal communication with an African art gallery owner, New York City, July 18, 2001.

5. See Moonan (2001).

6. See Steiner (1994).

7. Afrocentrism is a philosophically specific orientation to African and African American sociocultural life; it is a serious attempt to construct an epistemology based upon principles of African philosophy, principles that, according Molefe Asante, protect scholars from making interpretative errors—about African and African American social life—that devolve from Eurocentric categorizations. Asante says that Afrocentrism is primarily epistemological—a set of guidelines one can use to interpret a wide variety of data. Afrocentrists work in two domains, cultural aesthetic and social/behavioral, which cut across traditional disciplinary boundaries. In essence, "Afrocentricity is a perspective which allows Africans to be the subjects of historical experiences rather than the objects on the fringes of Europe. This means that the Afrocentrist is concerned with discovering in every case the centered place of the African" (Asante 1990, 2).

8. Personal communication with a museum curator, New York City, May 8, 2000.

9. See Errington (1998).

10. See Stoller (2001); Stoller and McConatha (2001).

11. Stoller (1999).

12. See Rouch (1956, 1967); Stoller (1999, 2002).

13. See Augé (1995).

14. See Baudrillard (1981); Taussig (1993); Stoller (2002).

15. See Marcus and Myers (1995); Marcus (1998); Myers (2002); Steiner (1994).

16. In a recent work, the philosopher Mark Taylor (2002) suggests that the complexity of (social) systems, based now upon complex networks rather than straightforward grids, has outpaced the capacity of social theories to explain contemporary interactive patterns. Systems of relations, including social relations, are far more complicated than contemporary social theories would suggest. He suggests that cultural analysts rethink their analytical categories. He urges them to explore other modes of categorization that are less dependent upon binary distinctions. One could argue that in separating

the spaces of African art and West African wood, I have followed this well-worn and increasingly irrelevant path. I have set up these categories, in part, to show how they are continuously transformed and reconfigured by various participants, themselves parts of complex social, economic and ideological networks. Such is the challenge of contemporary cultural analysis.

CHAPTER FIFTEEN

1. See Stoller and Olkes (1987).
2. See Stoller (1989a).
3. See Stoller (1989b, 1992, 1997).

CHAPTER SIXTEEN

1. Frank (1995), 84.
2. See Napier (2003).
3. Much of this material is taken from my book *Stranger in the Village of the Sick* (2004).

CHAPTER SEVENTEEN

1. This chapter is adapted from my book *Stranger in the Village of the Sick* (1994). The notion of the villages of the healthy and the sick are anthropological adaptations of Susan Sontag's more religious invocations of the "Kingdom of the Healthy and the Kingdom of Sick" in her book *Illness as Metaphor* (1978). The idea of a village of sick is also similar to Arthur W. Frank's notion of the remission society, which he introduces in his second book, *The Wounded Storyteller: Body, Illness and Ethics* (1995).

CHAPTER EIGHTEEN

1. There has been much discussion of divination in ethnographic reports on societies in West and Central Africa. Among the most celebrated texts are Adler and Zempleni (1972) on the Moundang of Chad, Bascom (1994) on the Yoruba of Nigeria, and Peek's (1991) collection on African divination systems. Shaw (2002) has produced a fine ethnography that describes how divination, among other practices, shapes memory and contours the historical imagination of the Temne of Sierra Leone. Shaw claims, quite rightly, that by linking past and present, most West African divination systems help to forge an atmosphere of completeness, harmony, and continuity. Shaw's broad approach to West African divination has striking parallels to the diagnostic processes central to Western medical practice. In times of physical crises, we seek out physicians, who, in order to make a diagnosis, order diagnostic tests, most of which entail some ritual elements

as well as some degree of risk. Tests are called "procedures" and are filled with ritualistic preparations—fasts, premedication, qualifying blood work, ingestion of barium. The iodine administered during a contrast CAT scan, after all, can produce a fatal allergic reaction.

2. This section is adapted from Stoller and Olkes (1987) and Stoller (2004a).
3. There are many studies on the relation of cancer to the onset of depression. Some of the more important studies include: McDaniel et al. (1995), Sheard and Maguire (1999), Barraclough (1998), Miller (2002), and Ly (2002).
4. See Stoller (2004a).

CHAPTER NINETEEN

1. Frank (1995).
2. Turner (1969), 98. See also Turner (1967).
3. The mission of the Lance Armstrong Foundation is focused on remission, what they call "survivorship."

CHAPTER TWENTY

1. Taussig (2006), viii.
2. See Jacques Derrida's difficult but incomparably brilliant books, *Of Grammatology* (1974) and *The Post Card* (1987).
3. Merleau-Ponty (1964), 45.
4. See Breton (1972).

CHAPTER TWENTY-ONE

1. See Geertz (1989).
2. See Said (1979), Marcus and Fischer (1985), Clifford and Marcus (1986), Pratt (1992), among many others.
3. See Marcus and Fischer (1985).
4. See Dwyer (1982), Crapanzano (1985).

CHAPTER TWENTY-TWO

1. See Frank (1995).
2. See Rodgers (2000).
3. See Drescher (2002).
4. See Sontag (1978), Alsop (1973), and Frank (1991).

CHAPTER TWENTY-THREE

1. Interview with Jean Rouch, 7 March 1990, Paris.
2. See Stoller (1992), 112.

3. See Thomas (1999).
4. "See" is used here, in a quite conventionally metaphorical way, to mean 'perceive' in its broadest sense. Ibid., 109.
5. Chittick (1989), ix.
6. Ibid., x.
7. Crapanzano (2003), 64–65.

CHAPTER TWENTY-FOUR

1. Taussig (2006), viii.
2. Benjamin (1968), 87.
3. Ibid., 108–9.
4. Taussig (2006), 62.
5. O'Brien (1990), 38.

EPILOGUE

1. Rouch (1978), 17–18.
2. These works are considered films of what Rouch called "ethnofiction," the first cases in which Rouch played with genre to confront the complexities of colonialism and racism. Rouch's films include (1953), *Les maîtres fous* (Paris: Films de la Pléiade, 1953–54); *Moi, un noir* (Paris: Films de la Pléiade, 1957); *La pyramided humane* (Paris: Films de la Pléiade, 1958–59 [released in 1961]); in collaboration with Edgar Morin, *Chronique d'un été* (Paris: Films de la Pléiade, 1960); *Petit à petit* (Paris: Comité de Film Ethnographique, 1969).
3. Rorty (1979), 369–70.

References

Allen, Catherine. 1988. *The Hold Life Has*. Washington, D.C.: Smithsonian Institution Press.

Alsop, Stewart. 1973. *Stay of Execution*. Philadelphia: Lippicott.

Amselle, Jean-Loup. 1971. "Parenté et commerce chez les Kookoro." In *Development of Indigenous Trade and Markets in West Africa*, edited by C. Meillassoux, 253–66. London: Oxford University Press.

Appadurai, Arjun. 1996. *Modernity at Large*. Minneapolis: University of Minnesota Press.

Appiah, Anthony Kwame. 1992. *In My Father's House*. London: Oxford University Press.

Armstrong, Lance. 2001. *It's Not About the Bike: My Journey Back to Life*. New York: Berkeley Trade.

Armstrong, Robert Plant. 1971. *The Affecting Presence: An Essay in Humanistic Anthropology*. Champaign-Urbana: University of Illinois Press.

Artaud, Antonin. 1958. *The Theater and Its Double*, translated by Mary Caroline Richards. New York: Grove Press.

Asante, Molefe Kete. 1990. *Kemet, Afrocentricity and Knowledge*. Trenton, NJ: Africa World Press.

Augé, Marc. 1995. *Non-Places: An Introduction to an Anthropology of Supermodernity*. London and New York: Verso.

Barraclough, B. 1998. *Cancer and Emotion: A Practical Guide to Psycho-Ontology*. 3rd ed. Chichester: John Wiley.

Bascom, William. 1994. *Ifa Divination: Communication between the Gods and Men in West African*. Bloomington: Indiana University Press.

Bastide, Roger. 1978. *The African Religions of Brazil*. Baltimore: Johns Hopkins University Press.

Baudrillard, Jean. 1981. *Simulations*. New York: Semiotext.

Bayart, Jean-François. 1993. *The State in Africa: The Politics of the Belly*, translated by Mary Harper. London: Longman.

Behar, Ruth. 1998. *The Vulnerable Observer: Anthropology That Breaks Your Heart.* Boston: Beacon Press.

Benjamin, Walter. 1968. *Illuminations*. New York: Schocken.

Blier, Suzanne Preston. 1994. *The Anatomy of Architecture*. Chicago: University of Chicago Press.

———. 1996. *African Vodun: Art, Psychology and Power*. Chicago: University of Chicago Press.

Bourdieu, Pierre. 1990. *The Logic of Practice*, translated by Richard Nice. Stanford: Stanford University Press.

Bourgois, Philippe. 1995. *In Search of Respect*. New York: Cambridge University Press.

Breton, André. 1972. *Manifestos of Surrealism*. Ann Arbor: University of Michigan Press.

Burawoy, Michael. 2000. *Global Ethnography: Forces, Connections and Imaginations in a Postmodern World*. University of California Press.

Calvino, Italo. 1996. *Six Memos for the Next Millennium*. Cambridge: Harvard University Press.

Castells, Manuel. 1996. *The Rise of Network Society*. Cambridge, Mass.: Blackwell.

———. 1997. *The Power of Identity*. Cambridge, Mass.: Blackwell.

———. 1998. *The End of the Millennium*. Cambridge, Mass.: Blackwell.

Charbonnier, Georges. 1959. *Monologue du peintre*. Paris: Juliard.

Charlick, Robert. 1991. *Niger: Personal Rule and Survival in the Sahel*. Boulder: Westview Press.

Chernoff, John Miller. 1979. *African Rhythm and African Sensibility. Chicago*: University of Chicago Press.

Clifford, James. 1988. *The Predicament of Culture*. Cambridge: Harvard University Press.

———. 1996. *Routes*. Cambridge: Harvard University Press.

Clifford, James, and George F. Marcus, eds. 1986. *Writing Culture*. Berkeley: University of California Press.

Chittick, W. C. 1989. *The Sufi Path of Knowledge: Ibn al-'Arabi's Metaphysics of the Imagination*. Albany: State University of New York Press.

Cole, Jennifer. 2001. *Forget Colonialism? Sacrifice and the Art of Memory in Madagascar*. Berkeley: University of California Press.

Comaroff, John, and Jean Comaroff. 1997. *Of Revelation and Revolution*. Vol. 2, *The Dialectics of Modernity on a South African Frontier*. Chicago. University of Chicago Press.

Coombe, Rosemary J., and Paul Stoller. 1994. "X Marks the Spot: The Ambiguities of African Trading in the Commerce of the Black Public Sphere." *Public Culture* 15: 249–75.

Crapanzano, Vincent. 1981. *Tuhami*. Chicago: University of Chicago Press.

———. 1985. *Waiting*. New York: Random House.

———. 2003. *Imaginative Horizons: An Essay in Literary-Philosophical Anthropology*. Chicago: University of Chicago Press.

Curtin, Phillip. 1975. *Economic Change in Precolonial Africa: Senegambia in the Era of the Slave Trade*. Madison: University of Wisconsin Press.

De Boeck, Filip. 1998. "Beyond the Grave: History, Memory and Death in Postcolonial Zaire/Congo." In *Memory and the Postcolony*, edited by R. Werbner, 21–58. London: Zed Books.

Deleuze, Gilles, and Felix Guattari. 1987. *A Thousand Plateaus: Capitalism and Schizophrenia*. Minneapolis: University of Minnesota Press.

Derrida, Jacques. 1974. *Of Gammatology*. Baltimore: Johns Hopkins University Press.

———. 1987. *The Post Card*. Chicago: University of Chicago Press.

Devisch, Réné. 1995. "Frenzy, Violence and Ethical Renewal in Kinshasa." *Public Culture* 7, no. 3: 593–629.

Dewey, John. 1929 [1980]. *The Quest for Certainty*. New York: Dover Books.

Drescher, Fran. 2002. *Cancer Schmancer*. New York: Warner Books.

Dumont, Jean-Paul. 1987. *The Headman and I*. Austin: University of Texas Press.

Dwyer, Kevin. 1982. *Moroccan Dialogues*. Baltimore: Johns Hopkins University Press.

Early, Gerald. 1997. "Dreaming of a Black Christmas." *Harper's* 294: 55–62.

Echard, Nicole. 1992. "Cultes de possession et changement social. L'exemple du bori hausa de l'Ader and du Kurfey (Niger)." *Archives de Sciences Sociales de Religions* 79, no. 2: 87–101.

Errington, Shelly. 1998. *The Death of Authentic Primitive Art and Other Tales of Progress*. Berkeley: University of California Press.

Evans-Pritchard, E. E. 1976. *Witchcraft, Oracles, and Magic among the Azande*. London: Oxford University Press.

Evens, Terrence M. S. 1996. "Witchcraft and Self-Craft." *Archives of European Sociology* 37, no. 1: 23–46.

Foner, Nancy. 2000. *From Ellis Island to JFK: New York's Two Great Waves of Immigration*. New Haven: Yale University Press.

Foner, Nancy, ed. 2001. *New Immigrants in New York*. New York: Columbia University Press.

Foucault, Michel. 1967. *The Archaeology of Knowledge*: New York: Harper & Row.

———. 1970. *The Order of Things*. New York: Harper & Row.

Frank, Arthur W. 1991. *At the Will of the Body: Reflections on Illness*. New York: Houghton-Mifflin.

———. 1995. *The Wounded Storyteller: Body, Illness and Ethics*. Chicago: University of Chicago Press.

Friedson, Steven. 1997. *Dancing Prophets: Musical Experience in Tumbuka Healing*. Chicago: University of Chicago Press.

Geertz, Clifford. 1983. *Local Knowledge*. New York: Basic Books.

———. 1984. "Anti-anti Relativism." *American Anthopologist* 86, no. 2: 263–78.

———. 1989. *Works and Lives: The Anthropologist as Author*. New York: Polity Press.

Goffman, Erving. 1981. *Forms of Talk*. Philadelphia: University of Pennsylvania Press.

Goodman, Nelson. 1978. *Ways of Worldmaking*. New York: Hackett Publishing Company.

Hale, Thomas. 1990. *Scribe, Griot and Novelist*. Gainesville: University of Florida Press.

———. 1999. *Griots and Griottes of the Sahel*. Bloomington: Indiana University Press.

Harvey, David. 1989. *The Condition of Postmodernity*. Cambridge, Mass.: Blackwell.

Hegel, G. F. W. 1975. *Aesthetics: Lectures on Fine Art*. Oxford: Clarendon Press.

Hopkins, A. G. 1973. *An Economic History of West Africa*. New York: Columbia University Press.

Horten, Robin. 1970. "African Traditional Thought and Western Science." In *Rationality*, edited by Bryan Wilson, 131–71. New York: Harper & Row.

Husserl, Edmund. 1970. *Logical Investigations*, translated by J. N. Findlay. London: Routledge and Kegan Paul.

Ihde, Don. 1976. *Listening and Voice: A Phenomenology of Sound*. Athens: Ohio University Press.

Jackson, Michael. 1998. *Minima Ethnographica: Intersubjectivity and the Anthropological Project*. Chicago: University of Chicago Press.

Jackson, Michael, ed. 1996. *Things As They Are: New Directions in Phenomenological Anthropology*. Bloomington: Indiana University Press.

Jeune Afrique. 1987. "Interview with Seyni Kountché." *Jeune Afrique* 1402: 67.

Kant, Immanel. [1790] 1966. *The Critique of Judgment*. New York: Hafner Publishing Company.

Lan, Ly K. 2002. "Depression in Advanced Disease: A Systematic Review. Part 1: Prevalence and Case Finding." *Palliative Medicine* 16: 81–98.

Lansing, J. Stephen. 2003. "Complex Adaptive Systems." *Annual Review of Anthropology* 32: 183–225.

Latour, Bruno. 1993. *We Have Never Been Modern*. Cambridge: Harvard University Press.

Lévi-Strauss, Claude. 1967. *Structural Anthropology*. Garden City, N.J.: Doubeday.

———. 1973. *The Savage Mind*, translated by John and Doreen Weightman. Chicago: University of Chicago Press.

MacDougall, David. 2006. *The Corporeal Image: Film, Ethnography and the Senses*. Princeton: Princeton University Press.

Marcus, George E. 1998. *Ethnography through Thick and Thin*. Princeton: Princeton University Press.

Marcus, George E., and Michael M. J. Fischer. 1985. *Anthropology as Cultural Critique*. Chicago: University of Chicago Press.

Marcus, George E., and Fred R. Myers. 1995. "The Traffic in Art and Culture: An Introduction." In *The Traffic in Culture: Refiguring Art and Anthropology*, edited by George E. Marcus and Fred R. Myers, 1–55. Berkeley: University of California Press.

Marcus, George E., and Fred R Myers, eds. 1995. *The Traffic in Culture: Refiguring Art and Anthropology*. Berkeley: University of California Press.

Masquelier, Adeline. 2001. *Prayer Has Ruined Everything: Possession, Power and Identity in an Islamic Town*. Durham and London: Duke University Press.

Mbembe, Achille. 1992. *Provisional Notes on the Postcolony*. *Africa* 61, no. 1: 5–37.

Mbembe, Achille, and Janet Roitman. 1995. "Figures of the Subject in Times of Crisis." *Public Culture* 7, no. 2: 323–52.

McDaniel, J. S., et al. 1995. "Depression in Patients with Cancer: Diagnosis, Biology and Treatment." *Archives of General Psychiatry* 52: 89–99.

McIntosh, Ann. 2006. *Conversations with Jean Rouch*. Cambridge, MA: Documentary Education Resources.

Meillassoux, Claude. 1991. *The Anthropology of Slavery*. Chicago: University of Chicago Press.

Mennan, Moustapha. 1986. *Islamic Economics: Theory and Practice*. Boulder: Westview Press.

Merleau-Ponty, Maurice. 1962. *The Phenomenology of Perception*, translated by Colon Smith. London: Routledge.

———. 1964. *The Primacy of Perception*. Evanston, Ill.: Northwestern University Press.

———. 1970. *Themes from the Lectures at the Collège de France, 1952–1960*. Evanston, Ill.: Northwestern University Press.

Miller, Douglas K. 2002. "Psychosocial-Spiritual Correlates of Death Distress in Patients with Life-Threatening Medical Conditions." *Palliative Medicine* 16, no. 4: 331–38.

Moonan, Wendy. 2001. "Antiques for Sale: African Art in Abundance." *New York Times*, June 22.

Morris, Brian. 1987. *The Anthropology of Religion: An Introduction*. London: Cambridge University Press.

Myers, Fred R. 2002. *Painting Culture: The Making of an Aboriginal High Art*. Durham. N.C.: Duke University Press.

Napier, A. David 2003. *The Age of Immunology: Conceiving a Future in an Alienating World*. Chicago: University of Chicago Press.

———. 1996. *Foreign Bodies*. Berkeley: University of California Press.

Narayan, Kirin. 1989. *Storytellers Saints and Sinners*. Philadelphia: University of Pennsylvania Press.

———. 2007. *My Family and Other Saints*. Chicago: University of Chicago Press.

Newman Andy, and Robert F. Worth. 2003. "Police Killing of Unarmed Man Is Investigated." *New York Times*, May 24, A22.

Newman, Kathryn. 1999. *No Shame in My Game*. New York: Free Press.

———. 2003. *A Different Shade of Gray*. New York: Free Press.

Nordstrom, Caroline. 1997. *A Different Kind of War Story*. Philadelphia: University of Pennsylvania Press.

O'Brien, Tim. 1990. *The Things They Carried*. New York: Broadway Books.

Olivier de Sardan, Jean-Pierre. 1976. *Quand nos pères étaient captifs*. Paris: Nubia.

———. 1984. *Sociétés Sonay-Zarma*. Paris: Karthala.

Peek, Phillip, ed. 1991. *African Divination Systems: Ways of Knowing*. Bloomington: Indiana University Press.

Plattner, Stuart. 1996. *High Art Down Home*. Chicago: University of Chicago Press.

Pratt, Mary Louise. 1997. *Imperial Eyes: Studies in Travel Writing and Transculturation*. New York: Routledge.

Price, Sally. 1989. *Primitive Art in Civilized Places*. Chicago: University of Chicago Press.

Ponty, William. 1906. "Rapport au Governeur General de l'A. O.F. Aix-en-Provence." Archives de l'Afrique Occidentale française.

Qashani, Abu al-Razzaq. 1984. *A Glossary of Sufi Technical Terms*. New York: Octagon Press.

Rabinow, Paul. 1985. *Reflections on Fieldwork in Morocco*. Berkeley: University of California Press.

Ravenhill, Philip L. 1996. *Dreams and Reveries: Images of Otherworld Mates among the Baule, West Africa*. Washington, D.C: Smithsonian Institution Press.

Rodgers, Joni. 2000. *Bald in the Land of Big Hair*. New York: HarperCollins.

Rorty, Richard. 1979. *Philosophy and the Mirror of Nature*. Princeton: Princeton University Press.

Rosaldo, Renato. 1989. *Culture and Truth*. Boston: Beacon Press.

Ross, Doran. 1998. *Wrapped in Pride: Ghanaian Kente and African American Identity*. Los Angeles: UCLA Fowler Museum of Cultural History.

Rouch, Jean. 1953. "Contribution à l'histoire des Songhay." *Mémoires de l'institut français d'Afrique noir* 29: [137]–259.

———. 1953–54. *Les maîtres fous*. Paris: Films de la Pléiade.

———. 1956. "Migrations au Ghana." *Journal de la Société des Africanistes* 26, nos. 1–2: 33–196.

———. 1967. "Jaguar." Paris: Films de la Pléiade.

———. 1978. "Jean Rouch Talks About His Films to John Marshall and John W. Adams." *American Anthropologist* 80, no. 4: 1005–20.

———. 1989. *La religion et la magic Songhay*. 2nd ed. Brussels: Free University.

Said, Edward. 1979. *Orientalism*. New York: Vintage.

Sassen, Saskia. 1991. *The Global City: New York, London, Tokyo*. Princeton: Princeton University Press.

———. 1994. *Cities in a World Economy*. Thousand Oaks, Calif.: Pine Forge/Sage.

——— 1996. "Whose City Is It? Globalization and the Formation of New Claims." *Public Culture* 8: 205–23.

Schutz, Alfred. 1962. *Collected Papers*. Vol. 1, *The Problem of Social Reality*. The Hague: Nijhoff.

Shaw, Rosalind. 2002. *Memories of the Slave Trade: Ritual and the Historical Imagination in Sierra Leone*. Chicago: University of Chicago Press.

Sheard, T., and P. Maguire. 1999. "The Effect of Psychological Interventions on Anxiety and Depression in Cancer Patients: Results of Two Meta-analyses." *British Journal of Cancer* 80: 1770–1780.

Shiller, Nina Glick, and Georges Fouron. 2001. *Georges Woke Up Laughing: Long Distance Nationalism and the Search for Home*. Durham, N.C.: Duke University Press.

Sontag, Susan. 1978. *Illness as Metaphor*. New York: Farrar, Strauss and Giroux.

Steiner, Christopher. 1994. *African Art in Transit*. New York: Cambridge University Press.

Steiner, Christopher. 1995. "The Art of the Trade: On the Creation of Authenticity in the African Art Market." In *The Traffic in Culture*, edited by George E. Marcus and Fred R. Myers, 151–66. Berkeley: University of California Press.

———. 2002. "Waiting to Inhale: Paul Stoller's Money Has No Smell." *Anthropological Quarterly* 75, no. 2: 381–93.

Stewart, Rory. 2006. *The Places in Between*. New York: Harvest Books.

Stoller, Paul. 2004a. *Stranger in the Village of the Sick: A Memoir of Cancer, Sorcery and Healing*. Boston: Beacon Press.

———. 2004b. *Sensuous Ethnography, African Persuasions and Social Knowledge*. *Qualitative Inquiry* 10, no. 4: 817–35.

———. 2003. "Circuits of African Art/Paths of Wood: Exploring an Anthropological Trail." *Anthropological Quarterly* 76, no. 2: 207–35.

———. 2002. *Money Has No Smell: The Africanization of New York City*. Chicago: University of Chicago Press.

———. 2001. "West African: Trading Places in New York." In *New Immigrants in New York*, edited by Nancy Foner, 229–49. 2nd ed. New York: Columbia University Press.

———. 1998. "Rationality." In *Critical Terms in Religious Studies*, edited by Mark Taylor, 239–56. Chicago: University of Chicago Press.

——— 1997. *Sensuous Scholarship*. Philadelphia: University of Pennsylvania Press.

———. 1995. *Embodying Colonial Memories: Spirit Possession, Power and the Hauka in West Africa*. New York: Routledge.

———. 1992. *The Cinematic Griot: The Ethnography of Jean Rouch*. Chicago: University of Chicago Press

———. 1989a. *Fusion of the Worlds: Ethnography of Possession among the Songhay of Niger*. Chicago: University of Chicago Press.

———. 1989b. *The Taste of Ethnographic Things*. Philadelphia: University of Pennsylvania Press.

Stoller, Paul, and Cheryl Olkes. 1987. *In Sorcery's Shadow: A Memoir of Apprenticeship among the Songhay of Niger*. Chicago: University of Chicago Press.

Stoller, Paul, and Jasmin Tahmaseb McConatha. 2001. "City Life: West African Communities in New York City." *Journal of Contemporary Ethnography* 26, no. 4: 651–78.

Strathem, Marilyn. 2005. *Partial Connections*. Lanham, MD: Atamira Press.

Tambiah, Stanley. 1994. *Magic, Science, Religion and the Scope of Rationality*. Cambridge: Cambridge University Press.

Taussig, Michael. 1993. *Mimesis and Alterity: A Particular History of the Senses*. New York: Routledge.

———. 2006. *Walter Benjamin's Grave*. Chicago: University of Chicago Press.

Taylor, Lucien, Barbash Illisa, and Christopher Steiner. 1993. "In and Out of Africa." Berkeley: University of California Film Extension.

Taylor, Mark. 2002. *The Moment of Complexity: Emerging Network Culture*. Chicago: University of Chicago Press.

Thomas, Nigel J. T. 1999. "Are Theories of Images Theories of the Imagination?" *Cognitive Science* 23: 207–45.

Torgovnick, Marianna. 1990. *Gone Primitive: Savage Intellects, Modern Lives*. Chicago: University of Chicago Press.

Turner, Victor. 1969. *The Ritual Process: Structure and Anti-Structure*. Ithaca, N.Y.: Cornell University Press.

———. 1967. *The Forest of Symbols: Aspects of Ndembu Ritual*. Ithaca, N.Y.: Cornell University Press.

Van Gennep, Arnold. 1961. *Rites of Passage*, translated by Monica Vizedon and Gabrielle Caffe. Chicago: University of Chicago Press.

Vitebsky, Piers 2005. *The Reindeer People: Livings with Animals and Spirits in Siberia*. New York: Houghton-Mifflin.

Vogel, Susan Mullin. 1997. *Baule: African Art, Western Eyes*. New Haven: Yale University Press.

Wilde, A. D. 1995. *Mainstreaming Kwanzaa. Public Interest* 119: 68–80.

Wittgenstein, Ludwig. 1953. *Philosophical Investigations*, translated by G. E. M. Amscombe. London: Blackwell.

Index

Adamu Jenitongo, 38, 50, 131, 140,
154–55, 156, 160, 173; death of,
38–40; and the *genji how*, 42–44.
See also Songhay; sorcery; spirit
possession
African art, 89–92, 106–10; collectors of, 107; concepts of 110–11;
marketing of, 110–14. *See also*
National Museum of African Art
Afrocentrism, 96, 187n. 7
al 'Arabi, Muhammad Ibn, 6, 128,
169, 177. *See also* Between
Alsop, Stuart, 163
Askia Mohammed Touré, 79, 87
Azande, 31–32, 48

Barthes, Roland, 21
Bayart, Jean-Francois, 184n.4
Behar, Ruth, 163
Benjamin, Walter, 171–72, 190n.2
Bernus, Suzanne, 20–22
Between, 3, 35, 134, 143, 144, 150;
as a phenomenon, 17, 27, 41,
49, 123, 174, 177–78; as a space,
91, 94, 110, 113, 115, 151, 171;
masters of, 34
Boubé, Mounkaila, 2–4, 57, 58
Breton, André, 152
Bourdieu, Pierre, 32, 74, 181n.8,
184n.1
Burawoy, Michael, 115

cancer, 120, 137, 143, 155; diagnosis
of, 120–21, 124–26, 129–32, 137–
38; lessons of, 152–53; narratives

of, 162–63; as war, 124–25, 126.
See also village of the sick
Chernoff, John M., 41, 184n.10
Chittick, William C., 169, 179n.3,
179n.4, 1990n.5
Chomsky, A. Noam, 13, 16, 180n.2
Collège de France, 19
Comaroff, John and Jean, 76, 184n.10
Crapanzano, Vincent 5, 167, 179n.3,
179n.5, 190n.7

De Boeck, Filip, 87, 185n.14
Dewey, John, 12
Dieterlen, Germaine, 174–75
Diori, Hamani, 83–84
divination, 138–42; analysis of
138–39, 188n.1
Dogon, 174–76
Dongo, 79, 84
Douglas, Mary, 13
Drescher, Fran, 163

embodiment, 28–35; and memory,
79–88; and rationality, 33
epoche, 30
Errington, Shelley, 99, 186n.1, 187n.9
ethnofiction, 176, 190n.2. *See also*
Rouch, Jean
ethnography, 154–59; and the personal, 155–56; and representation, 156; textual strategies of,
157–58
Evans-Pritchard, E. E., 16, 32, 48
Evens, Terrence M. S., 23–24,
1980n.8, 181n.2